01/03

THE ARCHITECTURE OF
PHILIP JOHNSON

THE ARCHITECTURE OF
PHILIP JOHNSON

foreword PHILIP JOHNSON

photography RICHARD PAYNE

essay HILARY LEWIS

text STEPHEN FOX

Bulfinch Press

AOL Time Warner Book Group

Boston | New York | London

Book design and composition by Judson Design Associates for
Anchorage Press, Houston, Texas

First Edition

ISBN 0-8212-2788-2

Library of Congress Control Number 2002102356

Bulfinch Press is a division of AOL Time Warner Book Group.

Printed in Hong Kong

It is embarrassing to see all the buildings I have ever built stretched out in one book like this. I had no idea I'd built so many buildings. I couldn't say (as I would like to) that this one's good and this one's bad. Like all architects, I am only interested in my next building. What did happen as I went through this book is that by leaving out the obvious (my own house and other well-known structures), several buildings struck me as worth a remark.

Technically the MoMA Sculpture Garden is landscape architecture, but it is organized as an architecturally arranged room. It is interesting to me to walk through the sequence of "rooms" to view the sculptures. In the reconstruction of the MoMA beginning in 2001, the garden was destroyed. It will, however, we trust, be rebuilt.

The Museum Building at the Munson-Williams-Proctor Institute in Utica is one of my best plans — in fact, one of my best buildings. Clear plan and good materials (granite and bronze).

The Nuclear Reactor in Rehovat, Israel, is my temple in the desert. Again the clear plan, with an inner courtyard. The warped panels covering the actual reactor sphere are a feature I have used very often in my later work, right up to the Cathedral of Hope in Dallas, which is still on the boards.

The Sheldon Memorial Art Gallery is a calm repetition of symmetrically placed arcuated features. The nine arches are identical, except that the center three are glass. Simple to the point of repetition, but clear and successful.

The New York State Pavilion at the 1964–65 World's Fair is now a ruin. In a way, the ruin is even more haunting than the original structure. There ought to be a university course in the pleasure of ruins.

The Kline Tower at Yale dominates its part of the campus by its size and site. It is known as my "Tootsie Roll Building" because of the cylindrical columns that emphasize each of its main façades. I have always had a weakness for round or curved surfaces. They catch light so much better than square or right-angle corners.

The RepublicBank (now Bank of America Center) in Houston was designed in a style reminiscent of Dutch Baroque gables. It makes a much less boring tower than the usual block.

The "Lipstick Building" is a nickname that stuck for my tower at 53rd Street on Third Avenue. What a thrill to drive through the streets of New York and find this relief from the square plan of the normal office tower.

The Gerald D. Hines College of Architecture at the University of Houston was the only building in my career that I unashamedly copied from another architect, Claude-Nicholas Ledoux, an eighteenth-century French genius. His building was also an educational structure. I changed a few little things along the way.

PHILIP JOHNSON
New Canaan, CT

THERE IS ONLY ONE ABSOLUTE TODAY AND THAT IS CHANGE. THERE ARE NO RULES, SURELY NO CERTAINTIES IN ANY OF THE ARTS. THERE IS ONLY THE FEELING OF A WONDERFUL FREEDOM, OF ENDLESS POSSIBILITIES TO INVESTIGATE, OF ENDLESS PAST YEARS OF HISTORICALLY GREAT BUILDINGS TO ENJOY.

NO RULES, JUST ART

Hilary Lewis

Philip Johnson has lived at the Glass House in New Canaan, Connecticut, for over fifty years. This forty-acre property captures Johnson's essence. Combining a sleek, urbane structure with a pavilion-dotted country landscape, the Glass House is the work of a postwar architect known for his support of modernism. Located in southern New England, where stone walls appear like natural formations, the property, like Johnson, brings together modernity and intellect while embracing tradition and history. This may seem contradictory, but unsurprisingly that is Johnson.

It was not until Johnson was thirty-four years old that he began studying architecture formally. However, this late start did not prevent his spending more than sixty years as a designer. Over the years Johnson has also worked as a curator, commentator, and teacher, which has contributed to his role as a central figure in architecture — a position he has held since 1932, when his first show at The Museum of Modern Art attracted the public's attention. Johnson's practice has taken many forms, with a variety of partners: Landis Gores, Richard Foster, and John Burgee, to name a few. Today his firm is Philip Johnson/Alan Ritchie Architects.

Johnson began as a modernist. His travels in the late 1920s included visits to the Bauhaus, where he met the great figures of the period, including Walter Gropius and Ludwig Mies van der Rohe. In 1930 he befriended the Dutch architect J. J. P. Oud. In later years, Johnson would work with Mies, most notably on the first show in New York on the great German architect, held at The Museum of Modern Art in 1947, and later on the Seagram Building in New York in the 1950s.

Johnson's appreciation of art and architecture came in part from his mother, Louise Pope Johnson, who loved art and learning. She regularly traveled with her children to Europe in order to show them great works of art. The first trip was when Johnson was thirteen. He made the crossing in 1919 when his father was called to diplomatic duty by President Woodrow Wilson. During that visit Johnson encountered great architectural monuments in Europe, such as Chartres Cathedral, an edifice that has left a lasting impression on him. Johnson has compared Chartres Cathedral with Frank Gehry's Guggenheim Museum in Bilbao, Spain: "Chartres is the first building I visited that made me cry. I thought all good architecture could do that. Bilbao is the most recent building I have seen that has brought me to tears."

Johnson began his studies at Harvard in 1923, where he followed an undergraduate program in philosophy and classics while retaining his interest in art. In Cambridge, Johnson had contact with the leaders of the Society of Contemporary Art, a group headed by Lincoln Kirstein and dedicated to showing modern art. Kirstein would later found the New York City Ballet and commission Johnson to design its performing space at Lincoln Center, the New York State Theater (1964). They developed a lifelong friendship, eventually leading to Johnson's building a monument to Kirstein at the Glass House — the Kirstein Tower (1985).

While still at Harvard, Johnson developed a link to The Museum of Modern Art, in part, through his sister, Theodate. She knew a young professor of art history at Wellesley College, where she was studying, whom she introduced to her older brother. The professor was Alfred H. Barr, Jr., whom Johnson would later refer to simply as "God." Barr, as the first director of The Museum of Modern Art, made the decision early on to bring in Johnson to direct what would later be known as the Department of Architecture and Design. The fact that Johnson had been traveling to Europe since 1919 and had already been to the Bauhaus in the late twenties explains in part why Barr chose him for this task.

When Johnson graduated from Harvard in 1930, he embarked on one of the seminal research trips of early twentieth-century architecture. Johnson and another friend from Harvard, the architectural historian Henry-Russell Hitchcock, traveled throughout Europe to see and document the "new" architecture of the 1920s. The results of that trip would become the source material for the groundbreaking show at The Museum of Modern Art *Modern Architecture — International Exhibition*, which opened in 1932. This show and its accompanying book, *The International Style: Architecture Since 1922,* have made a deep mark on the history of architecture and would add the term "International Style" to contemporary architectural discourse. Johnson is adamant in pointing out that it was Barr who coined the famous term. He describes his own role as "a precocious member of the team." Johnson, twenty-six, and Barr, his senior by only five years, were already arbiters of taste and ideas in architecture and design.

It is now difficult to imagine how different the landscape of American cities was in the early 1930s when Johnson and Hitchcock's work appeared at MoMA. The glass towers commonly associated with America's downtowns did not yet exist. In 1932 New York was celebrating its new skyscrapers: the Chrysler and Empire State Buildings. Art Deco was the rage. The flat-roofed structures of Mies van der Rohe, Walter Gropius, and Le Corbusier were a far cry from the streamlined styles then being built, and certainly bore no relation to the classic stone buildings of the teens and twenties. Yet, decades later the architecture presented in the International Style turned out to be the prevalent corporate style in the United States in the second half of the twentieth century. Johnson and Hitchcock turned out to be not only proselytizers but also visionaries.

Johnson's alliance with both Barr and Hitchcock would continue for many years. These two men influenced Johnson deeply, but in different ways. Barr was a leader and promoter determined to vault a new museum into prominence. He did this through critical aesthetic choices for the museum and its exhibitions. Johnson's admiration for Barr and his artistic sensibilities — "his eye" — is profound. He learned an enormous amount from working with Barr, whom Johnson credits for many elements in his projects, including the thoughtful placement of sculpture in the MoMA garden, which Johnson originally designed 1953, and the careful positioning in the Glass House of an oil painting attributed to Poussin. When Johnson elected to show design in addition to architecture at the museum beginning in 1933, Barr was his partner.

The exhibitions *Objects 1900 and Today* (1933) and *Machine Art* (1934) broke new ground in the New York museum world. Both of these shows presented everyday objects as art. (Some of these items remain within the collection at The Museum of Modern Art.) Johnson, in collaboration with Barr, showed audiences that modern objects could be art.

Hitchcock, on the other hand, was a pure architectural historian. His interests in pre-twentieth-century work affected Johnson's view of architecture. Working with Hitchcock, Johnson could not ignore the monuments of earlier centuries. This historian's attitude has remained with Johnson through today. He embraces the new while not only appreciating the past but also borrowing directly from it (and citing his sources). For example, in 1983 Johnson built RepublicBank (now Bank of America Center) in Houston, Texas, where he articulated the silhouette with a multitude of abstract gables. Johnson says that this design element came directly from his reading of Hitchcock's book on seventeenth-century Dutch architecture.

Johnson's work at The Museum of Modern Art marks a pivotal point in his career. It would have made sense for Johnson to continue at MoMA for decades after his success there in the early 1930s. However, he made a bold decision in 1940 to return to Harvard to study architecture, leaving his life in New York to take a chance as a designer. He left MoMA, where Barr shared his interest in the art of architecture. At Harvard, where Walter Gropius led the architecture program, the mentality was different. Other Bauhaus figures, such as Marcel Breuer, taught at the school. Johnson recalls that while he was not a great friend of Gropius, he was fond of Breuer. Johnson states, "I was a Mies man, not a Gropius man," and he had difficulty accepting Gropius's emphasis on the social aspects of architecture. Johnson preferred the artistry of Mies. Even at that time, Johnson adds, he was interested in bringing sculptural aspects into his architectural designs, then considered to be an inappropriate direction by the school's leadership.

Johnson is known for saying, "I would rather sleep all night in Chartres Cathedral and walk down the street to the john than spend the night in a Harvard house with back-to-back plumbing." He is referring here to the type of projects then given at the School of Design at Harvard — functionally oriented houses where economy of plumbing systems was considered more important than aesthetic considerations. This is no small quip on Johnson's part. It is his aesthetic position. Johnson appreciates architectural greatness over comfort and applies this attitude to his own work. Effect and monumentality trump the functional approach to design in his work, despite his Harvard training.

The impact of this on Johnson's architecture is clear in his early work, such as the house that he built for himself in Cambridge, Massachusetts, in 1942. This building is based on Mies's court houses, an urban housing solution. The residence on Ash Street is a loft-like living space with a wall of glass looking out on a small garden enclosed by a high wall. It was built by Johnson for his own use and would later be accepted as his master's thesis. However, for all it apparently owes to the work of his mentor Mies, this building also represented the way in which Johnson would at once absorb the designs of others and yet make the work his own. For example, the overhang at the wall comes from neither Mies nor Gropius. Ash Street marks the beginning of Johnson's blending of pure International Style tenets with his own sense of taste. The Glass House would take this much further, but Ash Street was the point of departure.

A composite of nearly every style Johnson has embraced since he began his practice in the early 1940s, the Glass House has been a work in progress for a half-century. The main pavilion (1949) functions as a home, not just an architectural concept. What makes the Glass House so good is not just how it combines Miesian and classical principles but how well the design takes advantage of its natural surroundings. Johnson says, "Trees are the basic building block of the place." Frank Lloyd Wright was known to have asked while visiting the Glass House, "Philip, am I inside or am I out? Do I take my hat off or leave it on?"

Johnson recalls that Wright's remarks were critical because the Glass House was so unlike Wright's own work. These differences did not keep the two men from forming a friendship. Johnson and Wright visited on many occasions at the Glass House since Wright was working on a residential project in New Canaan. Wright's ideas did make their way into Johnson's thinking, even if this was not obvious to Wright. Johnson believes in integrating landscape into his architecture. He shares Wright's conviction that this is possible only when you have "acreage, not a lot." In New Canaan, Johnson had the right mix of elements: rolling hills, a rocky promontory, old trees, and nineteenth-century stone walls. Far from a clean slate, the site for the Glass House is the premise for the design — the entire property, all forty-plus acres, is the Glass House.

Johnson is fond of saying that he is not a Miesian — not then, not now. He is not a strict disciple of Ludwig Mies van der Rohe, the great architect Johnson promoted and eventually worked with in New York. This assertion can appear disingenuous if one takes a cursory look at Johnson's early work.

AS A PREJUDICED PRACTITIONER OF THE ART, I CAN BE FREE TO BE AS NON-INTELLECTUAL AND UNINHIBITED AS I WISH. I MUST EXPLAIN THE WORD *NON-INTELLECTUAL.* I REALLY MEAN ANTI-WORD, BECAUSE THE WORD KILLS ART. THE WORD IS AN ABSTRACTION, AND ART IS CONCRETE. THE WORD IS OLD, LOADED WITH ACCRETED MEANINGS FROM USAGE. ART IS NEW. THE WORD IS GENERAL — ART IS SPECIFIC. WORDS ARE MIND — ART IS EYES. WORDS ARE THOUGHT — ART IS FEELING.

THE DAY OF IDEOLOGY IS THANKFULLY OVER. LET US CELEBRATE THE DEATH OF THE IDÉE FIXE. THERE ARE NO RULES, ONLY FACTS. THERE IS NO ORDER, ONLY PREFERENCE; THERE ARE NO IMPERATIVES, ONLY CHOICE; OR, TO USE A NINETEENTH-CENTURY WORD, TASTE; OR A MODERN WORD, TAKE: WHAT IS YOUR TAKE ON THIS OR THAT?

So much of it is clearly based on Mies. It is not just the house in New Canaan, certainly the place Johnson loves best, with its glass walls and steel frame, but so many other Johnson projects from the 1940s and 1950s that contain elements often associated with Mies.

So what does Johnson mean? That he departed from Miesian style when he turned to postmodernism? In truth, Johnson honestly rejects the Miesian label from the start, because he can so vividly see how his work differs from that of the German master builder. Indeed, the furniture in the Glass House is almost all by Mies. It was Mies after all who designed Johnson's 1930 apartment in New York, and Johnson still has those items. The Barcelona chairs, the daybed, and those Brno chairs are designs that frequently appear in the current pages of any design magazine. (It takes some effort to recall that when Johnson first acquired these they were contemporary pieces.) Johnson does not debate that he was passionate about Mies's work. But when it came time for Johnson to design buildings his work departed from that of Mies, despite the many similarities.

Mies himself appears to have understood. According to Johnson, Mies was very displeased with the Glass House, not because the design so heavily relied on Mies's principles, but because it so dramatically differed from them. The symmetrical façades, the central entrance, and the brick base that so firmly anchors the building were moves away from Mies's manner, not to mention that thick brick cylinder containing the fireplace and bathroom.

The plan of the building, according to Johnson, is "Georgian," a traditional house divided into rooms for various functions, albeit without dividing walls. Johnson is consistent in his claim. In fact he was quoted discussing the Georgian qualities of the Glass House even before the building was completed in 1949. Johnson was surprised when Mies declined an offer to spend the night at the Glass House. On reflection, Johnson understood Mies's dislike of what he had done, although at first he was disappointed by the reaction.

Johnson has continued to produce architecture that follows this pattern. He often embraces forms developed by others, but then transforms these in various ways. He has frequently been described as a designer who jumps from style to style and is known to incorporate ideas from a wide variety of sources. But he does have consistent elements in his architecture, one being his love of history. Well traveled and well aware of the history of buildings worldwide, Johnson finds inspiration in the mannerism of Giulio Romano and the classicism of the Treasury of Atreus. He gets ideas from the Turkish Baroque of Mimar Sinan and the spires of Chartres Cathedral. While Johnson certainly leans toward classical form, he is not exclusively reliant on any one historic style. But he enjoys pulling images from the past into his own work — all the better if they are recognized as such.

In his work today, the Pantheon and St. Peter's in Rome are influences, while just a few years back Johnson was revisiting the German Expressionism of Hermann Finsterlin. An earlier example is his revival of eighteenth-century French architecture in the form of Claude-Nicolas Ledoux at the University of Houston's Gerald D. Hines College of Architecture (1985). Johnson is eclectic in his choices but consistent in his insistence on the importance of looking at history.

Another passion for Johnson is what he calls "procession." By this he means the visual experience of moving through a building or a series of buildings. The way in which a building unfolds is critical to Johnson. He has written on the subject, most notably in "Whence and Whither," an article published in 1965 in *Perspecta, the Yale Architecture Journal.* As early as 1949, Johnson commented on the subject in an article on Frank Lloyd Wright's Taliesin. Johnson's commitment to procession is best seen in Johnson's work with landscape. Of course, there is the Glass House, but Johnson has produced other landscape architecture. In 1953 he created the garden at The Museum of Modern Art and would go on in 1974 to produce the Fort Worth Water Garden, a study of different presentations of water — from calm to cascading — all rolled into an urban park, smack in the middle of downtown. In all cases, Johnson was concerned with the experience of the viewer moving through these environments.

Scale is an area of interest as well. Johnson's first clear expression of this is his Pavilion (1962) at the Glass House, a playful structure that sits a few feet from the shore of a man-made lake beneath the main house. Like a classical folly in an English garden, the pavilion appears to exist primarily as something to be seen from afar. Up close, the pavilion can be seen for what it is, a six-foot-high structure that requires a man of average height to stoop inside. Johnson compares the little structure to a tree house, a place for play. To him it is, "full-scale, small-scale." Another example is Johnson's postmodern tower in Boston, 500 Boylston Street. Here Johnson used elements such as lampposts, which are clearly larger in scale than their surrounding architecture. This contrast is precisely what he wanted.

When prompted, Johnson admits that he has a personal affinity for the work of Marcel Duchamp. In part, it is this that leads to Johnson's use of incongruous juxtaposition of scales. Johnson's respect for Duchamp extends to a project completed in 2000 in Big Sur, California. Here he has produced a sculpture based on an amusing interpretation of a chess piece. The sculpture's formal name is the *Drunken Rook;* however, Johnson likes to refer to it as "Marcel."

Johnson likes the clever and the witty in architecture of all ages, even more so when it is combined with grandeur, such as the work of the Italian baroque master Francesco Borromini, whose manipulation of scale and geometric form is best known in his church in Rome, San Carlo alle Quattro Fontane (one of Johnson's favorites.) The oval plans of Johnson's buildings, the New York State Pavilion — originally constructed for the New York World's Fair in 1964–65 — and 53rd at Third (1986) in New York (known locally as the Lipstick Building), owe their form partly to Johnson's admiration of Borromini. With the unusually shaped skyscraper, Johnson wanted not only to make a mark on a busy New York avenue but to create a public space. The choice of an oval allowed Johnson to "create a city square out of an oval, a place on a Manhattan lot." As for wit, consider the terrazzo paving of the New York State Pavilion — an oversized Texaco map of New York State.

Often, Johnson looks toward Italian architecture for inspiration, although he makes use of the architecture of many other regions. For example, he prefers French Gothic to English and has been influenced by German architecture — especially by Karl Friedrich Schinkel — as was Mies. But when pressed about which architecture impresses him most, he emphatically states, "Italian, above all else." This declaration has made its way into his architecture directly. His New York State Theater at Lincoln Center in New York is loosely based on eighteenth-century German performance spaces. But if you visit its auditorium and look up you will see a design based on Michelangelo's Piazza del Campidoglio in Rome.

There is another aesthetic concept Johnson often incorporates into his designs, what he calls "safe danger." In New Canaan Johnson has used this in a variety of ways. He likes to point out that the main house itself should get the point across — a house made of glass is a precarious thing. Another example is the Kirstein Tower, whose high steps (and lack of railing) provide a challenging ascent to anyone who attempts it. The Sculpture Gallery (1970) in New Canaan has a similar quality. The building is based on a spiraling stairway that descends around a large atrium. Again, no railing. At the Fort Worth Water Garden there is a section where rushing water makes its way through a chasm of steps. Johnson intended that visitors climb them, even though at first glance they look ominous.

Johnson is an unabashed formalist. The appearance of the building, not its function, is what gets Johnson going. This places him well within historic precedent, but far outside the mainstream of his contemporaries. The prevalent attitude in architecture schools at the time Johnson trained stemmed from Walter Gropius, founder of the Bauhaus. Form was to follow function. But Johnson disagreed and has remained true to this attitude. Even when he first presented architecture at The Museum of Modern Art, he was interested in its form, its art.

Johnson's portfolio covers all building types. He began, as most architects do, with houses. Some of his earliest were for himself — Ash Street and the Glass House — but most were for various clients. Johnson has designed in excess of sixty houses. An early favorite is the Oneto house (1951) in Irvington, New York. One of his latest projects is a house for a speculative development in Sagaponack, New York, where Johnson is working in a style quite different from his Miesian roots. Here, he is creating a "village of Pantheons."

His work with museums has undergone a similar transformation. Johnson's additions to The Museum of Modern Art were Miesian as was his garden there. In the 1960s classical form dominated Johnson's civic buildings such as the Amon Carter Museum (1961) in Fort Worth, Texas, and the Sheldon Memorial Art Gallery (1963) in Lincoln, Nebraska. These buildings have arcuated façades and appear as modern temples for art. However, in a recent museum project in Guadalajara, Mexico, Johnson worked with Platonic solids — cubes, cones, pyramids and cylinders — warping and manipulating them. Johnson calls the project "Playing with Plato." Other new projects from Johnson have the same theme. Johnson's garden pavilion for a private estate in South Salem, New York, and his recently completed Trylons at Chrysler Center in New York are two projects in which he experiments specifically with the collision of pyramids in order to create interesting shapes, and perhaps even more important, interesting shadows.

Similarly in skyscrapers, Johnson has moved from his early work in 1958 with Mies at the Seagram Building in New York to buildings of greater personal expression. Even at Seagram, Johnson made his artistic mark with his memorable interiors for the Four Seasons restaurant. Classic, but not classical, they have a solidity that is more Johnson than Mies. One of Johnson's first tall buildings was a commission at Yale University, the Kline Biology Tower (1965). Here, Johnson used a favorite form — the thick cylinder — which has made an appearance in many Johnson buildings, not just at the Glass House. The school's students nicknamed the tower the Tootsie Roll Building. In a building of the same period, the Museum of Pre-Columbian Art (1963) at Dumbarton Oaks in Washington, D.C., thick cylinders are the basis for the building, which is actually loosely modeled after a school by Mimar Sinan, the sixteenth-century Turkish architect. Johnson likes curved surfaces for their ability to reflect light, to be sculptural. The result of using such forms at Kline is a monumental, yet playful building. In a more recent project for a house in Telluride, Colorado, Johnson has returned again to the idea of creating a structure from columns, this time in a plan where the columns seem to be placed randomly. He calls this design "the dancing cylinders."

Johnson's record as a designer of skyscrapers cannot be fully understood without looking at Johnson's extraordinary history with the developer Gerald D. Hines. Hines and his company have commissioned and built thirteen buildings with Johnson. He began his work with Hines in Houston, although he went on to do buildings with Hines in cities throughout the United States. The work in Houston is some of Johnson's most groundbreaking. Their first project was phase one of Post Oak Central (1975), which was soon followed by Pennzoil Place (1976). Pennzoil was a very public announcement by Johnson that he was "bored with the box." Two glass towers are separated by merely ten feet and are capped by sharp angles. Across the street from Pennzoil is now Bank of America Center (formerly RepublicBank), where Johnson's approach was completely different. As noted before, pointed gables decorate a massive triangular form. Both buildings are considered major features of the Houston skyline.

The third major skyscraper by Johnson in Houston for Hines is the Transco (now Williams) Tower (1983), a slender tower in an extraordinary

COULD WE NOT BE THE ARTISTS OF OUR ENVIRONMENT? IT SEEMS TO ME, PREJ-
UDICED THOUGH I KNOW I AM, THAT WE COULD REBUILD OUR COUNTRY CLOSER
TO OUR HEART'S DESIRE, SO THAT OUR CULTURE COULD OUTSTRIP ALL OTHERS
IN HISTORY IN BUILDING, AS WE DO IN SCIENCE AND TECHNOLOGY. ARE WE
LESS IN ANY WAY THAN THE ITALIANS OF THE QUATTROCENTO? I CAN'T BELIEVE
IT IS A MATTER OF INBORN TALENT, THAT WE ARE NOT AS GREAT AS IN THE
RENAISSANCE. IT IS A MATTER OF VALUES — OF WHAT WE IN AMERICA THINK IS
IMPORTANT. WE SPEND MONEY ON MILITARY HARDWARE, LIQUOR, HAIR-
DRESSERS, THE AUTOMOBILE; WE COULD, IF WE WERE SO INCLINED, SPEND
MONEY ON MAKING AMERICA BEAUTIFUL. IF WE THOUGHT IT IMPORTANT TO
BUILD MAGNIFICENTLY, I MAINTAIN WE COULD BUILD MAGNIFICENTLY. WE MAY
NOT MAKE IT IN OUR LIFETIME, BUT HOPE WE MUST. *ARTS LONGA, VITA BREVIS,*
LIFE IS SHORT, BUT ART IS LONG.

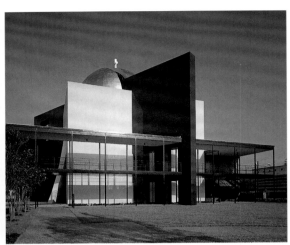

RIGID RULES DO HELP OUR BAD ARCHITECTS BUT DO NOT INHIBIT THE IMAGINATIVE. THAT IS WHAT IS SO WONDERFUL! NO SINGLE ARTIST IS CONSCIOUS OF THE RULES ANY MORE THAN OF HIS WELTANSCHAUUNG, HIS VIEWPOINT THROUGH WHICH HE LOOKS AT THE WORLD. HE JUST CREATES. ACTUALLY, HE STUGGLES *AGAINST* THE STYLE, *AGAINST* THE KNOWN, *TOWARD* THE UNKNOWN, *TOWARD* THE ORIGINAL. IT IS THIS TENSION BETWEEN STYLE AND CHANGE — KNOWN AND UNKNOWN — THAT KEEPS A STYLE ALIVE.

setting. Surrounded by a park, the tower is separated from any other tall buildings and is, of course, monumental. It is constructed out of a combination of stone and glass that often allows the building to blend with the sky. At the base, the property contains a horseshoe-shaped fountain at the far end designed by Johnson, called the Water Wall. The theatricality of the piece is heightened by the inclusion of a proscenium arch behind which water flows.

For all the buildings Johnson has designed, none may be associated with him more than the AT&T building (now Sony Plaza), completed in New York in 1984. Its distinctive silhouette and formidable entrance and lobby make this building the primary example of Johnson in the 1980s. Johnson says he simply wanted to reestablish the stone clad skyscraper in New York — which he did. There were many imitators. Despite the frequent comparisons between AT&T and a Chippendale highboy, Johnson maintains that he was looking for an interesting way to cap the building and looked to ancient models for doing so. He elected to use the broken pediment as seen at Petra in Jordan. In fact, he looked at several options before deciding on the now famous top. Of course, it was pure Johnson to place an exhaust vent within the pediment so that curling forms of steam sometime emerge from that signature space. AT&T is Johnson at his most postmodern, where he took elements from different periods of history and put them together in one grand, pink granite package. Today he is still eager to use historic forms, but not in the same sort of combinations.

Following this work in the 1980s, Johnson both named and embraced Deconstructivism. He worked on the show of that name at The Museum of Modern Art and tried his hand at creating buildings in that style. One of his most successful designs is The Chapel of St. Basils, completed in 1997 at the University of St. Thomas in Houston. This was a homecoming for Johnson, who had designed the campus in a Miesian style in 1957. The chapel is the key element in the composition, which is loosely based on Jefferson's Academical Village at the University of Virginia in Charlottesville.

Since that time, Johnson has enjoyed a period of great experimentation. Like many architects practicing now, Johnson is working with non-Euclidean geometry. But he is quick to remind us that while this form is popular with architects he admires such as Frank Gehry, Peter Eisenman, and Daniel Libeskind, Johnson's new work also stems from his admiration for Frank Stella and the much earlier designs of the German Expressionist Hermann Finsterlin. The two best expressions of Johnson's work in this area are Da Monsta, his visitors pavilion at the Glass House, and the Cathedral of Hope in Dallas, Texas, currently under construction. At the same time, Johnson is still reworking the Pantheon.

Johnson's early training in philosophy has had an effect on his attitude towards aesthetics. Johnson asserts that he is no fan of Plato and his statements on "the beautiful and the true." Johnson prefers another Greek philosopher, Heraclitus, who maintained that the only constant was change, a position well accepted by Johnson. His appreciation of Nietzsche's relativism is also significant.

This anti-Platonic stance is at the heart of Johnson's constant search for something new, something different, with little concern for neglecting some aesthetic principle. Surely, Johnson has come a long way since he and Barr began their catalog for Machine Art with an extended quote from Plato's *Philebus*. In addition to the comments from Plato, they included remarks from Le Corbusier, who had written eloquently about "forms under light." Johnson grew to eschew Plato, but he has remained true to Le Corbusier. Johnson understands the power of light on architectural form and works to incorporate this into his own designs. In 1980 at the Glass House, Johnson designed a small studio composed of basic geometric forms — primarily a cube and a cone. Initially, this building was painted white. After a while, Johnson and his color consultant, Donald Kaufman, chose a soft orange tone. Eventually, they decided to change the exterior again and use a muted brown. Johnson is now delighted with the effect of this darker hue. What he likes is the way in which the cone catches light more dramatically than the rest of the building, remarking that "in bright sun the cone is nearly white."

Johnson has never felt trammeled by rules, but even so he seems particularly liberated in his practice today. Age may have something to do with it. Johnson has publicly stated that real professional freedom probably doesn't begin until seventy, and in his case it may have come even later. At ninety-five, Johnson has had ample time to move beyond whatever professional strictures there may have been and is now quite happy to approach projects ranging from sculpture to cathedrals with a wide variety of design solutions.

With such a large portfolio of work, Johnson's legacy is somewhat subjective. Some will choose the obvious landmarks, the AT&T Building, the Glass House, and the work at The Museum of Modern Art. Others will look at Johnson's houses and other small-scale projects. But beyond the buildings themselves there is the central tenet of Johnson's many years of practice and participation in his chosen field. His greatest mark may be that future generations of architects who examine Johnson's work will feel a greater freedom and take a fresh look at the art of architecture.

HILARY LEWIS
New York, NY

PHILIP JOHNSON HOUSE

9 Ash Street | Cambridge | MA

1942 | Philip Johnson with S. Clements Horsley

Essential to the myth of Philip Johnson is the story of how he designed and built this small, one-story, flat-roofed, wood house while an architecture student at the Graduate School of Design at Harvard University. Johnson enclosed most of the site with a tall wood wall, treating the flag-stone-paved court as an extension of the interior living space. Interior space is contained in a glass-fronted enclosure, sixty-six feet long and twenty feet wide, facing due west. Ezra Stoller's photographs of the early 1940s, which show the court covered in snow, register Johnson's affinity for the provocative and the oppositional: the fragile glass house defied neighborhood convention with its high street wall, and an extreme climate with central air-conditioning.

MR. AND MRS. RICHARD E. BOOTH HOUSE

Bedford Village | NY

1946 | Philip C. Johnson

Built of exposed block, this small, flat-roofed, slab-walled pavilion-type house was Johnson's first commissioned building to be constructed. Johnson formularized Mies van der Rohe's approach to building organization by strictly differentiating between solid walls and transparent walls and by adhering rigorously to the roof-ceiling plane as a mirror of the floor plane. The house was not published until fifty-five years after it was built; Stover Jenkins and David Mohney note that a secondary building planned as part of the landscape organization of the house site was never built.

DAMORA

MR. AND MRS. EUGENE FARNEY HOUSE

Sagaponack | NY

1947 | Philip C. Johnson

The Farney House represents the approach to domestic spatial planning that marked almost all of Johnson's published postwar houses. His organization of compact bedrooms, no-nonsense bathrooms, and a cross corridor as a network of interlocked rectangles, his contrast of these closed private spaces with the glass-walled living and dining room, and his treatment of the house as a single, coherent figure, were to be reiterated through the mid-1950s. It is tempting to see the Farney House as a reinterpretation of Mies van der Rohe's unbuilt Resor House of 1938, with solid, wood-sheathed bays framing a long, central glazed bay, elevated above grade, and capped by the horizontal fascia of a flat roof.

Philip Johnson's Glass House is his most famous and most highly regarded building. It is a steel-framed, flat-roofed, one-room, glass-walled weekend house that
he built for himself in tandem with a flat-roofed, brick-walled guest house. The
design of the two houses, their relationship to each other, and their relationship
with the site — a grass shelf that looks out across a valley — were analyzed by
Johnson in an apologia he wrote, published in the *Architectural Review*. Johnson's
dependence on the architecture of Ludwig Mies van der Rohe was evident; yet he
went further in the *Architectural Review* to detail a range of historical art and
architectural associations that guided his design. The architectural historian
William Jordy ranked the Glass House with Charles and Ray Eames' Case Study
House #8 of 1949 and Mies van der Rohe's Farnsworth House of 1950 as the three
pivotal American houses of the midpoint of the twentieth century. Of these, it was
the Glass House that proved to be most connected to the architectural history of
the century's second half. Its problematic relation to originary sources, its obses-
sion with yet ambivalence about history, its modernist exaltation of technique and
radical rejection of limits combined with its conventional social elitism suggest the
contradictions that kept the Glass House at the forefront of twentieth-century
architecture. Beginning with alterations to the Guest House in 1953, Johnson
made a practice of adding new small buildings to the property, which he expanded
through purchase. In 1975 the American Institute of Architects awarded its 25-
Year Award to the Glass House. In 1986 Johnson conveyed the property to the
National Trust for Historic Preservation so that after his death it might be opened
to the public. In 1997, the Glass House property was listed in the National Register
of Historic Places and designated a National Historic Landmark. The Eipel
Engineering Company was structural engineer for the Glass House and the Guest
House; Richard Kelly was the lighting consultant.

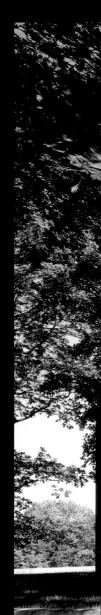

I CONSIDER MY OWN HOUSE NOT SO MUCH A HOME (THOUGH IT IS THAT TO ME)
AS A CLEARINGHOUSE OF IDEAS WHICH CAN FILTER DOWN LATER, THROUGH MY
OWN WORK OR THAT OF OTHERS.

GUEST HOUSE

New Canaan | CT

1949 | Philip C. Johnson Associates

Designed as a pendant to the Glass House, the Guest House provides insight into the pattern of Johnson's thought, which is binary, literal, and systematic. Containing just less than half the area of the Glass House, the Guest House is solid rather than transparent, cellular rather than unified, introverted rather than expansive, and practical rather than polemical. It is consistently used in photographs as a foreground frame for the Glass House, reproducing the spatial order that the Glass House projects onto its landscape. In his *Architectural Review* explication, Johnson naughtily described the Guest House as "descended from" the Baroque (by virtue of its symmetrical front elevation) and the buildings of Mies, anticipating the ideological consternation this pairing of opposites was likely to have aroused in 1950. Borrowings from Mies include the three circular windows on the uphill side of the house (looking away from the Glass House), each five feet in diameter.

GUEST HOUSE INTERIOR ALTERATIONS

New Canaan | CT

1953 | Philip Johnson

Johnson remodeled his Guest House internally by consolidating two of its three rooms. In the expanded bedroom, he constructed a pair of domical plaster vaults, supported on paired columns, that stood free of the ceiling and walls. Artificial light from concealed sources washed the walls, which were draped with moveable panels of printed Fortuny fabric. Carpeting and a low bed contributed to the room's atmosphere of sensuousness. The wire sculpture above the bed is by Ibram Lassaw. The plaster vaults were Johnson's first built work to experiment with curved surfaces.

PAVILION

New Canaan | CT
1962 | Philip Johnson Associates

Johnson built the Pavilion in a purpose-made pond downhill from the Glass House. It is a pre-cast concrete shelter of eight bays, each eight feet square and six feet high, grouped in a pinwheel configuration. Narrow channels of water slice through the floor of the Pavilion to connect to a tank in one of two unroofed bays. Ceilings are finished with gold leaf. The diminutive structure gave Johnson the opportunity to address certain "problems" associated with neoclassical architecture: adjusting for proportion and perceptions of scale in a deliberately undersized structure, and resolving the intersection of piers and fascias at salient and reentrant corners. The Pavilion enabled Johnson to pursue his modern fascination with generating plastically deformed volumes from plane surfaces, and of constructing materially austere structures that occupants experienced as sensually affecting and witty.

PAINTING GALLERY

New Canaan | CT

1965 | Philip Johnson

Built into a mound on an uphill slope to the northeast of the Glass House and the Guest House, Johnson's windowless art-storage gallery consists in plan of three circles of different diameters (and a small fourth circle at the entrance) whose circumferences overlap. Wall panels, hung from the flat ceiling, rotate around a thick cylinder at the center of each large circle. The wall panels do not rise as high as the ceiling, so that as they are rotated they clear rows of adjustable track lighting. Paintings, drawings, prints, and photographs can be hung on the panels. Johnson explained the design of the gallery to the art critic Francine du Plessix as resulting from his desire to explore practical solutions to the problem of storing works of art, as well as exploring the spatial consequences of stationing orthogonally arrayed panels in intersecting circular containers. Even in the context of anti-architecture, Johnson continued to work on spatial and haptic issues related to the Dumbarton Oaks, Kline, and New York State Pavilion projects. The Painting Gallery was equipped with low stools and tables on casters. These permitted Johnson and his guests to playfully experience sensations of bodily displacement. Lev Zetlin & Associates were structural engineers, Jaros, Baum & Bolles were mechanical engineers, and the E. W. Howell Company was the general contractor.

SCULPTURE GALLERY

New Canaan | CT
1970 | Philip Johnson

Built adjacent to the Painting Gallery, northeast of the Glass House, the brick-walled, steel-and-glass-roofed Sculpture Gallery is set into the sloping site to minimize its impact on the landscape. More so than in his larger commissions of the 1960s, Johnson deftly integrated characteristic concerns here. The scale of the Sculpture Gallery is ambiguous externally because the angled plan geometry works against the slope of the roof to confuse accurate perception. Internally, the gallery is open to the sky. The plan (a rectangle with segments of three right triangles emerging from it in a pinwheel-like whorl) expands spatially as visitors follow a diagonally organized processional route down flights of steps around a central well. The haptic experience of bodily suspension above the central well is maintained until the conclusion of the procession. The Sculpture Gallery is experienced as a play of tense oppositions that creates surprise and a sense of discovery. Its interior spatial organization is amphitheatrical, transforming a visit into a spatial performance. The skylit triangular alcoves create pockets in which to display sculpture. With their protruding angular forms they continue the exercise in spatial fragmentation that Johnson explored in the Painting Gallery. The Sculpture Gallery was the first completed building in which Johnson exchanged the preoccupations evident in his New Formalist work for an engagement with geometric deformation that marked the buildings he and his new partner John Burgee produced during the 1970s, what the critic Charles Jencks was to characterize as Late Modernism. Its visual economy, lack of pretension, and lack of superfluous architectural detailing forecast the attributes of the most assured body of work Johnson produced. The E. W. Howell Company was the general contractor.

LIBRARY/STUDY

New Canaan | CT
1980 | Philip Johnson

Johnson built the Library/Study as a personal retreat where he could concentrate on architectural design work. He explained his intention to Walter Wagner as exploring issues of space, scale, and light. Set on a downhill slope, the Library/Study is rectangular in plan and cubic in shape. Its implied geometric regularity is deformed by the inclusion of a cylindrical volume in one corner that, above the parapet line, becomes a truncated cone. The vertical protrusion of the cone is echoed by a slender, square chimney stack that rises on the diagonally opposite corner of the building. Johnson animated the static space of the cube geometrically by emphasizing the diagonal, which planimetrically expands the square into a golden rectangle. Internally, the truncated cone functions as a light chimney. Skylight is introduced as another element that animates static space by filling volumes, emphasizing walls as diverging rather than enclosing planes, and creating contrasting zones of light and dark in a single room. A single window frames a vista, converting the out-of-doors into a picture-like scene. Johnson's fascination with how geometry and daylight interact in constructing, and deconstructing, haptic sensations of spatiality is materialized in the Library/Study. Robertson, Fowler & Associates were structural engineers, Sanford Hess Associates were mechanical engineers, Claude R. Engle was the lighting consultant, and Louis Lee & Company was the general contractor.

GHOST HOUSE

New Canaan | CT

1984 | Philip Johnson

Positioned so that it is framed by the window in Johnson's Library/Study, the Ghost House is a steel framework screened with chain-link fencing, whose shape suggests a gabled house split in two. It is a site-specific work, incorporating the foundations of a no-longer-extant building. Johnson paid tribute in his choice of material to the Los Angeles architect Frank Gehry, who began to use chain link as an architectural material in the 1970s.

LINCOLN KIRSTEIN TOWER

New Canaan | CT

1985 | Philip Johnson

Johnson built this folly as a tribute to his friend, the dance impresario Lincoln Kirstein. It is a lookout tower, as well as a Neoplasticist exercise in advancing and receding planes and reentrant and salient angles. The tower's gestural composition evokes bodily movement and extension. Its construction of steel-reinforced concrete masonry units enabled Johnson to turn it into an ebullient exercise in cantilevering concrete block, a material without tensile strength that typically is used only in compression.

GATE HOUSE

Anticipating the transfer of his New Canaan homestead to the National Trust for Historic Preservation, Johnson designed a gatehouse to be used by the Trust as a visitors' orientation center. He and his associate John Manley designed the three-room building as a series of faceted and curved shapes derived from the wax sculptures of Frank Stella. As the critic Deborah Dietsch noted, Johnson played with experiences of perceptual disorientation in his design of an orientation center. The first of his deconstructionist works to be based on non-Euclidean geometry, the Gate House demonstrated Johnson's persistent fascination with what Jeffrey Kipnis described as warped planes, colliding shapes, and sensually evocative spaces. It also demonstrated his ability to extract more intensity from small buildings than larger, less tectonically articulate designs. The Gate House is constructed of two layers of steel mesh sandwiching a layer of polyurethane foam and sprayed externally with concrete. Ysrael A. Seinuk was the structural engineer, Claude R. Engle was the lighting consultant, and the Louis Lee Company was the

MR. AND MRS. G. E. PAINE, JR., HOUSE

Wellsboro | NY

1949 | Philip C. Johnson Associates

Jenkins and Mohney observe that the Paine House, following the Farney House, displayed Johnson's fascination with Mies's Resor House as a model. The Paine House was never published under Johnson's auspices, reflecting perhaps his dissatisfaction with the resolution of its design. Even so, its central glazed living space exhibited his predilection for static volumes and its detached guest wing represented what would become his characteristic means of accommodating multiple private spaces in the confines of the pavilion house type.

MR. AND MRS. JOHN DE MENIL HOUSE

3363 San Felipe Road | Houston | TX

1950 | Philip C. Johnson Associates with Landis Gores and Cowell & Neuhaus

The Menil House, built for the Franco-Texan art collectors and patrons Dominique Schlumberger and John de Menil, is a one-story house on a flat lot in the Houston subdivision of Briarwood. The house is configured around an open-air courtyard. It is closed on the north side facing the street, but open to the south through walls of glass that overlook a rear garden. The Menil House lacks the planimetric clarity of Johnson's early published houses. That, and John de Menil's decision to retain the couturier Charles James to design Surreal-influenced furniture and finishes for the interiors, resulted in the Menil House's exclusion from the canon of Johnson's work, despite Dominique and John de Menil's patronage. During the 1960s the Houston architects Howard Barnstone and Eugene Aubry added a steel-framed canvas canopy above the courtyard and remodeled the garage to serve as office and art storage space for Mr. and Mrs. de Menil's curatorial staff and collection. Aspects of the house are reflected in The Menil Collection art museum (1980–87), which Renzo Piano designed in Houston for Dominique de Menil after John de Menil's death in 1973. Since Dominique de Menil's death in 1997, the house has been owned by the Menil Foundation. It is intact and retains original finishes as well as hardware, lighting, kitchen, and plumbing equipment. The house was constructed by the Kaiser-Oaks Construction Company.

MRS. JOHN D. ROCKEFELLER 3RD GUEST HOUSE

242 East Fifty-second Street | New York | NY

1950 | Philip C. Johnson with Landis Gores and Frederick C. Genz

Designed for the New York collector and philanthropist Blanchette Hooker Rockefeller as a guest house and a place to display modern art, this one- and two-story house is a radical reconstruction of a long, narrow townhouse in midtown Manhattan. As Peter Reed observes, the front elevation appears to be based on a drawing by Mies van der Rohe for the Illinois Institute of Technology library. The ground floor is one room wide. A gallery—living room, entered from the street, overlooks an open-air courtyard spanned by a shallow reflecting pool. The walls, floor, and ceiling are white. Travertine stepping stones in the pool lead to a one-story bedroom at the rear of the site. The courtyard walls of the living room and bedroom are made of glass, so that the ground floor appears to be a continuous space outlined by the party walls of painted brick. Johnson designed much of the furniture for the house, as well as lighting fixtures and a luminous ceiling in consultation with Richard Kelly. Mrs. Rockefeller, a trustee and eventual president of The Museum of Modern Art, gave the house to the museum in 1958. The museum used it as a guest house until selling it in 1964 to Johnson's clients, Mr. and Mrs. Robert Leonhardt. The Eipel Engineering Company was the structural engineer.

MR. AND MRS. RICHARD HODGSON HOUSE

Ponus Ridge Road | New Canaan | CT

1951 | Philip C. Johnson Associates with Landis Gores

1956 | addition | Philip C. Johnson Associates

This one-story, flat-roofed house was built in two phases for Geraldine Reed and Richard Hodgson. Richard Hodgson, a graduate of the Harvard Business School, was president of Chromatic TV Labs when the house was built; he eventually became president of the Fairchild Camera and Instrument Corporation. The house is of brick bearing wall construction, with interior steel columns and a roof framed partially in steel and partially in wood. A central courtyard, open on the south, splits the house into parallel zones. Insertion of the courtyard enabled Johnson to create a sense of spaciousness and transparency while accommodating the kitchen, bedrooms, bathrooms, and studies of a family house. Johnson balanced the desire for transparency and spatial continuity with the practical requirements of designing a family house by adopting a pavilion plan. This isolated auxiliary rooms for the Hodgson's four children in a separate wing, built in a second phase in the 1950s, rather than trying to contain all the rooms in a single building, as at the Menil House. The use of black ceramic floor tiles and the implication that the wide reception hall was to double as the dining room reflected the influence of the Menil House. John Smith was the general contractor. The Hodgson House won an Honor Award from the American Institute of Architects in 1956.

MR. AND MRS. BURTON TREMAINE, JR., HOUSE

Madison | CT

1952 | alterations and additions | Philip C. Johnson Associates

Johnson rehabilitated a barn, dated to the 1770s and remodeled as a house in the early twentieth century, for Emily Hall and Burton G. Tremaine, who were important collectors of modern art. Like Johnson, Burton Tremaine, president of the Miller Company, a lighting systems manufacturer, was from Cleveland. The barn was cleared internally to become a single space, in which the historic timber framing and stone fireplaces were exposed and highlighted. Johnson replaced the forty-three-foot-long, south-facing side wall with wood-framed glass panels. These incorporated doors that opened to a new terrace. A freestanding counter at one end of the space contained kitchen equipment. Richard Kelly was the lighting consultant. Jenkins and Mohney identify this as one of a number of estate improvements Johnson carried out for Mr. and Mrs. Tremaine between 1952 and 1956.

MR. AND MRS. GEORGE C. ONETO HOUSE

Irvington-on-Hudson | NY

1951 | Philip C. Johnson Associates with Landis Gores

The Oneto House is a small, flat-roofed pavilion built on a shelf overlooking the Hudson River. The symmetrical exterior envelope encloses internal planning asymmetries that represent Johnson's effort to resolve potential conflicts between his desire for spatial openness and expansiveness and his clients' desire for the conventions of middle-class domesticity. Instead of an interior courtyard, Johnson used glass walls and terraces to expand indoor living space to the exterior. Offsetting the front of the house is a freestanding brick wall that shields the kitchen terrace from passersby and extends the lines of the house into the landscape. Interior partitions in the central living-dining room are finished with wood panels. The living-dining room and terraces are paved with flagstone. The Wolff Engineering Company was the structural engineer and Sears & Kopf were the mechanical engineers. In 1996 subsequent owners constructed additions to the house that altered it substantially. These were designed by Dennis Wedlick, a former employee of Johnson's.

SCHLUMBERGER ADMINISTRATION BUILDING

Schlumberger-Doll Research Center | Old Quarry Road | Ridgefield | CT
1952 | Philip C. Johnson Associates

John de Menil was in charge of Schlumberger Overseas and Schlumberger Surenco, two divisions of the Schlumberger oil field services corporation. His brother-in-law, Henri Doll, headed the corporation's research center, which Doll had established in Ridgefield, Connecticut, in the 1940s when Schlumberger operations were moved from Paris to the United States during World War II. Johnson designed this small, one-story, steel-framed building to contain the administrative offices of what is now the Schlumberger-Doll Research Center. The rectangularly planned building was designed to attach at one end to an existing one-story laboratory building. It was constructed above an underground parking garage. The scale, spatial organization, and architecture of the administration building are similar to those of the Hodgson House. Cellular offices are aligned, two per structural bay, along the side walls of the building, with larger executive offices at one end. A wide central bay extending through the building contains an open-air courtyard, a glass-walled library, and secretarial work stations. Corridors between the central bay and the offices are skylit. Along with extensive use of interior glass walls, skylighting was intended to enhance the ambiance of spatial openness in a closed, centrally air-conditioned building. The Eipel Engineering Company was the structural engineer, Richard Kelly was lighting consultant, James Fanning was the landscape architect, and Florence Knoll was the interior designer. Although the Houston architect Howard Barnstone expanded the Ridgefield complex with new research and office buildings between 1978 and 1985, the Administration Building remains in use by Schlumberger. The Schlumberger Administration Building won an Award of Merit from the American Institute of Architects in 1956.

MRS. ALICE BALL HOUSE

Oenoke Avenue | New Canaan | CT
1953 | Philip C. Johnson Associates

This small, flat-roofed, one-story house reiterates elements of the Oneto House, especially its use of a freestanding brick wall plane to punctuate external space. The Ball House attests to the constituency modern architecture attained in New Canaan in the 1950s, when Eliot Noyes, Marcel Breuer, John M. Johansen, John Black Lee, Frank Lloyd Wright, Edward Durell Stone, and Howard Barnstone, among others, designed single-family houses there that were similar in attitude and scale to those of Johnson's.

THE ABBY ALDRICH ROCKEFELLER SCULPTURE GARDEN

The Abby Aldrich Rockefeller Sculpture Garden is considered one of Johnson's masterpieces. It represents an original and highly refined application of Mies van der Rohe's practices for shaping modernist space to an urban garden meant for the exhibition of modern sculpture. Johnson was director of the Department of Architecture and Design at The Museum of Modern Art when the garden was designed and built. The garden occupies a space that was originally 110 feet wide and 202 feet long, on the north (rear) side of the original museum building, with frontage along East Fifty-fourth Street. It is separated from Fifty-fourth Street by a wall of gray brick, originally twelve feet high. From terraces on the south and west (adjacent to museum spaces), the garden steps down two feet. A long rectangular water channel, parallel to the Fifty-fourth Street wall, is divided into two offset segments by a stand of trees. This arbor subdivides the depressed portion of the garden into four zones in which works of sculpture can be exhibited. The paving consists of rectangular blocks of unpolished gray Vermont marble. Mirka Benes has documented the history of the sculpture garden's evolution; the landscape architect Laurie Olin has perceptively analyzed its formation and transformations. The garden was built as a memorial to Mrs. John D. Rockefeller, Jr., whose sons were important supporters of the museum. According to Alfred H. Barr, Jr., Nelson A. Rockefeller, president of the museum when Johnson began the project, was the donor. Johnson expanded the garden with the East Wing addition of 1964. It was modified during a subsequent expansion of the museum in 1984.

The Museum of Modern Art

11 West Fifty-third Street | New York | NY

1953 | Philip C. Johnson Associates with Landis Gores and George Hopkinson;

James Fanning | landscape architect

WHY SHOULD THE AIR AGE NOT HAVE THE GLOW OF THE RENAISSANCE AGE? THE
GRAND CENTRAL AND THE PENNSYLVANIA STATION, BEFORE THEY FELL OF EVIL
DAYS, WERE SPACES THAT MADE THE HEART SING, SPACES THAT NEVER GOT TOO
SMALL AS TRAFFIC EXPANDED, AS DID OUR AIRPORTS. WHAT WE HAVE LOST IS A
PUBLIC PASSION FOR GREATNESS. NO CATHEDRALS? NOT EVEN ANY GREAT

PUBLIC NUCLEAR PLANT? WHAT IS OUR GENERATION GOING VICARIOUSLY T
ENJOY AS IN OLD DAYS THE PALACE, THE CHURCH, OR THE ACROPOLIS? W
CANNOT ALL OF US ENJOY SLUM CLEARANCE AND PARKING LOTS. TH
QUESTIONS ARE RHETORICAL, THERE ARE NO ANSWERS. A CULTURE GETS TH
MONUMENTS IT DESIRES.

EAST WING, GARDEN WING, REMODELED SCULPTURE GARDEN, AND UPPER TERRACE

The Museum of Modern Art | New York | NY
1964 | Philip Johnson Associates
1984 | altered

Johnson's alterations and additions to The Museum of Modern Art consisted of a six-story, fifty-foot-wide annex facing Fifty-third Street on the east side of the original museum building, a new fire stair, a one-story, glass-faced corridor overlooking the Abby Aldrich Rockefeller Sculpture Garden that linked the East Wing to a new, two-story Garden Wing facing Fifty-fourth Street, and the raised Upper Terrace above the Garden Wing that extended the sculpture garden to the east. Johnson also reconfigured the ground floor of the original building, converting most of it into a spacious lobby that visually linked the Fifty-third Street entrance to the sculpture garden. This program grew out of an earlier Johnson scheme, prepared in 1958–59, for a boxy, solidly walled, eight-story building facing Fifty-fourth Street at the east end of the sculpture garden. The East Wing is faced with a curtain wall of black-painted steel and bronze-tinted solar glass. Johnson pursued his fascination with curvature by detailing the intersection of the curtain wall's horizontal spandrels and vertical mullions with quarter-round corners. Layers of shallow spatial recession animated the curtain wall faces of the wing. Johnson redesigned all the museum's gallery spaces. His most publicized interior was the Trustees Room on the top floor of the East Wing (1967). The eastward expansion of the sculpture garden behind the East Wing resulted in construction of the Upper Terrace, an unplanted roof deck paved with Vermont marble, sixteen feet above the level of the garden, used for the display of sculpture. Johnson's broad, turned, Schinkel-like flights of stairs connecting the garden and the terrace, and the elevated prospect of the garden available from the terrace, exemplified his notion of the "processional" element in architecture, an experientially based approach to design involving movement, perception, and bodily sensation. Zion & Breen were landscape architects for the garden. During the alterations and additions to the museum of 1980–84, the Garden Wing and Upper Terrace were reconstructed as a two-story building, eliminating the stairs and the open terrace. The fire stair Johnson added was also eliminated.

MR. AND MRS. ROBERT C. WILEY HOUSE

Sleepy Hollow Road | New Canaan | CT

1953 | Philip C. Johnson Associates

Confronting the dilemma of providing conventional domestic interiors and a structurally expressive, visually transparent modern living space, Johnson organized bedrooms and a children's play room in a raised basement of exposed rubble stone construction, embedded on three of its four sides in sloping terrain. The roof of what Johnson called the "podium" serves as a terrace, atop which a fifteen-foot-high, laminated timber-framed, flat-roofed cage, containing the living-dining-kitchen room, is cantilevered across the short dimension of the podium. The elevated living pavilion looks out onto a forest landscape. As at the Glass House, a circular swimming pool is juxtaposed with the rectilinearity of the house. Robert C. Wiley was Johnson's accountant and business associate. The Eipel Engineering Company was the structural engineer and Richard Kelly was the lighting consultant.

EZRA STOLLER © ESTO

EZRA STOLLER © ESTO

MR. AND MRS. RICHARD S. DAVIS HOUSE

1780 Shoreline Drive | Wayzata | MN

1954 | Philip C. Johnson Associates with Magney, Tussler & Setter

This one-story, two-part, pavilion-type house was designed for the collectors Phyllis Seaton Beckwith and Richard S. Davis. Richard Davis was a Harvard alumnus whose tenure had overlapped Johnson's in the early 1940s. At the time the house was built, Davis was curator of the Minneapolis Institute of Arts; he became director in 1956. Johnson clustered the kitchen, children's rooms, and two-car garage in the secondary part of the house, freeing the primary part for the owners' rooms and generous spaces for entertaining, which are separated with an interior, glass-walled winter garden. The two pavilions were arranged in an L-plan configuration. On the north (entrance front), they frame two sides of a motor court. On the east, they frame two sides of a limestone paved terrace containing a rectangular pool. The Davis House sits on a raised shelf overlooking Lake Minnetonka. The steel-framed, brick-walled house was finished with floors of Sicilian travertine. Interior partitions were of polished teak. Johnson designed the dining room chairs. The Eipel Engineering Company was the structural engineer, John Dillon was the mechanical engineer, and Richard Kelly consulted on the lighting design. The second owners of the house, Mr. and Mrs. David M. Winton, had Frank O. Gehry & Associates design a freestanding guest house on the property, completed in 1987.

METEOR CRATER PAVILION

Barringer Meteor Crater
Interstate 40 between Winslow and Flagstaff
Coconino County | AZ
1956 | Philip C. Johnson Associates

Isolated in its harsh desert landscape on the edge of Meteor Crater, this viewing pavilion was the replacement for a building by Johnson, completed in 1951 and destroyed in a windstorm in 1955. Its flatness and rectilinearity contrast with the dramatic topography of the crater rim, a sandstone and limestone upthrust, one hundred feet high, formed by the impact of a meteor that struck the high desert plateau and excavated the crater, which is 570 feet deep and over 4,000 feet in diameter. Although the setting is very different from Johnson's property in New Canaan, he pursued a similar strategy, playing the precision and civility of the pavilion against the emptiness and desolation of the landscape. As an observatory, Johnson's pavilion anticipated the ambitious earth art project begun by the artist James Turrell at Roden Crater, a cinder volcano crater north of Meteor Crater, in 1972. The clients, Emily Hall and Burton Tremaine, had Frank Lloyd Wright prepare a design for the structure in 1948 but chose to build Johnson's designs instead because they were more economical, according to Emily Tremaine's biographer, Kathleen Housley.

MR. AND MRS. ERIC H. BOISSONNAS HOUSE

Logan Road | New Canaan | CT

1956 | Philip C. Johnson Associates

This large, one-story house was built for Sylvie Schlumberger and Eric H. Boissonnas. Boissonnas was an official of Schlumberger; Mrs. Boissonnas was the sister of Dominique de Menil. Johnson planned the house within a grid of rectangular brick piers framing sixteen-foot square bays, eight wide and four deep, some containing garden courts and terraces. Looking out across the rear south-facing slope is the living room, a four-bay square twenty feet high and walled in glass. Axial composition and static spatiality are played against the hypnotic sensations generated by the expanses of undivided plate glass. Johnson accommodated the clients' eclectic array of furniture and designed the living room, in part, to contain Eric Boissonnas's pipe organ. Mr. and Mrs. Boissonnas sold the house in 1960 and commissioned Johnson to design a second house for them in France. The Eipel Engineering Company was the structural engineer.

CONGREGATION KNESES TIFERETH ISRAEL SYNAGOGUE

575 King Street | Port Chester | NY
1956 | Philip C. Johnson Associates

KTI Synagogue was designed as a combined sanctuary–social hall. It occupies a steel-framed rectangular volume 115 feet long, forty-seven feet wide, and forty feet high. Between the steel columns, the walls are constructed of five tiers of cast stone panels, each eight feet tall, with each row offset from the row above. Vertical slots between the panels, seven inches wide, are glazed with stained glass. From the center of KTI's long front, a freestanding, vaulted, elliptical entrance vestibule projects. A small, vaulted service wing is attached to the rear of the hall, on axis with the entrance vestibule. A low, demountable partition, framing one side of the passage connecting the vestibule and the rear wing, screens the 300-seat sanctuary from the social hall. The social hall and sanctuary are lit by the stained-glass slot windows. Suspended beneath the ceiling is a secondary ceiling of plaster handkerchief vaults spanning each of the structural bays. Against the back wall of the raised bema was a wire sculpture by Ibram Lassaw that is no longer in place. The Eipel Engineering Company was structural engineer, Richard Kelly the lighting consultant, John Johansen the stained-glass consultant, and Charles Middeleer the landscape architect. KTI Synagogue, like the Guest House remodeling and the Boissonnas House, marked Johnson's effort to explore the application of neoclassical compositional and space-shaping practices to modern architecture. Trees planted on either side of the entrance vestibule now obscure the front of the building.

MR. AND MRS. ROBERT C. LEONHARDT HOUSE

Lloyd's Neck | NY

1956 | Philip C. Johnson Associates

To configure this steel-framed, brick-faced, flat-roofed house to its waterfront site on the north shore of Long Island, Johnson organized living spaces in a pair of narrow parallel bars. A two-story bar containing bedrooms slides into the site. Sliding forward toward the view of the water, caged within an exposed steel bridging structure, is a long, glass-walled living and dining room, elevated above the downhill slope. Johnson cited Mies van der Rohe's sketch for a house on a hillside of about 1934 as the source for the design of the living room wing, with its diagonal chords. The owners, Mr. and Mrs. Leonhardt, bought the Rockefeller Guest House in 1964. In the 1990s, subsequent owners of the Leonhardt House extensively altered, refaced, and re-roofed the house to give it a more conventional appearance. The Eipel Engineering Company was the structural engineer, and Fred S. Dubin was the mechanical engineer.

EZRA STOLLER © ESTO

MASTER PLAN UNIVERSITY OF ST. THOMAS; STRAKE HALL, JONES HALL, AND WELDER HALL

3812-3900 Yoakum Boulevard | Houston | TX

1957–59 | Philip C. Johnson Associates with Bolton & Barnstone

Dominique and John de Menil persuaded the board of trustees of the small, ten-year-old University of St. Thomas, and its president, the Rev. Vincent J. Guinan of the Congregation of St. Basil, to retain Philip Johnson to prepare a campus master plan in 1956. Johnson's plan, adopted in 1957, encompassed three blocks in an early twentieth-century residential neighborhood. He proposed backing simply composed, two-story, steel-framed buildings onto surrounding streets so that they might face a central campus green space. The green is outlined with a two-story, steel-framed walkway structure, to which all the buildings are attached, an arrangement Johnson likened to Thomas Jefferson's Academical Village for the University of Virginia. Johnson proposed that a chapel be built at the north end of the site as a focal point and that the south end contain a tightly clustered group of women's dormitories. Johnson designed three initial buildings: Jones Hall, containing an auditorium and gallery, and the first phase of Strake Hall, a classroom building, both completed in 1958; and Welder Hall, the student center, completed in 1959. Severud-Elstad-Kruger was the structural engineer, and Fred S. Dubin was the mechanical engineer. During the 1960s, Jones Hall was the site of the university's Gallery of Fine Arts, directed by Jermayne MacAgy and, after her death in 1964, Dominique de Menil. Johnson designed what was to become the Rothko Chapel for Dominique and John de Menil as the university's chapel in 1964–67. It was to have been built at the south end of the campus, in place of the dormitories. (The chapel was built off-campus in 1970–71 after Johnson resigned the commission and the university determined it could not take responsibility for the project.) Between the mid-1960s and the early 2000s, the campus was built-out with two-story buildings that conform in their dimensions, architectural expression, and site-planning conventions to the principles of Johnson's master plan. These were designed by various Houston architects, with Johnson's office serving as consulting architect. Welder Hall was remodeled as a classroom building in 1978, losing its two-story-high central space. In 1997, Johnson completed the Chapel of St. Basil at the north end of the campus. The University of St. Thomas was Johnson's first multibuilding complex and, with the Tourre House, the last he designed according to Miesian practices. As built, the campus is more spatially open, and more uniform, than proposed in Johnson's 1957 master plan.

HARVEY RESIDENCE HALL

Seton Hill College | Seton Hill Drive | Greensburg | PA
1957 | Philip C. Johnson Associates

Built for a small college operated by the Pennsylvania Sisters of Charity, a Roman Catholic religious order, this is a three-story bar building. Harvey Hall is of reinforced concrete frame construction. Double-sash window units and brick spandrel and end wall panels in-fill the exposed concrete frame, as in some of Mies van der Rohe's less publicized buildings at the Illinois Institute of Technology. In 1990 Johnson designed a fine arts center for the college, but it was not built.

ASIA HOUSE

112 East Sixty-fourth Street | New York | NY
1959 | Philip C. Johnson Associates

Built during the presidency of John D. Rockefeller 3rd to provide exhibition, auditorium, and office space for the recently founded Asia Society, this seven-story building occupies the former site of townhouses on Manhattan's Upper East Side. According to Philip Johnson's associate John Manley, Richard Foster proposed turning a standard curtain wall inside-out to produce the crisply panelized façade of spandrel and vision glass set in an armature of white-painted steel. The result is like the cabinetwork in Johnson's Miesian buildings. Precise indentations between panels produce shadow lines, subtly energizing what would otherwise be a flat, reflective exterior surface. The Eipel Engineering Company was the structural engineer, and Fred Sutton was the mechanical engineer. After the Asia Society moved to new quarters in 1981, Asia House became the headquarters of the Russell Sage Foundation and the Robert Sterling Clark Foundation.

THE FOUR SEASONS

With the Glass House and the Abby Aldrich Rockefeller Sculpture Garden, the Four Seasons Restaurant ranks as one of the outstanding works of Johnson's early career. The client was Joseph Baum, whose firm, Restaurant Associates, operated the most imaginatively designed restaurants in New York in the 1950s and 1960s. The Four Seasons occupies the low rear wing behind the Seagram Building tower. It is accessible from East Fifty-second Street through a raised basement as well as from the lobby of the Seagram Building. The restaurant contains two large rooms: a bar and grill on the Fifty-second Street side of the wing and a dining room on the Fifty-third Street side. Between them, concealed from public view, is the restaurant's kitchen. Each public room is approximately fifty-eight feet square and twenty feet high. An especially perceptive description of the restaurant, published in *Interiors* magazine in December 1959, detailed the ways in which Johnson and his collaborators constructed modern interior settings that exuded luxury, sophistication, refinement, and power. Johnson explored for the first time in a completed work a broad range of interior design effects that would mark his work of the 1960s. Especially notable details were his design of the stair handrails and light-diffusing beaded draperies. Karl Linn was the landscape architect for interior plantings, Richard Kelly the lighting consultant, Emil Antonucci the graphic design consultant, and Ada Louise and Garth Huxtable the designers of tableware and serving equipment. William Pahlmann Associates were interior design consultants. The sculptor Richard Lippold executed a large piece above the bar composed of suspended bronze rods. A tapestry by Pablo Picasso and a painting by Joan Miró were installed in reception spaces. In 1989 the New York City Landmarks Preservation Commission designated the Seagram Building and the Four Seasons Restaurant as protected historical sites.

Seagram Building | 99 East Fifty-second Street | New York | NY
1959 | Philip Johnson with William Pahlmann Associates

A STYLE IS NOT A SET OF RULES OR SHACKLES, AS SOME OF MY COLLEAGUES
SEEM TO THINK. A STYLE IS A CLIMATE IN WHICH TO OPERATE, A SPRINGBOARD
TO LEAP FURTHER INTO THE AIR. THE ONUS OF DESIGNING A NEW STYLE ANY
TIME ONE DESIGNS A NEW BUILDING IS HARDLY FREEDOM; IT IS TOO HEAVY A
LOAD EXCEPT FOR THE GREATEST OF MICHELANGELOS OR WRIGHTS. STRICT
STYLE DISCIPLINE HINDERED NOT IN THE SLIGHTEST THE CREATORS OF THE
PARTHENON, NOR DID THE POINTED ARCH CONFINE THE DESIGNERS OF AMIENS.

MUNSON-WILLIAMS-PROCTOR INSTITUTE

310 Genesee Street | Utica | NY

1960 | Philip Johnson Associates with Bice & Baird

The Munson-Williams-Proctor Institute is a three-story, symmetrically composed art museum and performance center. The pavilion-type building is set in an open court on a site that slopes down from Genesee Street. The ground level, containing an auditorium, offices, support spaces, and the rear-facing parking lot entrance, is walled in glass. The upper two stories, entered from Genesee Street and containing the institute's art museum, are solidly walled with Canadian granite. Bronze-clad, reinforced concrete columns and girders carry the building's roof and floor plates, freeing the interior of structural columns. The museum levels are organized as a sequence of gallery rooms encircling the top-lit, two-story-high entrance court. A cantilevered scissor stair with symmetrically opposing runs connects the floor of the court with a second-level walkway hung from the roof. At the time the institute was planned and built, Richard B. K. McLanathan was the director of its art museum. Lev Zetlin was the structural engineer, Fred S. Dubin Associates were mechanical engineers, and the George A. Fuller Company was the general contractor. Bolt, Beranek & Newman were acoustical consultants, Richard Kelly was the lighting consultant, Knoll Associates were interior designers, Elaine Lustig was the graphic designer, and Charles Middeleer was the landscape architect. The Munson-Williams-Proctor Institute was Johnson's first freestanding art museum. It was built adjacent to Fountain Elms, an Italianate villa-type house of 1850. Johnson abandoned his dependence on Miesian practices at the Munson-Williams-Proctor to explore the use of neo-classical typologies as models for modern civic institutions in what came to be called the New Formalism. An addition of 1995 connected Johnson's building and Fountain Elms.

ROOFLESS CHURCH

North Street | New Harmony | IN
1960 | Philip Johnson Associates

Jane Blaffer Owen of Houston, a friend of Dominique and John de Menil, commissioned the design and construction of the Roofless Church, a seminal example of what came to be called an "art chapel," through the Robert Lee Blaffer Trust. Jane Owen's husband, Kenneth Dale Owen, was a great-great-grandson of the Welsh industrialist and social reformer Robert Owen, who had acquired the southwestern Indiana town of New Harmony, on the Wabash River, in 1825, from the Harmony Society, a German religious community led by Johann Georg Rapp. Robert Owen's effort to found an ideal community in New Harmony dissolved by 1827. But his remarkable children, including the social reformer Robert Dale Owen, a founder of the Smithsonian Institution, and the geologists David Dale Owen and Richard Owen, stayed. Following her marriage, Jane Owen committed her resources to the preservation of New Harmony. She built the Roofless Church as an ecumenical center and as a shrine to the Harmony Society. It is an open-air, brick-walled enclosure set on a flat site on the west edge of New Harmony overlooking the Wabash. Johnson evoked the classical temenos, a walled, open-air, sacred enclosure, in his design. As at the Abby Aldrich Rockefeller Sculpture Garden, Johnson used islands of planting to subdivide the granite-paved court. Centered at the south end of the enclosed court, on axis with a north-facing ceremonial gateway, is a wood-ribbed, shingle-surfaced, continuously curved baldachin sheltering Jacques Lipchitz's bronze *Our Lady of Joy*. The baldachin displayed Johnson's fascination with the topological distortions achieved by complexly curving a plane surface. Johnson's associate John Manley remembers that one of Johnson's draftsmen spent an entire year calculating the mathematics of the baldachin's curvature. The shape was generated from six intersecting circles surrounding a central circle, inscribed in a blocky Greek cross, a figure that refers to the ground plan of the Harmonist church. Johnson likened the resulting volumetric shape to a rose, another Harmonist symbol. Traylor Brothers Construction Company was the general contractor. Jacques Lipchitz modeled the gilded figures installed at the north gateway. A grass lawn has replaced most of the paving in the enclosed court. Jane Owen subsequently built the Atheneum (1979) and the Sarah Campbell Blaffer Pottery Studio (1978) nearby. Both were designed by Richard Meier. The Roofless Church won an Honor Award from the American Institute of Architects in 1961.

TAYLOR HALL, GARRISON HALL, AND ROTHSCHILD HALL

Sarah Lawrence College | Bronxville | NY

1960 | Philip Johnson Associates

Johnson designed the three-story dormitories, housing 150 students in one- and two-person rooms, as a precast, arcuated concrete frame in-filled with a brick curtain wall and tall casement and awning windows. The narrow, rectangularly planned building is divided into three bars. These are offset in plan as they step down the sloping site. A glazed stair and entrance well occur at each offset.

COMPUTING LABORATORY

Brown University | 180 George Street | Providence | RI
1961 | Philip Johnson Associates with Conrad Green

Johnson designed the Brown University Computing Laboratory as a modern stoa or loggia that combined practical uses with a memorial dedication. The laboratory was built with a gift from Thomas J. Watson, Jr., a Brown alumnus who was president and subsequently chairman of IBM, and his mother, Jeanette Kittridge Watson, as a memorial to Thomas J. Watson, the founder of IBM. IBM facilitated the university's acquisition of the computer the laboratory was built to hold. The building is of precast concrete construction. A red granite aggregate was mixed in the concrete, enabling the laboratory to defer to the granite surfaces of older university buildings. The pavilion-like laboratory is set back from the street. The two-story-high, glass-faced entrance lobby has a panelized interior wall on which a tapestry by Arshille Gorky, donated by Johnson, was installed.

AMON CARTER MUSEUM OF WESTERN ART (NOW THE AMON CARTER MUSEUM)

3501 Camp Bowie Boulevard | Fort Worth | TX

1961 | Philip Johnson Associates with Joseph R. Pelich

1964 | addition, Joseph R. Pelich with Philip Johnson Associates; demolished 1999

1977 | addition, Johnson/Burgee Architects; demolished 1999

John de Menil was responsible for introducing Philip Johnson to Ruth Carter Johnson (subsequently Stevenson), daughter of the Fort Worth newspaper publisher and entrepreneur Amon G. Carter and a trustee of the charitable foundation her father had established. In 1958 the foundation commissioned Johnson to design this small museum as a memorial to Amon Carter, in which his collection of works by the American artists Frederic Remington and Charles M. Russell could be exhibited. Johnson used the classical stoa as a model for the Amon Carter museum. He located the rectangular, two-story, steel-framed building at the crest of a sloping, triangular site. In front of the building's east-facing glass curtain wall, he laid out a stepped sequence of broad terraces that overlook Amon Carter Square Park and, in the distance, the skyline of downtown Fort Worth. Johnson faced the museum with fossilized limestone, a stone quarried in Texas that has the texture of travertine. Framing the inset glass curtain wall are limestone-cased piers. Their exaggerated taper and spike-like points led William Jordy to describe them as looking like the backdrop for a ballet performance, provoking the *Architectural Review*'s sarcastic characterization of the New Formalist phase of Johnson's career as his "ballet school manner." The cruciform piers and the arcuated fascia they engage introduce shallow concave volumes, plastically activating the entrance screen and giving the small, isolated pavilion the presence and historical resonance Johnson felt it needed to figure as a civic monument. Lev Zetlin was the structural engineer, Jaros, Baum & Bolles the mechanical engineers, Richard Kelly the lighting consultant, and the Menils' curatorial mentor, Jermayne MacAgy, the exhibition consultant. Johnson's office was responsible for the original interior and landscape design. Thomas S. Byrne was the general contractor. Johnson developed a close relationship with the museum and served several terms as a trustee. The museum's first director, Mitchell A. Wilder, defined an imaginative curatorial program based on Amon Carter's collection that, in time, required two sets of additions, which consumed the rest of the museum's small, buildable site. In 1996, the front curtain wall of bronze-tinted, single-pane, plate glass was replaced with insulating reflective glass, inhibiting the transparency of the original volume. Downhill from the Carter, to the east, are the Kimbell Art Museum by Louis I. Kahn (1972) and the Modern Art Museum of Fort Worth by Tadao Ando (2002).

MUSEUM FOR THE ROBERT WOODS BLISS
COLLECTION OF PRE-COLUMBIAN ART

Dumbarton Oaks | 1703 Thirty-second Street, N.W. | Washington | DC
1963 | Philip Johnson Associates

Although Johnson had experimented with circular figures and cylindrical volumes since the late 1940s, the museum for the Robert Woods Bliss Collection of Pre-Columbian Art, an addition to Dumbarton Oaks, a nineteenth-century country house set in a sixteen-acre park in Georgetown, was his first occasion to give form to this fascination in a constructed building. Robert Woods Bliss, a retired U.S. diplomat, and his wife, Mildred Barnes Bliss, gave their estate, Dumbarton Oaks, to Harvard University in 1940 to serve as a center for scholarly research on Byzantine and Medieval cultures as well as garden design (Beatrix Farrand designed the ten-acre gardens of Dumbarton Oaks for Mrs. Bliss in the 1920s). Johnson's gallery was designed on commission from Dumbarton Oaks's director, John S. Thacher, with Mr. and Mrs. Bliss's approval, to display Bliss's collection of Pre-Columbian artifacts from Mexico, Central, and South America. A free-standing addition to a new wing of the house (designed in the neo-Georgian style by Frederic Rhinelander King), it is a glass-walled pavilion tightly circumscribed with planting. Johnson evoked Byzantine and Turkish spatial themes in his circular version of a nine-square plan and in the low saucer domes capping each bay, although the combination of circular geometry and thick cylindrical columns was derived from the late work of Frank Lloyd Wright. In its conception as a sequence of glass-walled spaces in a landscape setting, the gallery can be compared to the Glass House. In its modular organization and emphasis on sensual experience, it can be compared to the Pavilion and the remodeled Guest House. The curvilinear shapeliness of the galleries (here, it was in the roof zone that a plane surface was plastically deformed to produce curved volumes), richly detailed finishes, the incorporation of water and vegetation in the voids between the circular galleries, and the use of transparent Lucite vitrines to exhibit objects created intense, and to judge from contemporary critiques, destabilizing erotic sensations. An unsigned article in *Architectural Forum* described the museum as "post-modern" and used coy rhetoric to insinuate the presence of a homosexual sensibility. The British *Architectural Review* was indignant at its theatricality. The most thoughtful critique, by the planner Stanley M. Sherman, appeared in the *AIA Journal*. Sherman discerned in the museum a static superficiality that yielded little to visitors' experience, once past the initial impressions; the building functioned more as an exercise in spatializing inversion than as an art museum. Sherman probed the dilemma that arrested Johnson's formalist experiments of the 1960s. His effort to Dionysianize the Apollonian at Dumbarton Oaks, like his efforts to generate shapes from planes, merge Miesian transparency with Wrightian mass and volume, and invest modern architecture with historical resonance involved syntheses that were willful rather than dialectical, for which buildings served as convenient pretexts rather than material and programmatic sources. Lev Zetlin & Associates were structural engineers, Jaros, Baum & Bolles were mechanical and electrical engineers, Richard Kelly was the lighting consultant, and the George A. Fuller Company was general contractor.

MONASTERY WING, ST. ANSELM'S ABBEY

4501 South Dakota Avenue, N.E. | Washington | DC

1963 | Philip Johnson Associates

The portion of this design that was constructed, a monastery for members of the English Benedictine Congregation, a Roman Catholic religious order that operates St. Anselm's Abbey School, was built during Father Alban Boutwood's tenure as abbot. An oversailing second-story, faced with precast concrete panels, rides above the elevated ground floor, carried on tapered, one-story cruciform columns. Lev Zetlin & Associates were structural engineers, and John McShain was the general contractor. Planning for a new complex on the congregation's forty-acre site in northeast Washington accompanied the elevation of St. Anselm's Priory to abbey status in 1961. Johnson's monastery wing was designed to link an existing chapel to a new abbey church, which was not built. The church was to be supported on a network of tapered, sculpturally articulated concrete columns and buttresses that formed the ninety-foot-tall, vaulted roof shell of the nave. Daylight, modulated by stained-glass curtain walls, was to have filtered into the church from either end and from wall planes layered between the columns and buttresses.

RADIO WRVA STUDIO

200 North Twenty-second Street | Richmond | VA

1968 | Budina & Freeman; Philip Johnson, consulting architect

Johnson was consulting architect on the design of a broadcast studio and office building for Radio WRVA; Wiley & Wilson were structural and mechanical engineers. Although located in Richmond's Church Hill district, an early nineteenth-century center city neighborhood that Paul S. Dulaney described in his book *The Architecture of Historic Richmond* as Richmond's equivalent of Georgetown or Beacon Hill, Johnson and Budina & Freeman treated the long, flat-roofed building as a modernist exception to Church Hill's historic fabric. The exterior shell of the pavilion-type building is of bush-hammered precast concrete. Openings are floor-to-ceiling slits, inserted into the wall planes with rounded corners. A slender, reinforced concrete pylon contained the station's transmitting and relay equipment.

Bequests from Mary Frances Sheldon and her brother, Adams Bromley Sheldon, provided the University of Nebraska, Lincoln, with funds to build an art museum. The Sheldons' gift stipulated that the university hire an architect of international stature; Philip Johnson was selected because he was a collector who could balance the requirements of art exhibition with the desire to create an architecturally distinctive building. Mrs. A. B. Sheldon, a member of the university's galleries coordinating committee, was closely involved with the design and appointment of the building. Like Johnson's other New Formalist work, the Sheldon Art Gallery is a symmetrically composed, boxlike building faced with sculptural piers that die into a repeating band of flattened arches. The glazed central bay contains the Great Hall, a fifty-foot-wide lobby, thirty feet high, spanned by cantilevered scissor stairs, like those in the Munson-Williams-Proctor Institute, that connect second-floor galleries across the Great Hall. Johnson continued the pier and arch system of the exterior into the Great Hall, rhythmically articulating its side walls and shaping ceiling coffers inset with gold-leaf plates. The exterior walls and those of the Great Hall are faced with Roman travertine. Double layers of gallery rooms fill the windowless bays. The north bay contains offices and support spaces on the ground floor; the south bay contains a 300-seat auditorium on the ground floor. Galleries for the permanent collection were finished with carpeted wall and floor surfaces. Aligned doorways that construct long views through the galleries, including views across the Great Hall, compensate for their lack of windows. The museum is set on a raised grass terrace on the university's campus. A sculpture garden, designed by the Houston architects Caudill Rowlett Scott, was installed to the west of the building in 1970. Johnson sought to construct monumentality through use of symmetry, grand scale, and honorific materials. He assigned special importance to the "elevating" experiences of ascending, descending, and crossing the stair-bridge, and the space-making properties of the aligned interior openings. Johnson's effort to construct static space, then animate it, is a recurring theme at the Sheldon. Like his fascination with spatializing planarity in much of his New Formalist work or spatializing inversion at Dumbarton Oaks, this hidden narrative on the erotic sensations of bodily displacement and projection recalls William Jordy's observation that Johnson's "classical" work of the early 1960s possesses a dream-like undercurrent. Lev Zetlin & Associates were structural engineers, Jaros, Baum & Bolles were mechanical engineers, and the Olson Construction Company was the general contractor. Johnson's influence on the Sheldon's sense of institutional style is evident from the design of the catalogue of the inaugural exhibition, which was the work of the graphic designer Elaine Lustig.

University of Nebraska, Lincoln
Twelfth Street and R Street | Lincoln | NE
1963 | Philip Johnson Associates with Hazen & Robinson

SHELDON MEMORIAL ART GALLERY

ARCHITECTURE, ONE WOULD THINK, HAS ITS OWN VALIDITY. IT NEEDS NO REFERENCE TO ANY OTHER DISCIPLINE TO MAKE IT VIABLE OR TO JUSTIFY ITS VALUE. WE MIGHT EVEN QUESTION WHETHER WORDS LIKE *VALUE* OR *MORALS* ARE APPLICABLE TO AN ARCHITECTURAL STYLE. THE INTERNATIONAL STYLE, FOR EXAMPLE, NEEDS NO ONE TO SAY IT WAS GOOD OR IT WAS BAD. GREEK AND GOTHIC STYLES WERE LOVED AND REVILED THROUGHOUT SUBSEQUENT AGES, AND NEITHER OPINION AFFECTED THE ARCHITECTURE ITSELF, BUT WERE COM-MENTS RATHER ON THE STATE OF MIND OF THE LOVER OR THE REVILER.

MR. AND MRS. HENRY C. BECK, JR., HOUSE

10210 Strait Lane | Dallas | TX
1964 | Philip Johnson Associates

Occupying a large lot in the Preston Hollow section of north Dallas near houses designed by Frank Lloyd Wright, Harwell Hamilton Harris, Edward Durell Stone, and O'Neil Ford, this house for Patricia Davis and Henry C. Beck, Jr., was based on plans prepared by the San Francisco architect Gardner A. Dailey. According to Frank Welch, Johnson recast Dailey's plans, organizing the ground floor with axes and cross-axes of movement and view that converge on a central reception hall containing twin curved stairs. Reception and service rooms, secondary spaces, and secondary buildings extend outward from this core, giving the house an irregular perimeter that Johnson sought to organize with a tiered system of precast concrete piers and arches derived from the design of his Pavilion. In its expansiveness the Beck House evokes Prussian neoclassical villa complexes. Johnson's effort to synthesize an upper-income domestic program, modern construction materials and techniques, and historical resonance — suburban sprawl versus classical decorum — was not rigorous. Henry C. Beck was an officer of his family-owned construction company. Mrs. Beck's sister was married to the brother of Jane Blaffer Owen of Houston, who recommended Johnson to Mr. and Mrs. Beck.

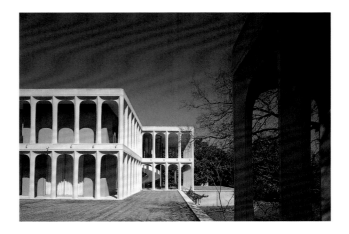

MR. AND MRS. ERIC H. BOISSONNAS HOUSE

Cap Bénat | Côte d'Azur | France
1964 | Philip Johnson Associates

After leaving the Schlumberger corporation in 1958, Eric Boissonnas joined his brother to develop Flaine, an Alpine ski resort in Haute-Savoie designed by Boissonnas's former New Canaan neighbor, Marcel Breuer, and Breuer's partner, Robert F. Gatje. On moving back to France from the United States, Sylvie and Eric Boissonnas commissioned Johnson to design a vacation house on the French Riviera, on a hilly site overlooking the Mediterranean. As Olga Gueft observed, Johnson treated the small compound as landscape design, positioning a slate-paved, canopy-covered, open-air court as the house's central living space. This is approached from a large, walled entrance courtyard that overlaps the roofed court at one corner. A long, walled outdoor passage connects the entrance court to two guest houses that step down the slope of the hill. A glass-walled pavilion that serves as an indoor living room, a kitchen-dining-service wing, and a master bedroom pavilion intersect three sides of the roofed court, leaving the fourth, south, side open to the sea. Working with the structural engineer Lev Zetlin, Johnson took advantage of the European propensity for building houses of reinforced concrete. Each of the enclosed pavilions is carried on external concrete columns (the living room pavilion on four centered columns). The canopy above the roofed court is a curved plane, a thin, hyperbolic paraboloid concrete "sail" supported at its four corners on tapered cylindrical columns. The disposition of windows and walls reflects not only the principal views but the need to shelter spaces from the mistral winds. By focusing on the house's site and avoiding historic models and monumentality, Johnson achieved a balance between program, construction, and architectural expression that is much more assured than in his other works of the early and mid-1960s.

EZRA STOLLER © ESTO

EW YORK STATE THEATER

During the spring of 1964, three major cultural buildings in New York City
designed by Johnson were dedicated: the additions to the MoMA, the New York
State Pavilion at the 1964–65 World's Fair, and the New York State Theater at
Lincoln Center for the Performing Arts. These marked recognition of Johnson as a
major American architect in his own city. Nelson A. Rockefeller was involved to
varying degrees in each project: as chairman of MoMA in 1958 when Johnson first
began work on its expansion, and after 1959 as governor of New York State, which
sponsored construction of the theater and the pavilion. The theater was built to
house the New York City Ballet, whose cofounders, the choreographer George
Balanchine and the impresario Lincoln Kirstein, had a long history of involvement
with Johnson in New York cultural circles, and the Lincoln Center Music Theater.
According to Edgar Young's history of Lincoln Center, Balanchine and Kirstein had
strong opinions on how the theater should represent itself to its public. The theater
building was boxlike in shape and clad in travertine. Except for the glass curtain
wall inset in the front portico, most of the rest of the building was windowless. The
2,729-seat theater was configured in an elliptical plan; continental seating was
installed on the orchestra level. Above the orchestra were five balcony tiers. A
large, tall stage house was bracketed by side-stage support spaces. Generous public circulation spaces emanated from the fifty-foot-high Grand Promenade on the
first tier level, one floor above the front entrance. The promenade was surrounded
by walkways at the levels of the upper seating tiers, which were suspended from
the roof structure on exposed steel cables. The New York State Theater represented Johnson's boldest effort to invent modernist analogues to classical architectural and decorative conventions. It projected a social vision of the theater's
audiences as glamorous urban elites whose public rituals occurred in a setting that
assimilated the classical to the modern, much as Balanchine's style of choreogra-
phy did. Johnson sought to explore the contradictions inherent in this program of
assimilation, especially in his witty attempt to produce decorative details that could
be read as Pop Art.

Lincoln Center for the Performing Arts | New York | NY
1964 | Philip Johnson Associates

MY PARTICULAR, INDIVIDUAL, NOT-TO-BE-COPIED METHOD IS TO SEARCH FOR THE REESTABLISHMENT OF ELEGANCE. I WOULD, WITHIN THE CONFINING LIMITATIONS OF OUR ERA, CREATE SOME TINY OASES OF MARBLE AND GOLD WHEREVER I CAN. THEY WOULD NOT BE LARGE, BUT THE HALLS, THE SUITES, THE FOUNTAINS, THE TERRACES WOULD BE AS GRANDIOSE AS THE CONFINING MORES OF OUR CENTURY WILL ALLOW. IT IS OBVIOUSLY NOT FOR ME TO MAKE THE AWESOME PILES OF LE CORBUSIER NOR HAVE I THE SPLENDID DISCIPLINE OF MIES VAN DER ROHE. NOR CAN I IMAGINE WHO IN THE SECOND GENERATION CAN FILL THEIR SHOES. BUT FOR ONE I DO NOT NEED TO CARE WHAT THEY DO. THE PROBLEM OF OUR GENERATION IS OURS. AND I WOULD LIKE SOME TINY PLACE IN THE SEARCH FOR THE ANSWERS.

Structural engineers for the New York State Theater were Severud Elstad Krueger Associates, mechanical engineers were Syska & Hennessy, the theater consultants were Ben Schlanger and Werner Gabler, the stage consultants were Donald Oenslager and Walter Unruh, the acoustical consultant was Vilhelm Lassen Jordan, the lighting consultant was Richard Kelly, and the general contractor was the Turner Construction Company. The artists Jasper Johns and Lee Bontecou were responsible for installations of works of art commissioned by Johnson and paid for by the Albert A. List Foundation. Pieces by other notable modern artists were installed under Johnson's direction. Johnson donated the pair of monumental Carrara marble figures in the Grand Promenade, enlargements of works by Elie Nadelman. In 1981–82, Johnson/Burgee, in collaboration with the acoustician Cyril M. Harris, Severud-Perrone-Szegezdy-Sturm, and Edwards & Zuck, carried out modifications to the performance space, including a new proscenium and an enlarged orchestra pit, to improve acoustical performance and dampen mechanical noises. Nonetheless by the end of the 1990s, Lincoln Center was examining the need to remodel the New York State Theater spatially and acoustically to make it more suitable for opera and to equip it with a backstage.

LINCOLN CENTER PLAZA AND FOUNTAIN

Lincoln Center for the Performing Arts | New York | NY
1964 | Philip Johnson Associates

NEW YORK STATE PAVILION

1964–1965 World's Fair | Flushing Meadows–Corona Park | Queens | NY
1964 | Philip Johnson and Richard Foster
1982 | interior renovation | Johnson/Burgee Architects

Dedicated the day before the New York State Theater, the New York State Pavilion was the largest state pavilion at the 1964–65 World's Fair and one of the few buildings to survive the exposition. Rather than conceiving the pavilion as a building, Johnson treated it as a circular, open-air plaza, 190 feet in diameter, paved with a map of New York State. Twelve hollow, reinforced concrete columns, one hundred feet high, supported a multicolored radial canopy, 300 feet in diameter at its widest, that shaded the plaza and an encircling, elliptically planned, one-story building with a continuous pedestrian terrace on top. To either side of the entrance to the pavilion were a cylindrical theater, the Circarama, and three cylindrical concrete columns carrying circular viewing platforms stationed at different heights. Johnson commissioned Peter Agostini, John Chamberlain, Robert Indiana, Ellsworth Kelly, Roy Lichtenstein, Alexander Liberman, Robert Mallory, Robert Rauschenberg, James Rosenquist, and Andy Warhol to install works of art on the exterior of the Circarama. At the time of the pavilion's completion, critics identified it as an example of Pop architecture, reflecting Johnson's awareness of current trends in contemporary U.S. art. The pavilion also embodied his interest in shaping open-air public space, collecting subsidiary structures beneath a tall canopy, and his fascination with circular geometries and expressive construction. Lev Zetlin & Associates were structural engineers, Syska & Hennessy were mechanical engineers, and Zion & Breen were landscape architects.

EZRA STOLLER © ESTO

EZRA STOLLER © ESTO

EZRA STOLLER © ESTO

EPIDEMIOLOGY AND PUBLIC HEALTH BUILDING

Yale University | 50 College Street | New Haven | CT
1964 | Philip Johnson and The Office of Douglas Orr

This eight-story building overlooks the Oak Street Connector, a depressed freeway, on a southern extension of Yale's campus that formed around the Yale Medical School and Yale–New Haven Hospital. Built to contain laboratories for scientific research, the upper six floors of the Epidemiology Building are carried on thick structural piers (containing mechanical and service chases in their hollow cores) above a two-story-high, recessed, glass-walled base. Secondary projecting bays alongside the piers contain small slot windows. The building is faced with a light-toned sandstone. It was built on property that the university acquired from the New Haven Redevelopment Authority, which had cleared a wide swath of real estate to facilitate freeway construction and the urban renewal of older, low-income, minority neighborhoods with upper-middle-income housing and new territory for institutional expansion.

MR. AND MRS. JAMES GEIER HOUSE

9100 Kugler Mill Road | Cincinnati | OH
1965 | Philip Johnson

From the New Formalism, Johnson turned to a trend of the mid- and late 1960s that represented its extreme opposite: anti-architecture — bermed buildings partially or wholly buried in the landscape. This one-story house for Anne Whittier and James A. D. Geier was built into a rolling landscape setting adjacent to a small lake. Johnson organized the floor plan in an irregular U shape, framing a pool that was constructed between contoured mounds as an extension of the lake. Glass-walled bedrooms and living room look onto the pool. The proportions and detailing of interior spaces, with their framed panels of floor-to-ceiling glass, make the Geier House look like Johnson's houses of the 1950s. Cylindrical canisters of Cor-ten steel, projecting through the house's sodded roof terrace, let skylight into windowless rooms. Exposed wall planes are of stone, capped by a thick, reinforced concrete fascia. At the time of the house's construction, James Geier was a vice-president of Cincinnati Milacron, Inc.

KLINE BIOLOGY TOWER

The Kline Biology Tower was part of a complex of five dispersed structures that Johnson and Richard Foster designed for Yale University's science quadrangle, Pierson-Sage Square. During the administration of Yale's sixteenth president, A. Whitney Griswold, the university commissioned new buildings from the leading modern architects of Johnson's generation: Louis I. Kahn, Eero Saarinen, Paul Rudolph, and Gordon Bunshaft of Skidmore, Owings & Merrill. Johnson treated the science center as a problem in site planning and architectural relationships. Pierson-Sage Square lay at the north end of Hillhouse Avenue, on a small summit. The fourteen-story Kline Biology Tower, Johnson's first completed high-rise building, is the centerpiece of his design. Johnson emphasized the tower's visual role in New Haven's urban landscape by positioning it to one side of a large, paved square at the crest of Pierson-Sage's hill. From the south, it framed the right-of-way of Hillhouse Avenue and vertically identified the Kline Science Center, as did towers associated with older clusters of Yale University buildings. Johnson outlined three sides of the square with a low, concrete-canopy-covered walkway that drew an existing, potentially disruptive laboratory building into a new urban composition. Johnson and Foster spaced brick-clad cylinders on ten-foot, six-inch centers to emphasize the building's height. Spandrels of Longmeadow sandstone, a material used on older Yale buildings, volumetrically activate its curtain wall. The cruciform plan of the tower, elongated parallel to the Hillhouse axis, intensified the perception of height, as did the fifty-one-foot-tall mechanical penthouse at the top of the building. Most of the tower floors contained laboratory spaces, vented through flues embedded in the exterior cylinders. The twelfth floor contained dining rooms and a kitchen. The biology library was located in the basement beneath the paved square, illuminated by an open-air, basement-level, garden court. Lev Zetlin & Associates were structural engineers for the Kline Biology Tower, Meyer, Strong & Jones were mechanical engineers, Zion & Breen were landscape architects, and the E. & P. Construction Company was general contractor. Johnson sought to construct spatial coherence at the Kline Science Center through site

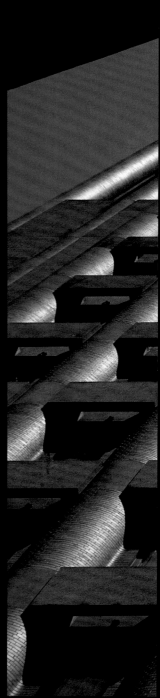

Yale University | Sachem Street | New Haven | CT
1965 | Philip Johnson and Richard Foster

WE LIVE IN A TIME OF FLUX. THERE SEEMS TO BE NO CONSISTENCY OF STYLE IN THE ARCHITECTURE OF THE SEVENTIES. SENSIBILITIES CHANGE FAST, BUT IN WHAT DIRECTION? THERE ARE NO NEW REGIONAL PRIDES, NO NEW RELIGIONS, NO NEW PURITANISM, NO NEW MARXISM, NO NEW SOCIALLY CONSCIOUS MORALITY THAT CAN GIVE DISCIPLINE, DIRECTION, OR FORCE TO AN ARCHITECTURAL PATTERN. TODAY WE KNOW TOO MUCH TOO QUICKLY. IT TAKES MORAL AND EMOTIONAL BLINDERS TO MAKE A STYLE. ONE MUST BE CONVINCED ONE IS RIGHT. WHO TODAY CAN STAND UP AND SAY: I AM RIGHT! WHO, INDEED, WOULD WANT TO?

planning and scale gradation; he sought to construct architectural coherence and institutional identity through stylistic and material coordination; and he sought to construct emotional engagement through sculptural buoyancy and textural modulation. Contemporary critiques of these efforts, especially a series of observations published in *Progressive Architecture* in 1967 and Johnson's interview with John Cook and Heinrich Klotz in *Conversations with Architects* in 1973, suggest, however, that the Kline Science Center operated at the level of a scenographic exercise. The completed structures failed to cohere programmatically and spatially on the terms Johnson set for them. Johnson's insistence on treating architecture as an exclusively formal exercise, and his failure to generate a totalizing system of architectural order akin to Mies van der Rohe's, meant that his New Formalist buildings had a persistently diagrammatic feel. This phenomenon, perceptively analyzed by Klaus Herdeg in his book *The Decorated Diagram: Harvard Architecture and the Failure of the Bauhaus Legacy* (1983), pertained not only to Johnson but to other leading American mid-twentieth-century modernist architects. The Kline Biology Tower represents the limits of Johnson's critique of mid-century modernism. The issues that were of such importance to him — monumentality, spatial and textural sensation, historical resonance, structural expressiveness — were pursued as though they were extraneous to the purposes for which the building was built. Instead of imbuing modern architecture with conceptual, experiential, and tectonic depth, Johnson's design practices seemed to detach and isolate these phenomena, giving his buildings the diagrammatic quality Herdeg analyzes.

KLINE GEOLOGY LABORATORY

Yale University | 210 Whitney Avenue | New Haven | CT
1964 | Philip Johnson and Richard Foster

The three-story Geology Laboratory was a supporting component of Johnson's Pierson-Sage Square science quadrangle. It was meant to be part of a three-structure subgroup on rising ground along Whitney Avenue on the east edge of the square, but the other two Johnson-designed buildings were never constructed. The flat-roofed, rectangularly planned building is set on a low plinth on its street front. Exterior walls are modulated with thick, regularly spaced cylinders clad in a purplish Pennsylvania iron spot brick. The cylinders frame recessed brick-clad bays. Spandrel panels of Longmeadow sandstone, lighter in tone than the brick, project between cylinders at the floor and roof levels, horizontally banding the Geology Laboratory. Johnson's exploration of curvature and volume took a different form here than in his preceding neoclassical works, but his purpose — to induce spatial depth using construction and finishing systems that tended to produce flat, unmodulated surfaces — remained the same. His choice of materials was keyed to the textures and coloration of adjoining nineteenth- and early twentieth-century university buildings. Henry-Russell Hitchcock noted a trace of "Miesian regularity" in the exterior composition of the Geology Laboratory, which Hitchcock linked to the project of constructing an "acceptable neutral vocabulary" for urban architectural groups. Johnson's pragmatism — the ease with which he dis-integrated interior programming and planning from site planning and tectonic expression — reduced the design of the Geology Laboratory to what Yale's architectural historian and critic Vincent Scully called "packaging." Johnson's overemphasis on the laboratory's labored exteriors and his lack of interest in its flexibly divisible interiors were noted by Hitchcock and others from the time the building was completed. Lev Zetlin & Associates were structural engineers, Meyer, Strong & Jones were mechanical engineers, and Zion & Breen were landscape architects. At the time the Kline Geology Laboratory was completed, it was the largest geological laboratory in the United States. This building, along with the other components of Johnson and Foster's Kline Science Center, was named for the donor, the Philadelphia businessman and Yale alumnus C. Mahlon Kline, president of Smith, Kline & French.

KLINE CHEMISTRY LABORATORY

Yale University | Prospect Street | New Haven | CT
1965 | Philip Johnson and Richard Foster

The Kline Chemistry Laboratory was the final component of Johnson and Foster's Kline Science Center to be built. It is a two-story, U-plan building that was, in effect, an addition to the north side of Sterling Chemistry Laboratory, a ponderous building of 1922 by the architects Delano & Aldrich, which faces Prospect Street on the west edge of Pierson-Sage Square. The chemistry laboratory's banded curtain wall employs the compositional and material attributes of the Kline geology and biology buildings. Johnson and Foster kept the wall planes of the chemistry building nearly flush with the vertical cylinders, emphasizing the continuity of the masonry curtain wall rather than its bay divisions and spatial depth.

HENRY L. MOSES INSTITUTE

Montefiore Hospital (now Montefiore Medical Center)

111 East Two Hundred Tenth Street | The Bronx | NY

1965 | Philip Johnson

This ten-story research laboratory tower figures strongly on a sloping, corner site. Johnson stacked cantilevered laboratory bays around a central elevator, stair, and toilet core in a Greek-cross-plan shape like that of the Kline Biology Tower. Brick-clad piers at the four inset corners of the tower visibly lift it above its entry steps and raised terraces. Projecting, vertical window bays illuminating laboratory spaces alternate with projecting, windowless service chases to emphasize the tower's rise. The formal and material economy, crisp assurance, and unpretentiousness of the Moses Institute give it the spatial and formal integrity that eluded Johnson in the Kline Science Center. The butt-jointed plate glass windows in the projecting bays proved vulnerable to differential pressure induced by the central air-conditioning system and had to be replaced with framed glazing. Lev Zetlin & Associates were structural engineers, Caretsky & Associates were mechanical engineers, Zion & Breen were landscape architects, and the Turner Construction Company was general contractor.

KUNSTHALLE BIELEFELD

Artur-Ladebeck-Straße 5 | Bielefeld | Germany

1968 | Philip Johnson with Architekt Professor Käsar F. Pinnau

Despite the popularity of the New Brutalism among leading U.S. architects in the late 1950s and 1960s, Johnson displayed little interest in this trend. The Yale Epidemiology Building and the Moses Research Institute preceded the Kunsthalle Bielefeld as his only built explorations of Brutalism. With its windowless, skylit top floor oversailing two lower floors, the Bielefeld art gallery exhibited the top-heavy profile of Le Corbusier's Dominican monastery of La Tourette, a building that was seminal for the Brutalist movement. Johnson's organization of reinforced-concrete wall planes terminating in thin rounded edges, so that, head-on, they read as piers supporting the top floor plate, contributed to the visual impression of a heavy mass raised on slender vertical supports (beneath the ground floor, these planes were carried on point supports). Characteristic of Johnson, the exterior detailing was precise and refined, with the concrete structure clad in sandstone. Johnson disposed wall planes around the perimeter of the gallery to create a pinwheel-like organization of interior exhibition spaces. Although it is not symmetrically composed, the Bielefeld building was quite similar in conception to the Munson-Williams-Proctor Institute: a central stair hall surrounded by subsidiary gallery rooms, set on a partially concealed, partially exposed basement-level podium containing an auditorium. The interiors are simply finished. Such details as the luminous ceilings and the stair rails show a continuity with Johnson's Miesian work of the 1950s, indicating how deeply embedded Miesian practices were in Johnson's consciousness. The glazed north side of the museum looks out across a small green park. Johnson designed a terrace facing the park and a rectangular reflecting pool extending forward from it. Severud, Perrone, Sturm, Conlin & Bandel were structural engineers, Jaros, Baum & Bolles were mechanical engineers, Bolt, Beranek & Newman were acoustical engineers, Elaine Lustig Cohen was the graphic designer, and John L. Kilpatrick was the lighting consultant. Rudolf August Oetker, a Bielefeld food corporation executive, was the donor of the gallery and Johnson's client.

MR. AND MRS. DAVID LLOYD KREEGER HOUSE (NOW KREEGER MUSEUM)

2401 Foxhall Road, N.W. | Washington | DC
1968 | Philip Johnson and Richard Foster

Johnson and Foster's opulent house for the Washington lawyer David Lloyd Kreeger and his wife, Carmen Matanzo y Jaramillo, was one of Johnson's most extravagant New Formalist work. Kreeger was chairman of the Government Employees Insurance Company when the house was built. Johnson designed the 24,000-square-foot house to facilitate entertaining and musical recitals and to display Mr. and Mrs. Kreeger's collection of nineteenth- and twentieth-century paintings and sculpture. Like the first Boissonnas House, the Pavilion in New Canaan, and the Beck House in Dallas, the Kreeger House exhibits Johnson's fascination with the dialectic of order and flexibility. Johnson worked with a grid of twenty-two-foot cubes, two-stories high, ceiled with shallow domical vaults, which he combined, subdivided, and hollowed out. An immense, double-volume loggia on the downslope, garden face of the house was linked to ground level by a turned Schinkel stair. Roman travertine was used to face the exterior walls and piers of the concrete-framed house as well as wall and floor surfaces in major interior spaces. Johnson supplemented the travertine with carpeting, used as wall covering on which to hang paintings. Lev Zetlin & Associates were structural engineers, Jaros, Baum & Bolles were mechanical engineers, John L. Kilpatrick was the lighting consultant, and Samuel A. Morrow was the interior designer. The George A. Fuller Company was general contractor. In the Kreeger House, Johnson recapitulated many of the themes that characterized his New Formalist work: the synthesis of modernism and classicism, the pursuit of monumentality, charging static space with perceptible sensation, generating spatial order from constructed geometry. In 1994, Mrs. Kreeger opened the house to the public as an art museum, the Kreeger Museum.

JOHN F. KENNEDY MEMORIAL

600 Main Street | Dallas | TX
1970 | Philip Johnson

Stanley Marcus, president of the Neiman Marcus specialty store, acting for the John F. Kennedy Memorial Citizens Committee, commissioned the design of an expiatory monument to be built by the citizens of Dallas near the site where President John F. Kennedy was assassinated on 22 November 1963. Delays in securing the site (a square block adjacent to the Victorian Romanesque-style Dallas County Courthouse, beneath which the county government had to first construct an underground parking garage) delayed completion until five years after the monument was designed. Johnson explained the design — a pair of U-shaped enclosures, constructed of post-tensioned, precast concrete and cantilevered from pairs of low piers — as an architectural trope for the "magnetism" of John Kennedy. The solemn rendition of this Pop conception was compromised by the small scale of the monument on its broad, open site (the U's frame a fifty-foot square; they stand thirty feet high) and the reduction of the architecture to articulation of the circular post-tensioning caps and tiptoe-like piers. Inside the monument, an inscribed granite plaque is embedded in a shallow recess in the pavement, as Mies van der Rohe had proposed for his Great War memorial in Schinkel's Neue Wache in Berlin of 1930. Robert E. McKee was the general contractor. The Kennedy Memorial was rehabilitated by the Sixth Floor Museum at Dealy Plaza in 2000. Philip Johnson/Alan Ritchie Architects consulted with the Dallas architects Corgan Associates; the general contractor was Phoenix I Restoration and Construction.

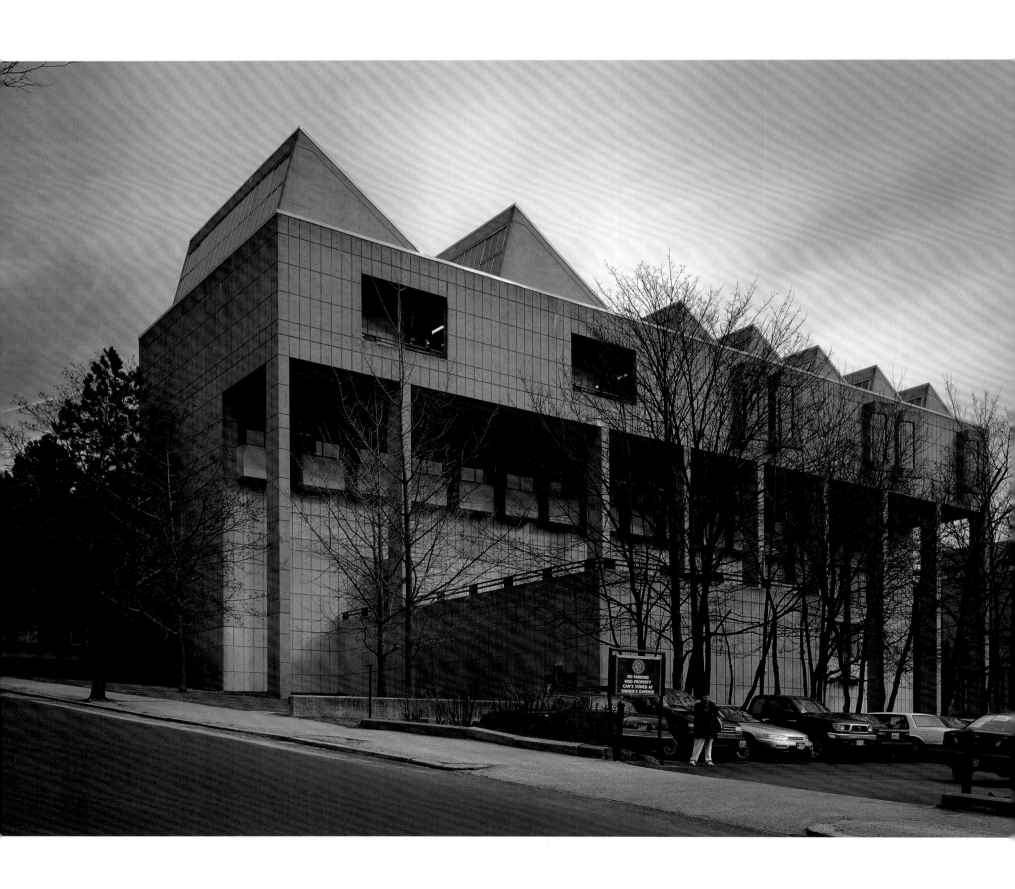

ALBERT AND VERA LIST ART BUILDING

Brown University | 64 College Street | Providence | RI
1971 | Philip Johnson with Samuel Glaser & Partners

The List Art Building contains Brown University's Department of Visual Art, the Department of the History of Art and Architecture, and the David Winton Bell Gallery. The five-story building is long and narrow, spanning a block between College and Waterman Streets on a steeply sloping site on Providence's College Hill. Johnson accentuated the narrowness and height of the building by locating the largest floor plate on top of the building, extending it out over the lower floors as a colossal portico supported on slender concrete piers. An auditorium occupies a block shot forward through the piers of the portico at ground level. Johnson contrasted the uniformly gridded wall surfaces of the cast-in-place concrete building with the varied treatment of window openings, which reflect the differing uses of internal spaces. Animating the building's profile are the handle-like concrete sunshade-reflectors at the fifth-floor level and north-facing skylights. These identify the top-floor painting studios. A service and circulation core is attached to the rear of the List Art Building. As with the Kennedy Memorial, a number of years elapsed between the time the List Art Building was designed and the time it was completed. Albert Goldberg & Associates were structural engineers, Buerkel & Company were mechanical engineers, Sasaki, Dawson & Demay Associates were landscape architects, and the Dimeo Construction Company was the general contractor.

THE ART MUSEUM OF SOUTH TEXAS

1902 North Shoreline Drive | Corpus Christi | TX

1972 | Philip Johnson and John Burgee with

Howard Barnstone and Eugene Aubry

Philip Johnson and John Burgee's first completed building was a small art museum on an unusual site, straddling the seawall that protects Corpus Christi's low-lying downtown from the occasional storm surges of Corpus Christi Bay. The building, which is constructed of white cast-in-place concrete, exposed outside and inside, consists of a fan-shaped auditorium, a rounded stair tower, and several gallery blocks grouped around a two-story-high entrance lobby and main gallery. Johnson and Burgee's organization of shapes figures strongly on the horizon line of grass, water, and sky at the edge of the city. From inside, deeply inset windows frame picture-like vistas of the downtown bayfront and of the bay. Daylight is admitted from concealed skylights as well as north-facing skylights that illuminate the largest of the top-floor galleries. The most arresting spaces in the building are not the activated main gallery, spanned by upper-level bridges, but the static museum shop and office spaces with their hypnotic views out. John de Menil recommended Philip Johnson to the oilman Edwin Singer and his wife, Patsy Dunn, Corpus Christi collectors who raised the funds to build the new museum building. As the museum's historian Alan Lesoff documented, Johnson so impressed himself on his clients' imaginations that he coordinated publicity for the opening, organized the opening festivities, and secured the services of David Whitney as guest curator for the inaugural exhibition, "Johns, Stella, Warhol: Works in Series," for which he loaned works from his collection. Cathleen S. Gallander, the director of the museum, was so strongly affected by Johnson and Whitney that she initiated a challenging program of exhibiting contemporary art. Cunningham & Lemus were structural engineers, Thomas John & Associates were mechanical and electrical engineers, Architectural Concrete Consultants were concrete consultants, Kilpatrick & Gellert were lighting consultants, and the Burnett Construction Company was the general contractor. Mr. and Mrs. Singer were instrumental in supporting design and construction of the Watergarden of 1988, designed by the landscape architects Zion & Breen in front of the museum as a spatial focus for the civic buildings grouped around the museum in Bayfront Arts and Science Park. In 1997 the Art Museum of South Texas became part of Texas A&M University, Corpus Christi, in a consortium of community art institutions called the South Texas Institute for the Arts. Legorreta Arquitectos of Mexico City designed an annex to be built to one side of the museum in 2001.

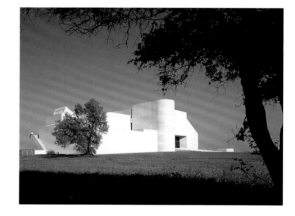

BURDEN HALL

Harvard Business School | Harvard University | Soldiers Field | Boston | MA
1972 | Philip Johnson and John Burgee

Burden Hall, a 1,000-seat auditorium, was designed to function as one, two, or three large lecture halls for the Harvard Business School's Boston campus. The fragmented, angular plan and faceted brick wall planes of the steel-framed building give it the sort of nonfigural appearance Johnson sought in his anti-architecture. To minimize its impact on the site, the bulk of the building was buried. The auditorium's conception as a flexible, changeable space proved problematic in operation. Zetlin, Desimone, Chaplin & Associates were structural engineers, Jaros, Baum & Bolles were mechanical and electrical engineers, Ranger, Farrell & Associates were audiovisual consultants, and John L. Kilpatrick was lighting consultant. George A. Fuller & Company were general contractors.

ROY R. NEUBERGER MUSEUM OF ART

State University of New York, Purchase | 735 Anderson Hill Road | Purchase | NY
1972 | Philip Johnson and John Burgee

The Neuberger Museum was a component of a new campus for the State University of New York outside the town of Purchase. The New York architect Edward Larrabee Barnes was responsible for the campus plan, which grouped buildings to either side of a wide paved concourse. Rows of maple trees and a continuous canopy structure lined each side of the concourse. Campus buildings were allotted long, narrow slots of ground so that buildings met the canopy structure on their shorter side and spread out on their long dimension perpendicular to the concourse. All campus buildings were required to use a mixed blend of dark brown brick as exterior facing. Barnes secured commissions for Johnson and Burgee; Venturi & Rauch; Gwathmey, Henderson & Siegel; Paul Rudolph; Gunnar Birkerts & Associates; and The Architects Collaborative. The presence of the canopy structure preempted the opportunity to design a façade. Johnson and Burgee accepted the relative anonymity implicit in this condition and shifted rectangular, brick-faced, box-like gallery bays, some two stories high, others one story, to either side of an axis that runs the long dimension of the building. This axis defines a processional route through the museum, which they treated as an enfilade. The enfilade's implication of symmetrical composition is contradicted by the shifted planning of individual gallery bays, resulting in a balance between experiential continuity and Johnson's preference for spatially defined rooms in which to exhibit art. Because building budgets required economy, the steel-framed Neuberger Museum is simply finished. Weiskopf & Pickworth were structural engineers, Segner & Dalton were mechanical and electrical engineers, Peter Rolland was the landscape architect, Kilpatrick & Gellert were lighting consultants, and P. M. Hughes & Sons, Inc. was the general contractor.

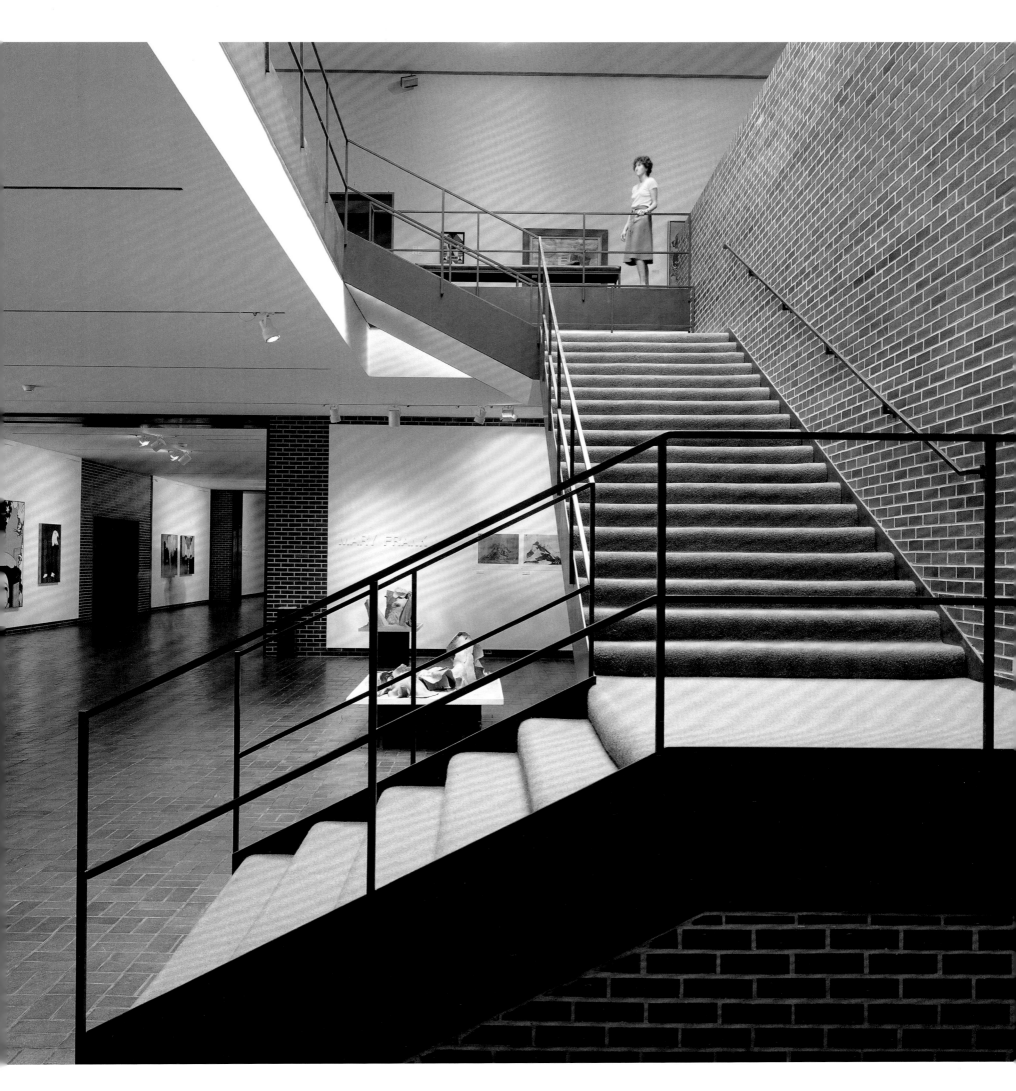

TISCH HALL

New York University | 40 West Fourth Street | New York | NY
1972 | Philip Johnson and Richard Foster

Tisch Hall, a ten-story academic building, was one of several projects that Johnson and Foster began to plan for New York University's Greenwich Village campus on the south and east sides of Washington Square in 1964. Stern, Mellins, and Fishman recount the controversies over New York University's expansion plans, undertaken by its president, James M. Hester, which accounted for the long interval between design and completion of Johnson and Foster's NYU commissions. As at the Kline Science Center, Johnson and Foster sought to use architecture to give NYU a new, unifying identity. In place of Kline's protruding cylinders, NYU's emblematic curtain wall, also of Longmeadow sandstone (chosen for its compatibility with Greenwich Village's nineteenth-century architectural fabric), contained hollow, semi-cylindrical recesses between vertical window bays. These rose all the way to Tisch's tall attic floor, which contained athletic playing courts. The slab-shaped Tisch Hall is set back from West Fourth Street behind a raised, planted plaza containing a Victorian Gothic finial, a fragment of NYU's first building.

FAÇADE OF ANDRÉ AND BELLA MEYER PHYSICS HALL

New York University | 4 Washington Place | New York | NY

1972 | Philip Johnson and Richard Foster

Johnson and Foster proposed refacing a number of existing NYU buildings with the sandstone curtain wall they developed for NYU's Bobst Library. Together with a uniform parapet line 150 feet above the street, this would have impressed the blocks east and south of Washington Square with buildings that Ellen Perry quoted Johnson as saying "are fairly anonymous... maybe even dull" since he wanted them to read as continuous urban fabric. Meyer Hall was the only NYU building to be refaced.

HAGOP KERVORKIAN CENTER
FOR NEAR EASTERN STUDIES

New York University | 50 Washington Square South | New York | NY
1973 | Philip Johnson and Richard Foster

Adhering to a pattern visible since the 1960s, Johnson's most assured building at NYU was his smallest. The Center for Near Eastern Studies occupies a single townhouse lot at the corner of Washington Square South and Sullivan Street. It respects the siting and height of adjacent five-story buildings. Yet its tense, granite-faced wall planes, deeply embrasured upper-level windows with their diagonally sloped sills and corner orientation, and the inset, two-story-high entrance portal off Sullivan Street give it a rhythm, scale, and sense of volume that sets it apart as a modern building. The Kevorkian Center works as both urban fabric and architectural exception. As Paul Goldberger observed in 1973, it possesses "a monumentality that is at least as powerful, and surely less strained, than that of the library." Michael Forstl was Johnson and Foster's associate-in-charge, Zoldos & Silman were structural engineers, Robert K. Bedell was mechanical and electrical engineer, and the Roberts Nash Construction Corporation was the general contractor.

ELMER HOLMES BOBST LIBRARY

New York University | 70 Washington Square South | New York | NY
1972 | Philip Johnson and Richard Foster

Johnson and Foster's Bobst Library, which faced the south side of Washington Square, represented their model for endowing NYU and Washington Square with the urban coherence and monumental scale that Johnson judged neither to possess. A uniform skyline and uniform façades that impressed with their materials and depth, rather than their composition, were posited on the library block as urbanistically correct. To compensate for the library's external solemnity, Johnson opened up the interior with a one-hundred-foot square central court, 150 feet high, ringed by tiers of balconies. Opposed stair runs traced insistent diagonals up the south wall of the court. Overlooking both the court and Washington Square were stacked, double-volume, glass-walled reading rooms. Book stacks, offices, and classrooms occupied single-floor-height levels on the other three sides of the court. Johnson further activated this phantasmagoric interior, whose openness was in startling contrast to the library's external stolidity, with his decorative finishes: an optically stunning court floor paved in black, gray, and white polished marble, and slender cruciform aluminum balusters on the handrails of the balconies that were gold anodized. Severud-Perrone-Sturm-Bandel were structural engineers, Jaros, Baum & Bolles were mechanical and electrical engineers, Kilpatrick and Gellert were lighting consultants, and the Diesel Construction Company was the general contractor.

IDS CENTER

The IDS Center restored Johnson's critical reputation in the aftermath of the New Formalism. With this complex he produced a designed yet unpretentious and lively public space of the type he had long championed. The four-building complex occupies a city block in downtown Minneapolis with frontage on the city's main shopping street, the Nicollet Avenue pedestrian mall. It consisted of a fifty-seven-story, 775-foot-high office tower, the nineteen-story, 285-room Marquette Inn, the eight-story 770 Marquette Building, and a two-story F. W. Woolworth Company variety store These were constructed above a 525-car underground parking garage and grouped around the Crystal Court, a 23,000-square-foot, air-conditioned winter garden at the center of the block, accessible from street level as well as from the second-level Skywalk system of pedestrian concourses that bridge streets to connect buildings in downtown Minneapolis. Paul Goldberger noted how Johnson internalized the diagonal geometry of his Sculpture Gallery to shape space in the Crystal Cour in plan and section. Johnson and Burgee generated diagonals by faceting the plan geometry of the office tower to minimize its visual bulk on the skyline, producing multiple corner offices in the process. Faceted planning also yielded a stepped plan configuration in the hotel's corridors that was much remarked. Johnson and Burgee's associate John Manley proposed that the steel-framed, glass-walled, and acrylic-roofed canopy above the Crystal Court also be stepped in section. Its ascent to a height of 121 feet imbued this space with a diagonal rise. The buildings of the IDS Center were sheathed in a silver-blue reflective glass curtain wall. Vertica mullions were closely spaced to animate the curtain wall at close range and intensify the play of reflections at reentrant angles. The cable-suspended balconies inside the Crystal Court and the panelized balcony handrails were detailed in characteristic Johnson manner. The formal simplicity and discipline of the IDS Center and the systematic way in which the complex was shaped in plan and section to

IT IS TIME TO RE-CREATE THE STREET AS A CENTERING DEVICE, INSTEAD OF THE SPLITTING DEVICE IT HAS BECOME. IN OUR TALK OF MALLS, PIAZZAS, AND SHOPPING CENTERS, WE TEND TO FORGET THE BEAUTY OF THE TOGETHERNESS OF THE STREET. THERE CAN BE HOPE THAT THE GREAT ART OF TOWNSCAPE IS NOT DEAD. SOMEDAY, PEOPLE ARE AGAIN GOING TO WANT PROCESSIONALS, ARE AGAIN GOING TO WANT TO DANCE IN VILLAGE SQUARES. AND WHEN THEY WANT THEM, THEY WILL GET THEM, AND LIKE EASTER ON FIFTH AVENUE, LET THE AUTOMOBILE TAKE CARE OF ITSELF.

accentuate public space gave it a consistency and rigor missing from Johnson's large public buildings of the 1960s. Johnson and Burgee's integration of site planning, pedestrian circulation, and a mixture of uses made the IDS Center seem like a model for urbanistically engaged high-rise buildings. Indicative of the critical esteem with which the complex was received, the IDS Center won an Honor Award for design from the American Institute of Architects in 1975. IDS Properties, a subsidiary of Investors Diversified Services, was the client for the IDS Center. Severud-Perrone-Sturm-Conlin-Bandel were structural engineers, Cosentini Associates were mechanical engineers, Eitingon & Schlossberg were electrical engineers, Philip Johnson and John Burgee were interior architects, Kilpatrick & Gellert were lighting consultants, Ranger Farrell was the acoustical consultant, E. O. Tofflemire was the curtain wall consultant, Hauser Associates were the graphics consultants, and the Turner Construction Company was the general contractor. Despite the reputation of the IDS Center in design circles, it was linked to a financial crisis Investors Diversified Services began to experience before the complex was completed. Although largely a result of changing market conditions, IDS's crisis was blamed in part on substantial cost overruns incurred during the design and construction of its headquarters complex. In 1980 IDS sold the complex to Oxford Properties. The possibility that Oxford might make inappropriate alterations to the complex led the Minneapolis Heritage Preservation Commission to consider designating it a Minneapolis historic landmark in 1984. This proposal was tabled when Oxford and the commission agreed that Oxford would submit any proposed changes for the commission's comment.

BOSTON PUBLIC LIBRARY ADDITION

Boylston Street and Exeter Street | Boston | MA

1972 | Philip Johnson and John Burgee and Architects Design Group

Like the NYU buildings, Johnson and Burgee's addition to the Boston Public Library was not completed until eight years after design work began. Therefore, like the NYU buildings, it exhibited strong traces of the New Formalism, combined with Johnson's smooth interpretation of the New Brutalism. An addition to McKim, Mead & White's Boston Public Library of 1895, a landmark of nineteenth-century American monumental classical architecture, Johnson and Burgee's library was designed to respect the height and scale of the 1895 building. It is surfaced in pink Milford granite, the material with which the 1895 library was built. The addition was planned on a nine-square grid, with vertical structural piers and secondary stairs organized along the lines defining the nine squares. The central fifty-eight-foot square was a skylit court, sixty-five feet high. An important design issue was to provide much more space than did the 1895 building yet contain it in a volume of similar dimensions. This requirement led to William LeMessurier's structural design for a steel roof and floor superstructure suspended above a reinforced concrete substructure containing a two-level basement and, on the first and second floors, expansive, open-stack reading lofts. The exterior of the building was a literal translation of its interior spatial organization. Tall, wide-span, publicly accessible spaces on the first and second floors and the vertically compressed stack levels above were countered by the vertical piers housing columns and stairs. Johnson and Burgee treated the exterior wall surfaces as a smooth skin. Wide arches identified the second-floor reading room and echoed the arched windows of reading rooms in the 1895 building. Horizontal slits identified the fourth-floor offices. The oversailing profiles of the tilted second-story walls and the projecting fifth- and sixth-level stack bays acknowledged the extent to which the New Brutalism had become a distinctly Bostonian version of modern architecture in the 1960s, although they masked the building's composite structural system. Johnson and Burgee sheathed the walls of the central court with Milford granite to emphasize the play of geometries. Johnson's proportioning of openings and the double-run stairs and his Miesian detailing of stair handrails gave the central court its monumental scale and austere dignity. Le Messurier Associates were structural engineers, Francis Associates were mechanical and electrical engineers, Architectural Interiors were interior designers, Ranger Farrell was the acoustical consultant, Walter Kacik was the graphics consultant, Kilpatrick & Gellert were lighting consultants, and Vappi & Company was the general contractor.

NIAGARA FALLS CONVENTION AND CIVIC CENTER

305 South Fourth Street | Niagara Falls | NY

1974 | Philip Johnson and John Burgee

In contrast to Johnson's New Formalist buildings with their aspirations to classical monumentality, the Niagara Falls Convention and Civic Center was designed as a monumental work of infrastructure. Its 355-foot-long steel arches bridge between limestone-faced steel abutments. The arches are tied together structurally with sixty-two-foot-long butterfly trusses. Operating at an urban scale, the center incorporates a city street, which is threaded through the abutments beneath the great arch. The convention center terminates a five-block-long pedestrian concourse in Niagara Falls' eighty-two-acre Rainbow Center urban renewal district, just above the falls of the Niagara River. The center was built by the City of Niagara Falls and its urban renewal agency. The New York State Urban Development Corporation managed the development of the precinct, which includes the Wintergarden by Gruen Associates and Cesar Pelli. Johnson and Burgee's convention center and the Wintergarden lie at opposite ends of the concourse designed by M. Paul Friedberg & Associates. Containing a multipurpose sports and entertainment arena, a 2,000-seat ballroom, a 400-seat theater, and smaller meeting rooms, the convention center was planned as a meeting and cultural center for residents of and visitors to the U.S.-Canadian border city. By refraining from historical thematization, Johnson and Burgee achieved a persuasive demonstration of public monumentality, architecturally integrated with the city. Lev Zetlin & Associates were structural engineers for the convention and civic center, Syska & Hennessy were mechanical and electrical engineers, and Pigott Construction International was the general contractor. Abraham Geller, Raimund Abraham, and Giuliano Fiorezoli were architects of E. Dent Lackey Plaza in front of the convention and civic center.

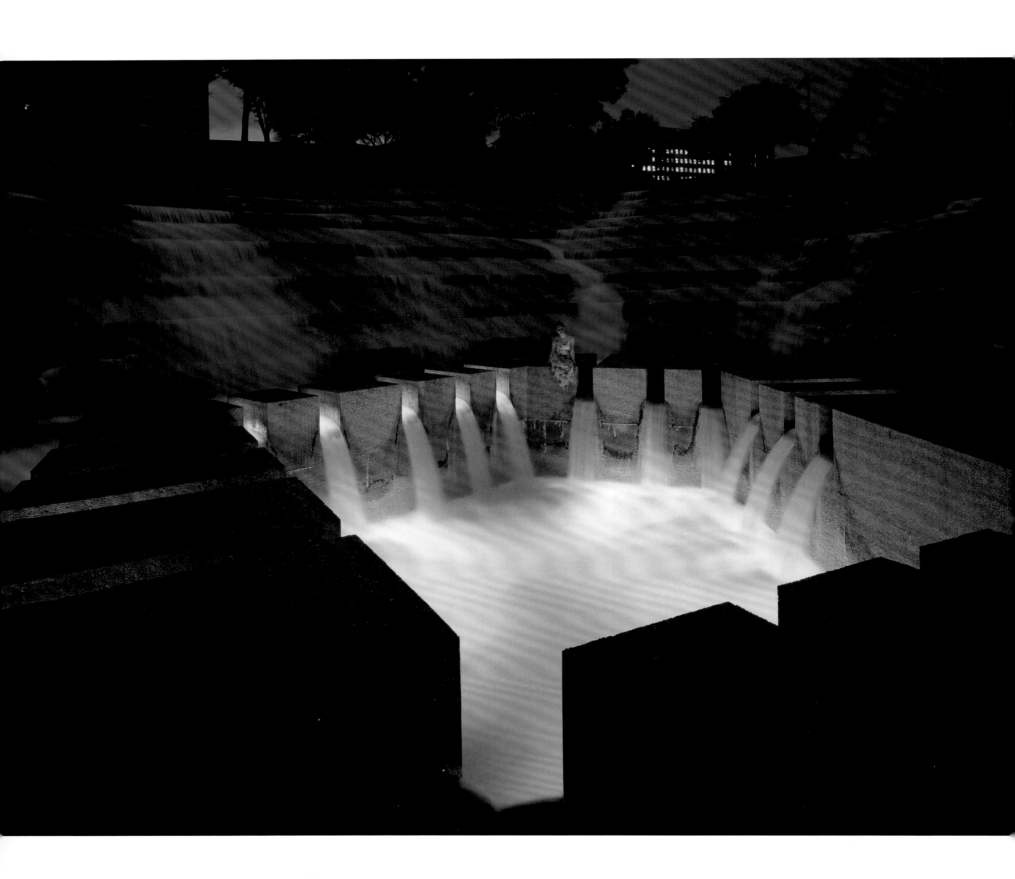

FORT WORTH WATER GARDEN

Fourteenth Street and Houston Street | Fort Worth | TX

1974 | Johnson/Burgee Architects

Ruth Carter Stevenson and the Amon Carter Foundation were Johnson/Burgee's clients for a four-and-a-half-block, seven-acre public landscape in downtown Fort Worth. Occupying a residual site within the city's street grid, between the back of a convention center and an elevated freeway, the Water Garden consists of three water-focused landscapes in addition to a central plaza, a lawn, and a hill. Johnson/Burgee used diagonal alignments to absorb the geometry of a curved access street behind the convention center. From this incursion, they developed the different sectors of the park, which are organized like large-scale outdoor rooms. Stepped terraces of warm-toned, cast-in-place concrete were the spatial element used to hollow out or elevate the downtown blocks. Johnson shaped the park's internal landscapes to reflect different characteristics of water. The most sculptural is the Cascade, a dramatic chasm into which water, and pedestrians, rush precipitously. The most serene is the Quiet Pool, enclosed by sloped walls and bald cypress trees. In contrast to Johnson's Pavilion, the Fort Worth Water Garden investigated erotic responses to water and sensations of bodily displacement in relation to changes in elevation without relying on modular repetition, figural composition, or historical quotations. Diagonal alignments propel pedestrians through the site without constructing obvious spatial hierarchies. Desimone & Chaplin were structural engineers, J. S. Hammel Engineering was the mechanical engineer, and Gaynor & Sirmen were associate mechanical engineers.

MORNINGSIDE HOUSE

1000 Pelham Parkway South | The Bronx | NY

1974 | Johnson/Burgee Architects

Morningside House, a pair of five-story buildings containing assisted living spaces for the elderly, was built on either side of Lurting Avenue facing Pelham Parkway in the Bronx. The two buildings were shaped to their sites, where Lurting intersects the Pelham Parkway at an angle. Both buildings have irregular U plans focused on protected inner courtyards. They are constructed of exposed, vertically striated, cast-in-place concrete, which is detailed as continuous horizontal spandrels that step up or down into the zone of continuous, horizontal ribbon windows in response to interior conditions. Zoldos-Silman were structural engineers, and Jaros, Baum & Bolles were mechanical engineers.

ONE POST OAK CENTRAL

2000 Post Oak Boulevard | Houston | TX

1975 | Johnson/Burgee Architects and S. I. Morris Associates

TWO POST OAK CENTRAL

1980 Post Oak Boulevard | Houston | TX

1979 | Johnson/Burgee Architects and Richard Fitzgerald & Partners

THREE POST OAK CENTRAL

1990 Post Oak Boulevard | Houston | TX

1982 | Johnson/Burgee Architects and Richard Fitzgerald & Partners

One Post Oak Central, the first component of a three-phase office building complex, was Johnson/Burgee's first commission from Gerald D. Hines Interests, the Houston-based real estate developer and investment builder. I. S. Brochstein, the founder of a Houston architectural woodwork and furniture production studio that had manufactured the woodwork for the Amon Carter Museum, specified that Hines retain Johnson/Burgee to design this complex on a seventeen-acre tract Brochstein owned near the Galleria, the shopping mall, hotel, and office center Hines built in stages beginning in the late 1960s. After an initial proposal was rejected by Hines's lenders as being too complex, Johnson/Burgee responded with three separate towers facing Post Oak Boulevard, bracketed by a multilevel, U-plan parking garage. The towers represented Johnson's architectural version of the artistic practice of works in series. One Post Oak Central represented the primary condition — a twenty-two-story slab with front and rear setbacks, faceted corners, and alternating horizontal bands of charcoal aluminum spandrels and silver reflective glass — which went through progressive geometric deformations in buildings Two and Three. One Post Oak Central, which was built speculatively and therefore economically, stood out by virtue of its shaped profile and sleek curtain wall. Colaco Engineers were structural engineers, I. A. Naman + Associates were mechanical engineers, and Claude R. Engle was the lighting consultant.

For Two Post Oak Central, Johnson/Burgee deflected One Post Oak Central into a parallelogram plan configuration. Colaco Engineers were the structural engineers and I. A. Naman + Associates were the mechanical engineers.

Completing the trio of office buildings, Three Post Oak Central takes the works-in-series approach to its logical conclusion by being a right triangle in plan while maintaining the setbacks and curtain wall posited with One Post Oak Central. When I. M. Pei & Partners designed the Warwick Post Oak Hotel across Post Oak Boulevard from Post Oak Central, they aligned the front of the hotel on the diagonal site line of Johnson/Burgee's buildings Two and Three.

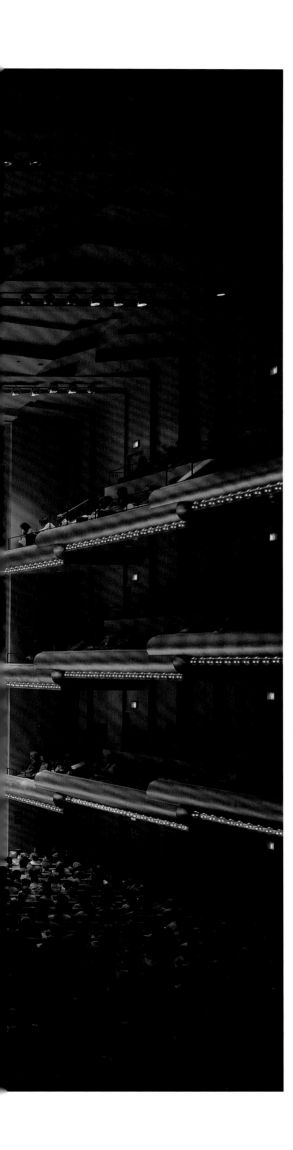

AVERY FISHER HALL INTERIOR

Lincoln Center for the Performing Arts | New York | NY

1976 | Johnson/Burgee Architects

Johnson/Burgee worked with the acoustical engineer Cyril M. Harris to completely reconstruct the stage, auditorium, and backstage of Philharmonic Hall, the New York Philharmonic Orchestra's home and the first theater in Lincoln Center to be completed. Only the building's exteriors and public circulation spaces were left intact. Harrison & Abramovitz's original auditorium and stage, which were judged acoustically flawed and had already been altered, were demolished and replaced within a six-month period. Designed to Harris's acoustical specifications, the 2,741-seat hall was configured within a rectangularly planned enclosure symmetrically focused on the stage, a wedge-shaped parallelogram in plan. Shallow balconies rise in three tiers above the auditorium. These step down in section as they approach the stage and are faced with embedded, horizontally aligned cylinders finished with gold leaf. The ceiling is composed of angled plaster facets. The cylinders and facets perform acoustically by breaking up sound. John Manley drew the ceiling facets at full scale so the drawings could be used as templates for the plasterers. Johnson/Burgee framed the stage with a proscenium and finished the angled walls and raked ceiling of the stage with panels of English oak plywood. Despite the liberal use of gold leaf, the interior of Avery Fisher Hall was not as gaudy or pretentious as that of the New York State Theater. Its dignity, restraint, even the sense of increased intimacy with which Johnson/Burgee endowed the redesigned hall, demonstrated that in abandoning the thematization of history, Johnson produced architecture that was more coherent than his formally ambitious but unintegrated designs of the 1960s. Cyril Harris was the acoustical consultant for Avery Fisher Hall, Claude R. Engle was the lighting consultant, Emil Antonucci was the graphics consultant, Robert Brannigan Associates were the theatrical consultants, Ammann & Whitney were the structural consultants, and Syska & Hennessy were the mechanical consultants.

NZOIL PLACE

Pennzoil Place, a pair of thirty-six-story office buildings in downtown Houston, was built by Gerald D. Hines Interests, with the Pennzoil Companies and the Zapata Corporation as chief tenants. Pennzoil Place followed the IDS Center as a landmark in Johnson's career because it represented a different way of conceiving the design of tall office buildings. Johnson/Burgee discarded the ethos of economy that provided the ideological and performative basis for U.S. skyscraper design in the 1950s and 1960s, replacing it with a new architectural ethos based on striking imagery and marketable appeal. Hines Interests so successfully exploited this appeal that they added two floors to each tower during construction to satisfy the demand for space in the buildings. The formal coherence of Pennzoil Place gives it visual authority. Johnson/Burgee internalized the diagonal line in plan and section. They spatialized the experience of the processional by playing the folded glass planes of the canopies above the lobbies against the inflected wall planes of the reflectively symmetrical towers. Peter Papademetriou remarked on Johnson's conceptual debt to the work of the Minimalist sculptors Robert Morris and Tony Smith, evident in the formal precision with which he essayed diagonality. The ten-foot slot between the towers is another Minimalist device that serves an urbanistic purpose by framing a view of the classical tempietto atop an adjoining 1920s skyscraper. By wrapping the towers in a bronze anodized aluminum curtain wall animated with a narrowly spaced grid of mullions, by surfacing the sloped greenhouses in a silver reflective glass that reveals its supporting steel space-frame structure, and by meeting the ground with parapets of flame-finished pink granite, Johnson/Burgee maintained a minimalist material economy while using each material to practical advantage. The congruence between their resolution of practical problems and the generation of new spatial possibilities internally and urbanistically was also achieved in the delivery of professional services. Hines's economic construction of the deal depended on Johnson/Burgee's sharing architectural authority with a Houston firm on terms that made it economical to hire a

SURELY ARCHITECTURE IS THE ORGANIZATION FOR PLEASURE OF ENCLOSED SPACE. AND WHAT MORE MAGNIFICENT ENCLOSURE THAN A TOWN, A PLACE, A PLACE WHERE SPIRIT IS CUDDLED, MADE SERENE, MADE AT HOME AMONG HIS FELLOW SPIRITS, MADE PROUD, HAPPY, OR EXCITED DEPENDING ON THE CERE- MONY, THE DAY, THE HOUR.

"prestigious" architect to design office buildings that had to perform economically like speculative projects rather than owner-occupied corporate buildings such as IDS. Johnson/Burgee worked so flexibly within the limitations of this practice and added such value to Hines's projects with their designs that Pennzoil positioned them to compete with such larger offices as Skidmore, Owings & Merrill (which originally had the Pennzoil Place job but lost it because the chairman of the Pennzoil Companies found their designs too staid). Unlike IDS, whose financial problems were linked to its headquarters building, Pennzoil Place succeeded as a real estate venture. Ada Louise Huxtable, architecture critic for the *New York Times*, pronounced it building of the year and in 1977 it received a design award from the American Institute of Architects. Pennzoil Place caused Gerald Hines to be acclaimed a patron of architecture and it propelled Johnson/Burgee into a new phase in their career as skyscraper architects. Although not a postmodern design stylistically, Pennzoil replaced the modernist economy of limits in high-rise architecture with a postmodern economy of profitable imagery to become, as John Pastier noted, the harbinger of American skyscraper design by 1980. Ellisor Engineers were structural engineers, I. A. Naman + Associates were the mechanical engineers, and Zapata Warrior Constructors were the electrical engineers. Gensler & Associates were responsible for the interior design of the Pennzoil Companies' floors.

CENTURY CENTER

120 South St. Joseph Street | South Bend | IN
1976 | Johnson/Burgee Architects

Located in downtown South Bend on the banks of the St. Joseph River, Century Center was built by the City of South Bend as a multipurpose civic and convention center that contains a theater, an art center, and an automobile museum. Johnson/Burgee organized different program spaces, administered by different organizations and agencies, on two levels around a high-ceilinged central court that overlooks the St. Joseph River. Triangular concrete-framed, skylit canopies traverse brick-paved concourses linking the upper street level to the lower river level. These concourses frame the central court and distribute visitors to the center's components. Johnson likened these processional concourses to the streets of a city. The diagonally arrayed processional, the diagonally roofed and skylit public concourse, the tall central collection space, and a designed landscape — an island that functions as a river terrace — bespeak preoccupations characteristic of Johnson's work. Alan Ritchie was the principal in charge of the project in Johnson/Burgee's office. Skilling, Helle, Christiansen, Robertson were structural engineers, Cosentini Associates were mechanical and electrical engineers, Hapert, Neyer & Associates were foundation and soils consultants, Robert A. Hansen Associates were acoustical consultants, Claude R. Engle was the lighting consultant, North American Signs were the graphics consultants, and Sollitt Construction Company was the cost consultant and the construction manager.

GENERAL AMERICAN LIFE INSURANCE COMPANY BUILDING

700 Market Street | St. Louis | MO
1976 | Johnson/Burgee Architects

The corporate headquarters of the General American Life Insurance Company is a six-story building in downtown St. Louis that displays Johnson/Burgee's fascination with combining diagonal and circular geometries. The building is a square in plan, sliced into two triangles by a diagonal incision containing secondary stairs, with a central, cylindrical void containing three elevators and two stairs at its center. To further complicate the geometric composition, one of the triangular pieces is elevated forty-five feet above ground level on a grid of structural columns, so that it appears to levitate above the site. The lower portion of the cylindrical lobby "rotunda" is exposed inside the resulting portico; its upper half is exposed on the back side of the building as a figural element, where it engages the levitated triangle. The dark, reflective glass curtain wall, criss-crossed by a network of lighter mullions as at Asia House, reinforces the primacy of the building's activated geometries. The rotunda lobby with its sculptural elevator towers, the bridges that link each tower to the upper floors, and the rounded subsidiary stairs, all faced with brick, accentuate the sculptural qualities of the 107-foot-high, top-lit interior and thematize the processional experience. Johnson/Burgee were interior designers for the open-plan office spaces. Severud-Perrone-Sturm-Bandel were the structural engineers, William Tao Associates were the mechanical and electrical engineers, and McCarthy Brothers were the general contractor. The General American Building demonstrates how Johnson continued to explore the architectural possibilities of geometric transformation in the 1970s, under the dispensation of Minimalist art and with a certain awareness of the work of the British architect James Stirling.

THANKS-GIVING SQUARE

Pacific Street and Ervay Street | Dallas | TX
1976 | Johnson/Burgee Architects
1996 | addition | Philip Johnson, Ritchie & Fiore, Architects

Johnson/Burgee pursued their engagement with geometrical transformation in the design of Thanks-Giving Square, a landscape complex occupying a narrow triangular block formed by the intersection of two street grids in downtown Dallas. Johnson/Burgee configured the site with a sequence of walkways that slide down into the block from street level between the sloped planes of a bermed landscape. These compose the Meditation Garden, which is walled off from surrounding streets. The walks are integrated with water channels fed by an inclined sluice. At the eastern tip of the triangle is a concrete frame containing bells. At the northern tip is the square's only building, the nondenominational Chapel of Thanksgiving. The chapel is a helical structure of white cast-in-place concrete that rises from a logarithmic spiral into an Archimedean spiral. The chapel wall is a continuously folded plane cantilevered above its interior. The interstices of the fold are roofed with a system of skylights above panels of stained glass executed by the French artist Gabriel Loire. A long-span walkway bridges the sluice fountain to connect the chapel entrance to the park. Below the chapel, at basement level, is a circular hypostyle space, the Hall of Thanksgiving and Exhibit Area, which contains patriotic displays. Also beneath the park are a hub of the downtown pedestrian tunnel system and a truck terminal. Thanks-Giving Square was the project of the Dallas philanthropist Peter Stewart. Stewart's Thanks-Giving Square Foundation raised funds to build and operate the chapel and park. Johnson/Burgee dignified and legitimized Stewart's surrealistically earnest

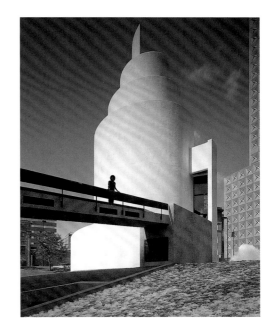

program with the rigorous formal abstraction of their design. Monumentality, historical archaism (Johnson cited the helical, ninth-century minaret of the Great Mosque in Samarra, Iraq, as the model for the chapel), the deformation of a plane surface into a curved volume, the construction of landscape, the orchestration of processional movement and of bodily displacement through sensations of sinking (descent into the park), levitating (the entrance bridge), and swirling (the interior of the chapel) persisted as imaginative themes from which Johnson shaped the architecture. At Thanks-Giving Square, they were condensed to produce a temenos that was spatially activated rather than static, as at the Roofless Church. A comparison of these two unconventional religious precincts (one ecumenical, the other non-denominational, both imbued with strong civic and representational content) demonstrates that despite shifts in his architectural interests, Johnson continued to rely on a recurring array of themes to emotionally engage presumed publics in a social context in which no consensus exists on what constitutes the proper public expression of religious sentiment. Datum Structures Engineering was the structural engineer, Herman Blum was the mechanical engineer, J. S. Hammel Engineering was the fountain consultant, Claude R. Engle was the lighting consultant, the Henry C. Beck Company was construction manager, and Manhattan Construction Company was the general contractor.

FINE ARTS CENTER (NOW DOROTHY AND DEXTER BAKER CENTER FOR THE ARTS)

Muhlenberg College | 2400 Chew Street | Allentown | PA

1977 | Johnson/Burgee Architects and Wallace & Watson Associates

Johnson/Burgee organized the Baker Center as a spatialization of the processional way. Aligned on the diagonal, it conforms to the downward slope of the site from Chew Street. The gallery is top-lit through a gabled steel-and-glass skylight that provides a horizontal datum, against which the slope of the site can be perceptually measured. The programmatic components of the center (the college's art, music, and theater and dance departments, as well as performance spaces and the Martin Art Gallery) occupy contiguous, parallel bars that slide past each other. Inside, residual triangular spaces provide transitions between the ramped floor of the processional gallery and adjacent instructional and performance spaces. The white painted brick surfaces of the center, the dark, brick-paved floor of the gallery, and the peaked skylight recall Johnson's Sculpture Gallery. Johnson/Burgee and Wallace & Watson Associates were interior designers, Wallace & Watson Associates were structural engineers, T. A. Coughlin & Coston were mechanical and electrical engineers, Robert A. Hansen Associates were acoustical engineers, John L. Kilpatrick was the lighting consultant, Robert Brannigan was the theater consultant, and the Somers Construction Company was the general contractor.

80 FIELD POINT ROAD BUILDING

80 Field Point Road | Greenwich | CT

1978 | Johnson/Burgee Architects

This small, suburban office building externalizes the interior geometries of the General American Building. Thick spandrel panels of pink Canadian granite framing horizontal strip windows appear to have been cleaved by a concave semicircular bay faced with a curtain wall of bronze-toned reflective glass in aluminum frames. A freestanding, granite-faced tower contains a special elevator, linked by a corridor bridge to the fourth-floor office of the client. Desimone+Chaplin & Associates were structural engineers, and Sanford O. Hess & Associates were mechanical engineers.

FAÇADE OF 1001 FIFTH AVENUE

New York | NY

1978 | Johnson/Burgee Architects and Philip Birnbaum & Associates

As part of a negotiated compromise that permitted the H. J. Kalikow Company to construct a twenty-three-story apartment building designed by Philip Birnbaum & Associates on Fifth Avenue across from The Metropolitan Museum of Art, Kalikow retained Johnson/Burgee to design the building's façade. It is a limestone plane that rises to a false front, framing vertical channels containing a metal-and-glass curtain wall. Horizontal belt courses are aligned with those of the building's neighbors, a townhouse on one side and McKim, Mead & White's twelve-story 998 Fifth Avenue apartment building on the other. Johnson/Burgee's façade for 1001 Fifth Avenue was their first completed venture into postmodernism.

TERRACE THEATER

Kennedy Center for the Performing Arts | Washington | DC
1979 | Johnson/Burgee Architects

When the Kennedy Center, designed by Edward Durell Stone, opened in Washington, D.C., in 1971, only two of its three theaters were completed. The third hall was left as an unimproved shell. A gift of $3 million from the government of Japan made it possible to build the third theater, the Terrace Theater, containing 500 seats. Working with the acoustical engineer Cyril M. Harris, Johnson/Burgee produced a design that used geometrical transformations to achieve acoustical results. Cylinders set in pockets in the side walls increase in diameter from front to rear; the angled ceiling planes likewise change rake and interval from back to front. Johnson's choice of colors — rose, silver, and purple — contrasted with the red and gold scheme of Stone's existing interiors. Harris was the acoustical consultant, Skilling, Helle, Christiansen & Robertson were the structural engineers, Syska & Hennessy were the mechanical engineers, and Claude R. Engle was the lighting consultant.

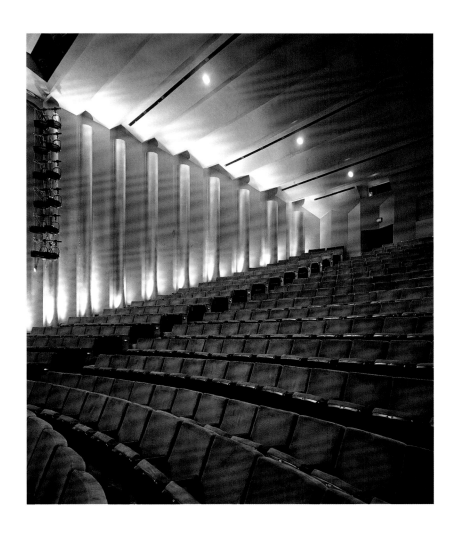

FAÇADE OF MARSHALL FIELD & COMPANY (NOW SAKS FIFTH AVENUE)

Galleria | 5115 Westheimer Road | Houston | TX
1979 | Johnson/Burgee Architects and S. I. Morris Associates
Dallas Galleria | 13250 Dallas Parkway | Dallas | TX
1983 | Johnson/Burgee Architects

Johnson/Burgee designed a façade for the Marshall Field & Company specialty store, built as part of an expansion of Gerald D. Hines Interests' Galleria in Houston. Both ends of the front wall curl away from the block-like building to advertise the façade's screenlike condition. The curved plane is faced with fossilized Texas limestone. Black granite outlines the entrance portal, which is highlighted by a giant inset panel of gold mosaic tile. At Johnson's instigation, the artist Claes Oldenburg proposed installation of a series of large-scale, free-form, color panels intended to be read as drips of paint flicked onto the façade by an unseen hand and called *Paintsplats (On a Wall by P. J.)*. Marshall Field's rejected the proposal. Marshall Field & Company represents the limitations Johnson/Burgee encountered as they became involved in producing architecture within the constraints of commercial real estate development practices. When Johnson's sophisticated sense of whimsy did not correspond to his clients' aspirations, the opportunity to start over was foreclosed by the financial constraints of the project. Marshall Field's, however, reproduced Johnson/Burgee's façade on its Dallas store when Hines built the Dallas Galleria in 1983. Colaco Engineers were structural engineers, I. A. Naman+Associates were mechanical engineers, and Claude R. Engle was the lighting consultant.

CRYSTAL CATHEDRAL

Built for the Rev. Dr. Robert H. Schuller, a minister of the Reformed Church in America and pastor of the Garden Grove Community Church, in a suburb of Los Angeles, the Crystal Cathedral joined the IDS Center and Pennzoil Place as one of Johnson/Burgee's most acclaimed works. It is a 2,990-seat church, structurally supported on an exposed, white-painted, steel space frame and clad entirely in silver reflective glass. In plan, the church is an attenuated diamond shape, elongated on its east-west axis. The glass roof is faceted into mono-pitch planes. The worship space, which occupies the entire aboveground volume of the church, is focused on a stepped tribune in the north facet of the plan. Four parallel rows of pews face the tribune. Additional seating is organized in concrete-framed balconies, supported on immense concrete cylinders, in the east, west, and south points of the plan. Their ascent to narrow points dramatically spatializes the church's triangular geometry, as does the corresponding descent of the roof facets above. The balconies hover above access spaces, some open-air, and accentuate the exhilarating sensation of entering the transparent worship space, which is 415 feet long, 207 feet wide, and rises to a height of 128 feet. Aligned on center along the central aisle is a raised water channel containing low fountain jets. The tribune, which is faced with polished, Rosso Alicante marble, contains seating for musicians, the pulpit, and two towers containing an organ and other technological equipment. The height and gestural composition of the towers provide visual focus and scale gradation. Adjacent to the pulpit, which is at the east end of the tribune rather than on-center, are ninety-foot-high segments of the wall that part to permit the preacher to gesture to worshippers parked in their cars in the church parking lot, listening to sermons on their car radios. The church was designed so that worship services could be broadcast. The Crystal Cathedral was a structural tour-de-force. Johnson/Burgee proposed use of a

Garden Grove Community Church | 12141 Lewis Street | Garden Gro'
1980 | Johnson/Burgee Architects with Albert C. Martin Associates

CREAN TOWER AND MARY HOOD CHAPEL
Garden Grove Community Church | Garden Grove | CA
1990 | Philip Johnson and Gin Wong Associates

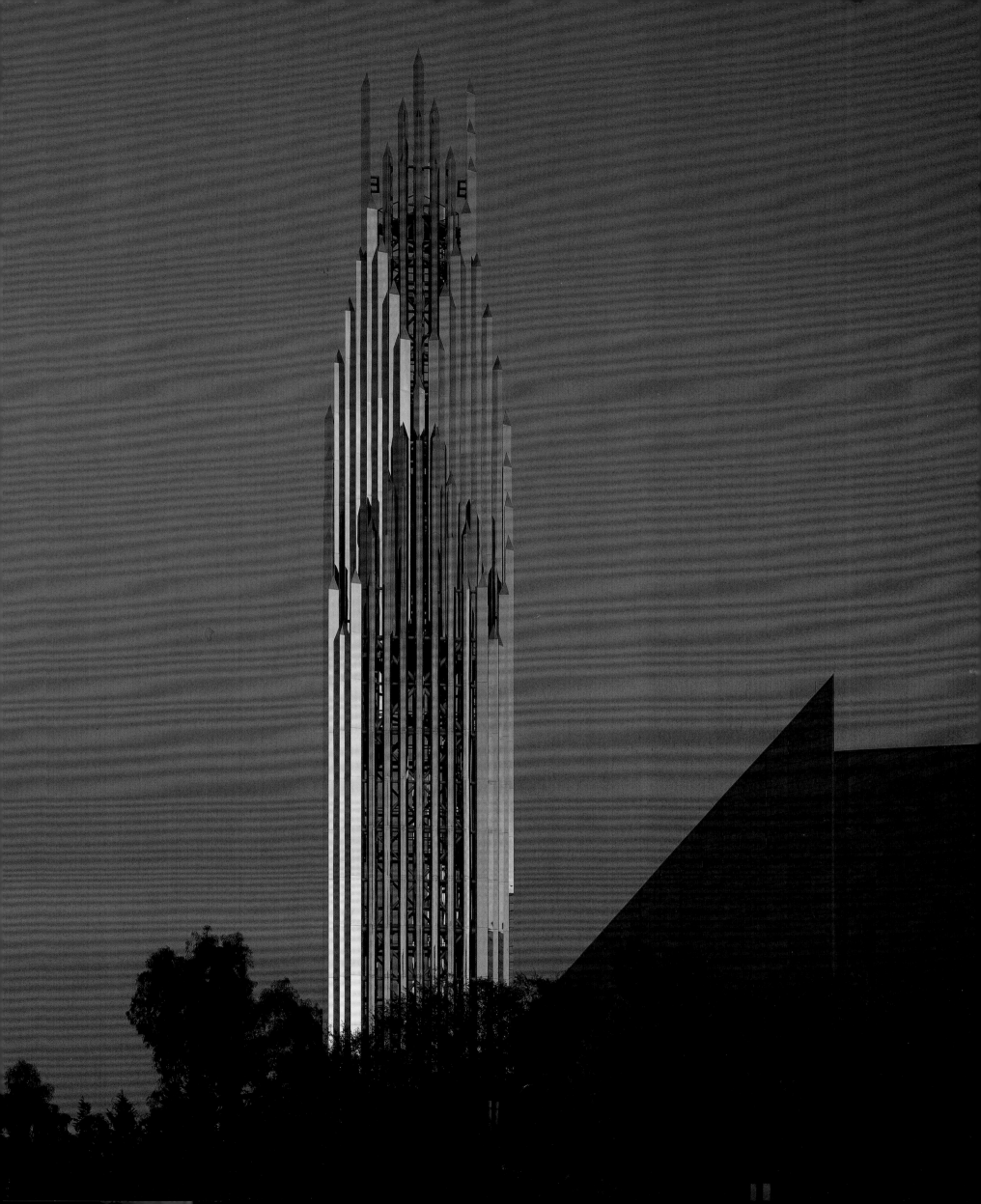

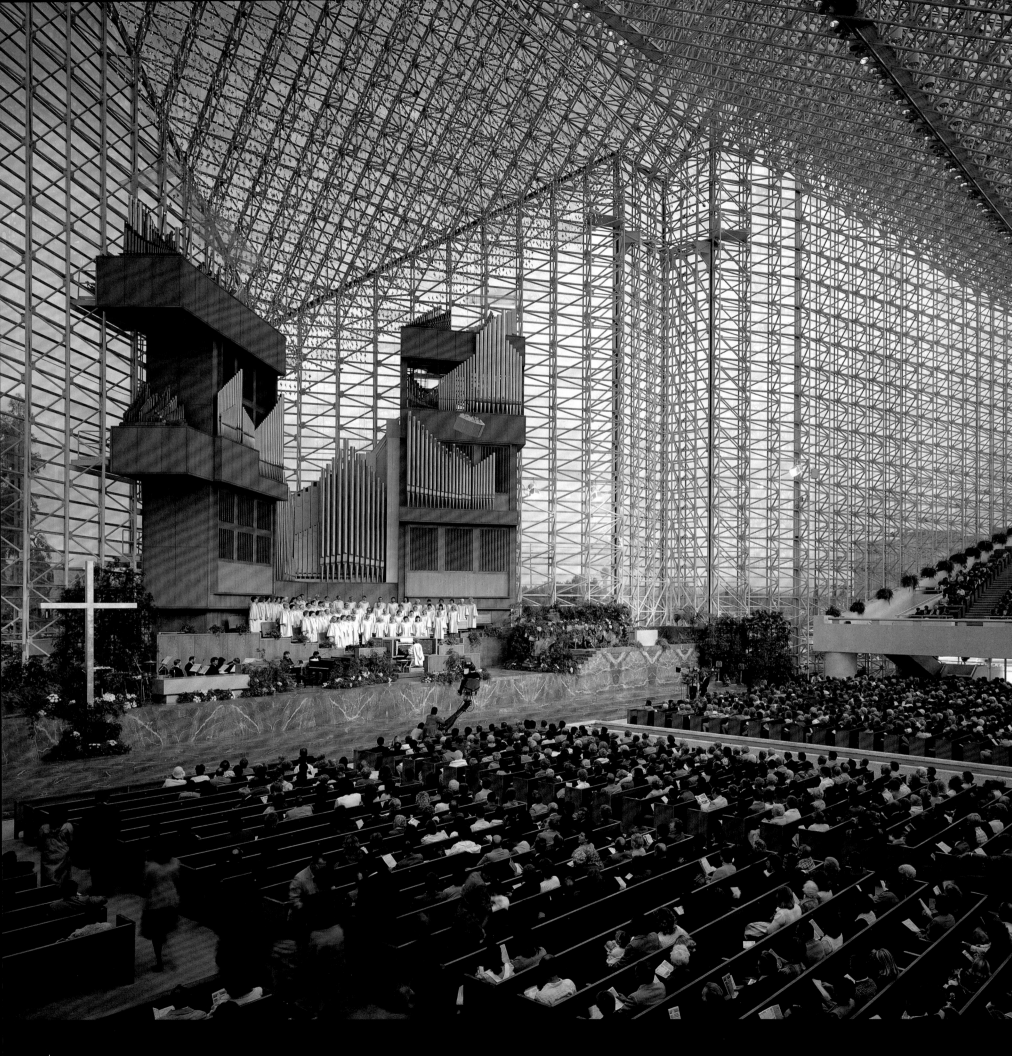

NOW, I DO NOT PROPOSE THAT WE APPROPRIATE TOMORROW THE 20 TO 50 MIL-
LION IT WOULD TAKE IN TODAY'S MONEY TO BUILD THE EQUIVALENT OF THE
PARTHENON. IT IS NOT IN THE CARDS. BUT TO BE MORE MODEST, SHOULD WE NOT
APPROPRIATE SOME OF OUR BILLIONS TO MAKE OUR HOUSES, OUR CITIES BEAU-
TIFUL, IF NOT FOR POSTERITY AND IMMORTALITY LIKE THE GREEKS, THEN FOR
OURSELVES FOR THE SAME SELFISH REASON WE DRESS WELL, DECORATE OUR
BEDROOMS, AND GROW GARDENS? CALL IT BEAUTIFICATION IF YOU WILL, CAN
WE NOT BE SURROUNDED BY BEAUTY? SOMEONE IS GOING TO REMIND ME OF
THE HORRENDOUS COST OF DOING ALL THIS. HOW ABOUT THE COST OF NOT DOING
IT? THE COST OF OUR DIRT, POLLUTION, TRAFFIC JAMS, DELAY, MENTAL ANGUISH?
THEY ARE IMMEASURABLE.

steel space frame instead of columns and beams to make the openness of the interior possible. All of the supporting structure is in the planes of the walls and ceilings; there are no structural supports in the space. The worship space was not equipped with air conditioning and only with minimal heating; instead operable vent windows stimulate internal air movement. Elements of the design — the importance of natural light and water, the dramatic framing of the preacher, and the inside-outside connection — were components of the congregation's existing church, adjacent to the Crystal Cathedral, designed for Dr. Schuller by Richard Neutra in 1959. With the Crystal Cathedral, Johnson achieved the architectural equivalent of a popular hit. The stunning emotional response the church elicited from visitors, the sense of spatial intimacy in the midst of dazzling transparency and spatial expansiveness, seemed to vindicate Johnson's search for modern monumentality and the construction of emotionally transformative spatial experiences. Even such critics as Barbara Goldstein and John Pastier, who noted the merely expedient design of the structural system, the prosaic detailing of the curtain wall, poor acoustics, and obstructed sight lines, conceded the extraordinary impact the space had on visitors. Severud-Perrone-Sturm-Bandel were structural engineers, Cosentini Associates were mechanical and electrical engineers, Klepper-Marshall-King Associates were acoustical consultants, Eugene Tofflemire was curtain wall consultant, Claude R. Engle was lighting consultant, Rolf Jensen was life safety systems consultant, and the Richard Beeson Company was the landscape consultant. A joint venture of C. L. Peck Contractor, Morse/Diesel, and the Koll Company was the general contractor.

Built alongside the Crystal Cathedral, the Crean Tower is 286 feet tall. It is composed of triangular, reflective, stainless steel fins, organized in plan as three nested squares with chamfered corners, with the middle square rotated on the diagonal. The tower contains a carillon. At the base of the tower, fitted inside it, is the small, domed, skylit, twelve-sided Mary Hood Chapel. The walls of the chapel are composed of closely spaced marble cylinders and five-sided trapezoidal piers stationed at the intersection between facets. The tower and chapel demonstrated Johnson's continuing fascination with combining shapes and layering geometries.

TATA THEATRE, NATIONAL CENTRE FOR THE PERFORMING ARTS

Dorabji Tata Road | Nariman Point | Mumbai | India

1980 | Johnson/Burgee Architects with Patell & Batliwala

Johnson/Burgee designed the 1,040-seat Tata Theatre for the performance of traditional Indian music, dance, and drama. They collaborated with the acoustician Cyril M. Harris to produce a performance space that would not require electronic amplification. Johnson/Burgee also provided a master plan for development of the theater's waterfront site as a cultural center for performance, art exhibition, art training, and scholarship. A diagonally aligned bar contains the lobby, which is 330 feet long and thirty-one-feet-nine-inches high. It is tangent to the faceted, fan-shaped theater, which is focused on a low, thrust stage. The lobby, the theater, and the stage house were treated as discrete volumes. They were set on a high-raised, reinforced concrete substructure, walled with Malad stone, and capped by a thick, oversailing, concrete parapet. The National Centre for the Performing Arts was funded by the Sir Dorabji Tata Trust and the Mumbai-based Tata group, India's foremost industrial group. Tata Consulting Engineers were structural engineers, Tata Consulting Engineers and Syska & Hennessy were mechanical engineers, Cyril M. Harris was the acoustical engineer, Dale Keller & Associates were interior design consultants, and the E.C.C. Corporation was the general contractor.

ONE SUGARLAND OFFICE PARK

15200 Southwest Freeway | Sugar Land | TX

1981 | Johnson/Burgee Architects and Richard Fitzgerald & Partners

Designed for Gerald D. Hines Interests, One Sugarland Office Park is a three-story, speculatively built office building facing a freeway in Sugar Land, a sprawling, "edge city" suburb of Houston. Johnson cited Karl Friedrich Schinkel's Feilner House in Berlin of 1829 as the source for One Sugarland's buff brick and cast-stone curtain wall. The building is a gable-fronted central block symmetrically framed by skewed, gable-capped wings. It was to have formed half of a reflectively symmetrical pair of buildings. There were to have been three such pairs, backing up to Oyster Creek and facing surface parking lots and the freeway. Johnson/Burgee's effort to construct an identity for the office park (it is adjacent to First Colony, a 9,700-acre planned community developed by Hines and Royal Dutch Shell, which opened in 1978) did not surmount the inherent limitations of the project. Although joined by other office and professional buildings that defer to the scale, materials, and style theme of One Sugarland Office Park, Johnson/Burgee's formal site plan proved insufficiently flexible and was not adhered to. Therefore, One Sugarland Office Park failed to construct a strong sense of place. Architecturally, it does not differ appreciably from other speculative office buildings in the vicinity. Goulas/Shaw Engineers were structural engineers and Cooke & Holle were mechanical engineers.

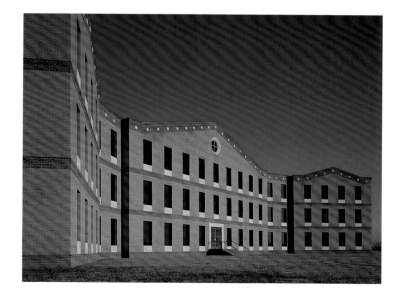

101 CALIFORNIA STREET BUILDING

101 California Street | San Francisco | CA

1982 | Johnson/Burgee Architects and Kendall/Heaton Associates

Gerald D. Hines Interests was Johnson/Burgee's client for the forty-eight-story office building at 101 California Street in the financial district of San Francisco. The tower appears to be a circle in plan, with a shallow notch incised at a right angle into its north face. The circular shape is suggested by stepped bays that facet the curtain wall. The reentrant walls of the notch and the stepped bays are solidly paneled in pink Spanish granite. The tower is set back in three shallow stages near its top. At the foot of the tower, structural columns, eighty-eight feet high, are revealed. A tilted disc, a version of the triangular greenhouse sheds above the lobbies of Pennzoil Place, is inserted beneath the tower and between the columns. A granite-faced base building, aligned with Market Street, cuts across the site on the diagonal, sliding beneath and seemingly through the tower. The big, screen-like openings of the seven-story base provide gradation in scale between the lower level of the complex and the tower. One-hundred-one California is treated as minimal sculpture on the skyline. At grade level, it becomes a monumental, space-absorbing building that bounds a triangular open plaza. Gillman-Colaco were structural engineers, I. A. Naman+Associates were mechanical engineers, Zion & Breen Associates were landscape architects, Claude R. Engle was the lighting consultant, and the Swinetron & Walberg Company was the general contractor.

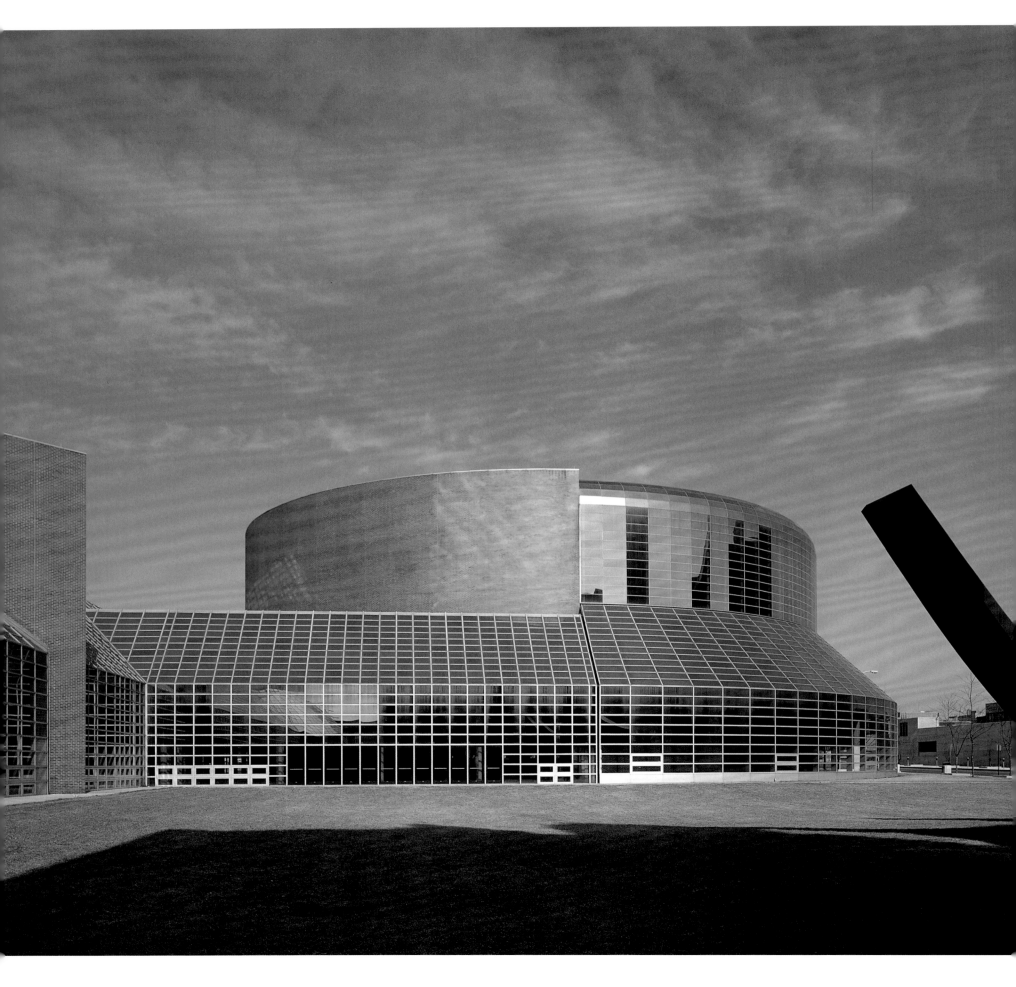

PEORIA CIVIC CENTER

201 Southwest Jefferson Avenue | Peoria | IL

1982 | Johnson/Burgee Architects and Lankton Ziegele Terry & Associates

Johnson/Burgee retrieved devices associated with Century Center in Fort Bend for their design of a civic and convention center on a cleared, multiblock site in downtown Peoria adjacent to City Hall, a classically detailed sandstone building. The three program spaces — the Arena, capable of seating 12,000 people, the Exhibit Hall, and the 2,224-seat Civic Center Theater — are organized in separate, brick-faced buildings configured in an L-plan around City Hall. They are linked by the Foyer, a linear, shed-roofed enclosure surfaced with reflective glass set in a pronounced aluminum grid. The rectilinearity of the major program blocks is qualified by rounded protrusions that introduce spatial and visual incident. The theater was the most architecturally developed building. It contains a dramatic, three-story lobby with a glass-fronted elevator and encircling promenade balconies, akin to the lobby of the General American Building. The auditorium, with its outward-stepping proscenium frames and continental seating, continues the design approach of the Terrace Theater at Kennedy Center. Two tiers of balconies and boxes are faced with illuminated decorative screens. In 1983 Ronald Bladen's steel sculpture *Sonar Tide* was installed on the Civic Center grounds. Robertson, Fowler & Associates were structural engineers, Cosentini Associates were mechanical engineers, Jules Fisher & Paul Marantz were the theater lighting consultants, Christopher Jaffe was the acoustical consultant, and Claude R. Engle was the lighting consultant.

NEIMAN MARCUS

Stockton Street and Geary Street | San Francisco | CA
1982 | Johnson/Burgee Architects

The San Francisco branch of the Dallas-based Neiman Marcus specialty store was built on a key site facing a corner of Union Square in the retail district of downtown San Francisco. Johnson/Burgee's building provoked controversy because its construction entailed demolition of The City of Paris, a retail building on the site designed by the San Francisco architect Arthur Brown, Jr. To appease public indignation over the demolition, Neiman Marcus dismantled and re-erected the skylit rotunda of The City of Paris in a cylindrical glass entrance tube at the corner of Stockton and Geary Streets, facing Union Square. The rest of Johnson/Burgee's boxlike building contained a variety of framed openings of different scales. On the top floor, a glass vault brought skylight into an upper-level sales area. The store is faced with a patterned façade of red granite tiles, alternately polished and flame-finished and rotated on the diagonal to give the street walls a feeling of weightlessness, not unlike the patterned walls associated with the Philadelphia architects Venturi, Rauch & Scott Brown. Whisler-Patri were architects for the reconstruction of The City of Paris rotunda, Skilling, Helle, Christiansen & Robertson were structural engineers, Magill-Cloyd Engineers were the mechanical engineers, and Claude R. Engle was the lighting consultant. In 1999, San Francisco preservationists mounted a campaign to prevent Neiman Marcus from effacing the building with radical alterations.

TRANSCO TOWER AND WATER WALL (NOW WILLIAMS TOWER)

2800 Post Oak Boulevard | Houston | TX

1983 | Johnson/Burgee Architects and Morris Aubry Architects

1984 | Water Wall | Johnson/Burgee Architects and Richard Fitzgerald & Partners

The sixty-four-story Transco Tower was designed for Gerald D. Hines Interests on a green-field site across the street from Hines's mixed-use complex, the Galleria. It was designed to function as two stacked office buildings, one containing the headquarters of Transco, an energy corporation, the other containing rental office space and the offices of Hines Interests. In addition to the tower, Johnson/Burgee designed a parking garage and the Water Wall, a fountain set on axis with the south face of the tower and separated from it by an allée of live oak trees. Johnson cited the Beekman Tower, a setback skyscraper of the 1920s visible from his office in the Seagram Building, as his inspiration for the tapered shaft of the Transco Tower. The slender, setback building is faced with a curtain wall of silver reflective glass set in a gridded aluminum frame. Slender V-shaped bays, faced with bronze reflective glass, protrude through the silver field in the central registers of each face. As implied shadow lines, the dark glass bays accentuate the tower's vertical rise. A low, fabric-surfaced pyramidal cap at the summit of the tower contains telecommunications equipment and a decorative rotating beacon. Johnson/Burgee collaged a colossal, granite-faced entrance portal onto the Post Oak Boulevard base of the building to mark the formal entrance; most people arriving at the Transco Tower enter from the rear parking garage or from the Galleria, both of which are connected to the building by overhead pedestrian bridges. The formal economy of the Transco Tower makes it a compelling presence in the Post Oak district of Houston. Because it is much taller than other nearby towers, it figures strongly as an isolated landmark. The building evokes the condition of postmodern urbanity. Its shape unequivocally symbolizes the architecture of the metropolis, but its hollow reflectivity and turf terraces attest to its posturban landscape setting. Formal restraint and authoritative proportions make Transco

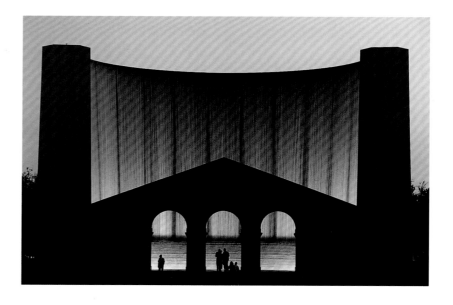

Tower one of Johnson/Burgee's most compelling explorations of the condition of postmodernity. Where their practice would tend, however, is represented by the Water Wall. It is a hollow, semicircular enclosure, sixty-four feet high, surfaced on its inner and outer faces with an exposed aggregate that "shreds" water as it cascades down from the upper rim of the wall. Watching the cascading water, viewers experience a sensation of bodily displacement, as if they were rising. Johnson/Burgee's installation of a triple-arched pedimented screen, which Johnson called a *scœnœ frons*, confused their effort to introduce spatial framing, spatial layering, and scale gradation, since its ersatz neoclassicism is unrelated to the architecture of the fountain or the tower. By displacing thrill-inducing design from the Transco Tower onto its fountain, however, Johnson/Burgee allowed the tower to retain a dignity that enhances its stature. CBM Engineers were structural engineers for the buildings and Madeley Engineers were structural engineers for the fountain. I. A. Naman+Associates were mechanical engineers, Zion & Breen Associates were landscape architects, Claude R. Engle was the lighting consultant, and CMS Collaborative was the fountain consultant. J. A. Jones Construction Company was the general contractor.

NEW CLEVELAND PLAY HOUSE

8500 Euclid Avenue | Cleveland | OH

1983 | Johnson/Burgee Architects with Collins & Rimer

Johnson/Burgee added two theaters and attendant public and service spaces to the premises of Cleveland's resident professional theater company, the Cleveland Play House, the oldest regional theater in the United States. That the Play House was a brick-faced Lombard Romanesque style complex built in 1927 gave Johnson/Burgee the opportunity to design their additions in a streamlined, postmodern, round-arched style. Johnson/Burgee's two theaters, the 124-seat Studio One, an experimental theater without fixed seating, and the more traditional, proscenium-focused Bolton Theater, containing 548 seats, were lined up to the west of the 1927 Play House in front of a defunct retail store that the Play House was able to incorporate into its complex. A linear sequence of lobbies, configured as geometrically shaped pavilions, faces Euclid Avenue: the domed entrance pavilion with its arcuated and pedimented loggia, a conically roofed octagonal lobby in front of the 1927 Play House, and a flat-roofed lobby in front of the Bolton Theater, behind which the stepped, gabled roofs of the theater and stage house rose. The interior of the Bolton Theater was Johnson/Burgee's most consistently finished space. It is in the tradition of their Terrace Theater and Peoria Civic Center Theater. The New Cleveland Play House displayed Johnson/Burgee's return to formalism under the dispensation of postmodern contextualism. Their inability to produce new traditional design with the conciseness of scale and particularity of detail of the 1927 building made the New Play House look merely expedient on close inspection. Robertson, Fowler & Associates were structural engineers, Cosentini Associates and Byers, Urban, Klug, White & Associates were mechanical engineers, Claude R. Engle was the lighting consultant, Brannigan Lorelli was the theatrical consultant, Klepper Marshall King Associates were the acoustical consultants, William A. Behnke Associates consulted on site development, and the R. P. Carbone Construction Company was the general contractor.

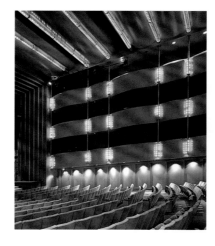

UNITED BANK OF COLORADO TOWER AND PLAZA (NOW WELLS FARGO CENTER)

1700 Lincoln Street | Denver | CO

1983 | Johnson/Burgee and Morris Aubry Architects

Gerald D. Hines Interests built the fifty-story United Bank of Colorado Tower and its plaza, a glass-vaulted galleria stretching through an adjacent city block to connect with downtown Denver's most famous modern skyscraper, the Mile High Center of 1956, an early work of I. M. Pei. The United Bank Tower was Johnson/Burgee's last Late Modern work. It pays homage to Frank Stella's Protractor paintings of the late 1960s with offset curved profiles that earned it its nickname: the cash register building. The curtain wall, like the exterior facing of the Neiman Marcus store, is a deliberately weightless pattern of square windows and recessed spandrel-level panels punched through a skin of flame-finished Swedish red granite. Johnson/Burgee detailed the galleria as a composition of stacked Stella vaults that engage, without obscuring, the Mile High Center. The United Bank Tower wittily claimed a place on the skyline of downtown Denver with its shaped profile while simultaneously articulating the repetitive nature of office lease space with its patterned curtain wall. Recessing the window glass and inserting the recessed panels at spandrel level animated the curtain wall at close range. CBM Engineers were structural engineers, I. A. Naman+Associates were mechanical engineers, and Claude R. Engle was the lighting consultant.

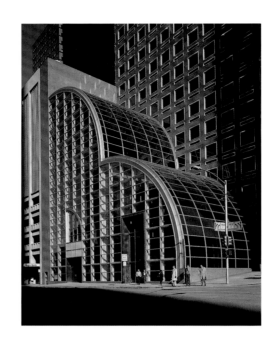

REPUBLICBANK CENTER (NOW BANK OF AMERICA CENTER)

700 Louisiana Street | Houston | TX

1984 | Johnson/Burgee and Kendall/Heaton Associates

Gerald D. Hines Interests built the fifty-six-story RepublicBank Center in downtown Houston across Louisiana Street from Pennzoil Place for the Houston branch of a Dallas-based bank holding corporation. The building occupies an entire city block. It consists of the 772-foot-tall office tower on the west half of the block and a separate 136-foot-tall banking hall on the east half. Concealed within the north half of the banking hall was a two-story building already on the site, which was not demolished but encapsulated. The roof of the existing building established the second-floor level of the banking hall. A flamboyant exercise in postmodern eclecticism, RepublicBank's style theme was the scrolled gables characteristic of seventeenth-century Dutch architecture. The tower was set back in three stages. Each stage terminates in a series of subsidiary, gable-like setbacks, which are punctuated with numerous pinnacles surfaced in lead-coated copper. Johnson/Burgee detailed the curtain wall of the tower with alternating major and minor vertical piers. The base of the building is largely without windows. Instead, colossal arched portals frame entrances on the east and west sides. The base walls are articulated with staged layers of Swedish red granite, as might be found in a stone-built building. CBM Engineers were structural engineers, I. A. Naman + Associates were mechanical and electrical engineers, Gensler & Associates were interior architects for RepublicBank (although Johnson/Burgee detailed the interior architecture of the ground floor), Calvin L. Kort was the elevator consultant, and David Gibson was responsible for the model office.

PPG PLACE

Third and Fourth Avenues and Market Street | Pittsburgh | PA
1984 | Johnson/Burgee Architects

Built to house the headquarters of PPG Industries (an outgrowth of the Pittsburgh Plate Glass Company), PPG Place is a six-building complex centered on a block-square corporate plaza in the Golden Triangle, the historic center of downtown Pittsburgh. The site is bounded on the north by Market Square, a public square of eighteenth-century origin, and consists of portions of six city blocks assembled by Pittsburgh's Urban Redevelopment Authority. Johnson/Burgee designed a forty-story, square-planned tower, 635 feet high, as the dominant building. It faces PPG's corporate plaza to the east and is abutted on the west by the Winter Garden, a glass-walled and roofed concourse. Johnson/Burgee lined the other three sides of the plaza with lower office buildings. All components are faced with variations of an aluminum-framed, silver reflective glass curtain wall from which the complex derives its architectural identity. As at the IDS Center and the Transco Tower, Johnson/Burgee imaginatively modified accepted practices in curtain wall design to give PPG (which manufactures curtain wall assemblies) a historically resonant, postmodern image. By projecting alternating square and V-planned bays between the buildings' steel structural columns, Johnson/Burgee imbued the walls of reflective glass with a rippling, vertically accentuated spatial depth enhanced by the play of distorted reflections. The corners of the forty-story tower were built out to form more complexly faceted configurations. As projections crested above the parapet lines of the

buildings they terminated in elongated pyramidal caps. The caps recalled Gothic pinnacles, an association supported by the major and minor pierlike aspect of the vertical projections. Johnson/Burgee wittily shaped the modern, industrially fabricated curtain wall to echo historic architecture (the tower resembles the profile of Victoria Tower at the Houses of Parliament in London) without, however, distorting the curtain wall's constructional logic. The complex met the low, nineteenth-century commercial houses of Market Square with a combination of proportioned assurance and postmodern surreality. Johnson/Burgee lined the buildings framing the corporate plaza with inset arcades along the sidewalks. The plaza was detailed with different colored granites, organized with diagonally aligned runners. At the center of the plaza, Johnson/Burgee designed a Rationalist truncated obelisk on a low, stepped base, all of pink granite. Unlike RepublicBank Center, its architectural aspirations were worked out in terms of the way a skyscraper office building was built in the 1980s. Johnson/Burgee cleverly subverted the banal, reflective glass curtain wall to explore its potential for constructing corporate and civic identity. Tishman Realty & Construction Company of Pennsylvania was development manager for PPG Place. Glenn Garrison, Anne Asher, and James Martin were Johnson/Burgee's senior staff members on the project. Robertson, Fowler & Associates were structural engineers, Cosentini Associates were mechanical engineers, W. A. Di Giacomo & Associates were electrical engineers, Claude R. Engle was the lighting consultant, Calvin Kort was the elevator consultant, Edison Parking was the parking consultant, Cerami & Associates were the acoustical consultants, Vignelli Associates were graphic designers, Cope Linder Associates were retail consultants, Zion & Breen Associates were landscape architects, Curtain Wall Design and Consulting and PPG Industries Commercial Construction Group were curtain wall consultants, and Mellon-Stuart/Blount was the general contractor.

DADE COUNTY CULTURAL CENTER (NOW METRO-DADE CULTURAL CENTER IN MIAMI)

101 West Flagler Street | Miami | FL

1983 | Johnson/Burgee Architects with Connell, Metcalf & Eddy

The Dade County Cultural Center, built for the metropolitan government of Miami and Dade County, consists of the blocklike, three-story Miami-Dade Public Library, a two-story bar building for the Historical Museum of South Florida, and an L-plan, one- and two-story building for the Miami Art Museum. They are grouped atop a raised, fourteen-foot-high parking podium and outline a tile-paved terrace. Like the New Cleveland Play House, the Dade County Cultural Center was a neotraditional design. Johnson cited the work of the Florida architect Addison Mizner, who practiced in Palm Beach in the 1920s, and the Prussian neoclassical architect Ludwig Persius as formal sources for the simply composed, minimally windowed buildings, which were faced with stucco and capped with red tile roofs. The library was treated as a figural, symmetrical building. An inset arcade runs beneath the east front and south side of the building. The other two buildings are treated as architectural dependents of the library. The interior plan diagrams of all three reflect Johnson's predilection for crisply proportioned rectangular spaces. To compensate for the center's elevation above the street, the walls of the parking garage along West Flagler Street are battered and faced with fossilized Texas limestone, which is similar in texture to Florida coral stone. The sidewalk is outlined with a double row of royal palm trees. At the midpoint of the block a stair leads from Flagler Street up to the front of the library. A second, more gradually inclined and canopied ramped access way down to Northwest First Avenue is paralleled by a broad water cascade that steps down in stages behind the art museum. The Dade County Cultural Center aroused criticism in Miami when the design was released in 1978 because it was traditional rather than modern, unlike other components of the downtown Government Center, of which it is a part. Ironically, Johnson/Burgee's design anticipated Miami's emergence in the 1980s as an architectural center for what might be termed progressive traditionalism, embodied especially in the urban planning theory and practices promulgated by Andrés Duany and Elizabeth Plater-Zyberk as the New Urbanism. Connell, Metcalf & Eddy were structural and mechanical engineers as well as associated architects. Claude R. Engel was the lighting consultant.

AT&T BUILDING (NOW SONY PLAZA)

550 Madison Avenue | New York | NY

1984 | Johnson/Burgee Architects and Simmons Architects

Designed as the headquarters of what was then the United States' major telecommunications corporation, the thirty-seven-story, 647-foot-tall AT&T Building marked Johnson/Burgee's embrace of postmodernism. The notoriety occasioned by the design's publication in 1978 catapulted Philip Johnson to the status of a popular cultural celebrity. The AT&T Building occupies an entire block front on Madison Avenue between East Fifty-fifth and East Fifty-sixth Streets. Johnson/Burgee treated the base of the building as a colossal, sixty-foot-high loggia, 134 feet high at the central, vaulted entrance bay. The office floors, five through thirty-three, rose to a tall attic capped by a raked parapet split at its apex by a circular incision that earned the building the nickname of "Chippendale skyscraper" for its likeness to eighteenth-century highboys. The uncertain spacing of major and minor vertical mullions in the curtain wall and a lack of setbacks made the tower an inert presence on the crowded skyline of midtown Manhattan. Eviscerating the center bay further depleted the compositional energy of the shaft, although it was a compositional theme that reappeared in subsequent Burgee/Johnson skyscrapers. Johnson and Burgee emphasized the ground level of the AT&T Building rather than its shaft. Apart from a compact entrance lobby enclosing the central elevator core (proportioned to contain AT&T's corporate icon, *The Genius of Electricity* of 1916, by the sculptor Evelyn Beatrice Longman), the ground floor was almost completely open as a publicly accessible hypostyle hall. Parallel to Madison Avenue but behind the building was a glass-vaulted, midblock galleria, one hundred feet high, framed by a four-story rear building containing retail and service spaces. The AT&T Building was sheathed in flame-finished pink Stony Creek granite, detailed to look as though it were load-bearing despite the wide, flat spans of the loggia bays. Johnson/Burgee finished interior circulation spaces with an array of rich materials, notably the flamboyant Breccia Strazzema marble walls of the skylobby, with its circular window set inside the central arch of the main entrance. Because of its long construction period, the AT&T Building had been somewhat eclipsed by the Transco Tower, RepublicBank Center, and PPG Place by the time it was completed. Its historical

importance derives from its role in legitimizing postmodern historical eclecticism as a mainstream architectural practice, and, secondarily, from Johnson/Burgee's effort to provide public spaces that looked as lavish and solidly constructed as those of the great, early twentieth-century eclectic skyscrapers of Manhattan, as the British critic Reyner Banham noted in an unexpectedly appreciative assessment. Its urban importance derives from AT&T's extraordinary provision of publicly accessible space at sidewalk level. These spaces were the portions of the building most subject to change after AT&T sold it to the Japanese entertainment corporation Sony in 1992. Sony retained Gwathmey, Siegel & Associates to enclose much of this space for retail and corporate display purposes. According to the critic Mark Alden Branch, the base of the building benefited from these alterations, which absorbed surplus space and gave the underside of the building spatial definition linked to movement and use. The AT&T Building forecast the path Johnson/Burgee (and Burgee/Johnson) pursued in their postmodern office building designs of the 1980s. Flamboyant, historically derived imagery, a predilection for monumental scale and durable facing materials outside and exaggeratedly grand, ostentatiously finished, but empty elevator lobbies inside, and inattention to compositional refinements were the attributes of their prolific postmodern architectural production. Alan Ritchie and Rolf Hedlund in Johnson/Burgee's office and Russell Patterson with Simmons Architects were the senior architectural staff. Robertson & Fowler Associates were structural engineers and Leroy Callender was the associate engineer, Mueser, Rutledge, Johnston & Desimone were the foundation consultants, Cosentini Associates were the mechanical engineers, ISD were interior designers, and the Frank Briscoe Company Crow/Briscoe joint venture and HRH Construction Company were the general contractors.

580 CALIFORNIA BUILDING

500-580 California Street | San Francisco | CA

1984 | Johnson/Burgee and Kendall/Heaton Associates

Located several blocks up California Street from 101 California, 580 California Street is a twenty-three-story speculative office building occupying a compact square allotment. Designed for Gerald D. Hines Interests, it is an exercise in postmodern contextualism, incorporating iconic elements of San Francisco architecture to construct a San Franciscan architectural identity. The faceted window bays, with their frosting of cast aluminum, the two-over-two windows in the corner bays, and the mansard roof — a sloped glass curtain wall with cast aluminum cresting and finials — echo the Victorian house fronts for which San Francisco is famous. The tower engages the sloping sidewalk with an inset, monumentally scaled arcade. The tower is faced with a light colored Sardinian granite. Draped, faceless figures cast in fiberglass, the work of the sculptor Muriel Castanis, are stationed on the parapet line above the cylindrical piers that separate the bay window stacks. The 580 California Building represents Johnson/Burgee at their least capricious. It demonstrate the postmodern possibility of a locally resonant architecture that grounds new construction in familiar images and spatial types while acknowledging major differences in scale, use, and status. Skilling, Helle, Christiansen & Robertson were structural engineers, I. A. Naman+Associates were mechanical and electrical engineers, Claude R. Engle was the lighting consultant, and Steven T. Baird Architects & Associates were the ornamental metal consultants.

FIVE HUNDRED BOYLSTON STREET BUILDING

Five Hundred Boylston Street | Boston | MA

1985 | John Burgee Architects with Philip Johnson and Kendall/Heaton Associates

Gerald D. Hines Interests and the New England Life Insurance Company were the clients for what was to have been a two-building complex in the Back Bay district of Boston, adjacent to such landmarks as Trinity Church by H. H. Richardson and I. M. Pei & Partners' John Hancock Building. Burgee/Johnson's design was so harshly criticized in Boston before the complex was built that Hines retained Robert A. M. Stern Architects to design the second tower. Five Hundred Bolyston Street is an exercise in neo-Victorian classicism. The twenty-five-story office slab is bisected by a glazed central bay culminating in a Crystal Palace–like arcuated register. To give the complex monumental scale, Burgee and Johnson treated pairs of floors as single layers framed by what they called a supergrid, aggressively maximizing the building's presence. Figural planning was intended to shape urban spaces between six-story wings that frame an entrance court on Boylston Street and in the elevator lobby. Five Hundred Bolyston holds the street edges, defers to adjacent buildings in terms of scale and massing, and attempts to construct an accessible, spatially buoyant sequence of public places that engage the building to the city. But rather than a collage of new and old energized by its architectural contradictions, the stylistic fulsomeness of the complex makes its thin granite and glass curtain walls seem meretricious. LeMessurier Associates/SCI were structural engineers, Cosentini Associates were mechanical engineers, Zion & Breen Associates were landscape architects, and Claude R. Engle was the lighting consultant.

ARCHITECTURE BUILDING

Burdette Keeland, a professor of architecture at the University of Houston, was instrumental in securing the design commission for the College of Architecture Building for Johnson. The three- and four-story building is big in scale and volume. It contains trays of studio loft space surrounding a central court, eighty feet high and capped by a skylight. Built astride a campus street along one edge of the campus, the building is visible from a nearby elevated freeway. Johnson made the building stand out among its architecturally prosaic neighbors by appropriating the image of the House of Education, an unbuilt design by the eighteenth-century French architect Claude-Nicolas Ledoux, inflating it in scale, jettisoning all architectural detail, and packaging it as a postmodern landmark. Despite caustic criticism by faculty and students, Burgee/Johnson's design was built. Its size, symmetry, and imageability succeed in giving the architecture building monumental stature while not hindering its internal operation as a design studio and academic building. CBM Engineers were structural engineers, Cook & Holle were mechanical engineers, and Claude R. Engle was the lighting consultant.

University of Houston | Houston | TX

1985 | John Burgee Architects with Philip Johnson and Morris Aubry Architects

TO MANY, THE IDEA OF A RETURN TO AN INTEREST IN HISTORY IS A SLAP AT THE WHOLE MODERN MOVEMENT, CAPITAL M, CAPITAL M. I CLAIM THAT IT IS NOT. IN THE TIME OF THE BAUHAUS AND THE TIME OF THE EARLY DAYS AT HARVARD, HISTORY WAS NOT CONSIDERED A PROPER STUDY. AND TODAY, HOW DIFFERENT! WE FIND OURSELVES NOW ALL WRAPPED UP IN REMINISCENCE. WE CANNOT TODAY NOT KNOW HISTORY. IT'S A STIMULATING AND NEW FEELING OF FREEDOM.

53RD AT THIRD BUILDING (LIPSTICK BUILDING)

885 Third Avenue | New York | NY

1986 | John Burgee Architects with Philip Johnson

Built by Gerald D. Hines Interests, 53rd at Third, or the Lipstick Building as it came to be popularly known, is a stack of thirty-five elliptical floor plates interrupted by two setbacks. Rather than rising on a central vertical axis, the floorplates engage an external elevator core on the west, rear, side of the building so that they rise eccentrically when seen from Third Avenue. Although this necessitated the presence of structural columns within the lease space, use of the curvilinear geometry meant that the building could contain more space under local planning regulations than would have been allowed if it had a more conventional rectangular plan configuration. Burgee and Johnson emphasized the horizontal layering of office lease space with their banded curtain wall, which superimposes ribbons of reflective glass windows above two-toned spandrels. The spandrels are composed of horizontal layers of Swedish Imperial granite, flame-finished above, polished below, accentuated with speed lines of stainless steel. Thick cylindrical columns with bulbous caps, wrapped in granite and stainless steel, protrude from beneath the recessed, high-ceilinged, glass-walled ground-floor lobby. The Lipstick Building, as Michael Sorkin observed, was a Houston or Dallas building transposed to midtown Manhattan. Burgee and Johnson made it work in the architecturally dull context of Third Avenue by scooping out urban space sculpturally with its curving shapes and making it sparkle amid the dour 1960s and 70s curtain walls. The Office of Irwin Cantor was structural engineer, Cosentini Associates were mechanical engineers, Claude R. Engle was the lighting consultant, and Zion & Breen Associates were landscape architects. Hines had its New York offices in this building. John Burgee moved the Burgee/Johnson office from the Seagram Building to the Lipstick Building, where it remained until its dissolution, when Johnson returned to the Seagram Building.

THE CRESCENT

Cedar Springs Road and Pearl Street | Dallas | TX
1985 | John Burgee Architects with Philip Johnson and Shepherd+Boyd USA

The Crescent is a mixed-use retail, hotel, and office complex built just beyond the northern edge of downtown Dallas on a triangular ten-acre site in a corridor of mixed office, retail, and residential uses. Burgee and Johnson's professional collaborator, the Dallas architect Phillip W. Shepherd, was a co-investor in the project and its managing partner. The Rosewood Corporation of Dallas was the general partner. Its Victorian French Mansard styling theme notwithstanding, the Crescent works spatially as an urbane complex of buildings. It successfully mixes pedestrian spaces and on-site vehicular circulation and parking space, it provides a measured sequence of publicly accessible outdoor and indoor spaces, and it marks a point of transition between the downtown core and the low- and midrise Cedar Springs and Oak Lawn districts. The buildings' limestone-faced walls and slate roofs imbue it with material substance. Its expensively finished ground level set a precedent that Kohn Pedersen Fox and their collaborators affirmed in the nearby complex of the Federal Reserve Bank of Dallas of 1992. Vincent Ponte was urban planning consultant for the Crescent, Ellisor & Tanner were structural engineers, Brady, Lohrman & Pendelton were mechanical engineers, Steven T. Baird Architects & Associates were ornamental ironwork consultants, Claude R. Engle was the lighting consultant, Zion & Breen Associates were landscape architects, and HCB Contractors was the general contractor. Kalef Alaton et Cie. designed the interiors of the Hotel Crescent Court.

TWO FEDERAL RESERVE PLAZA

33 Maiden Lane | New York | NY

1985 | Johnson/Burgee Architects

Built adjacent to the magisterial Federal Reserve Bank of New York Building by York & Sawyer, Johnson/Burgee's twenty-eight-story speculative office building sports a postmodern castellated theme. Because the site in lower Manhattan was irregular, Johnson/Burgee used projecting cylindrical bays to minimize the impact of the building's nonorthogonal geometry and animate its surfaces. The curtain wall is constructed of two tones of brick, a buff color for vertical stacks and a mixed blend of brown for spandrels. At street level, the building has a tall, vaulted, open-air pedestrian passage cut through it, parallel to the side street, Nassau Street. The Whitney Museum of American Art maintained a branch gallery in the basement of the building opened in the late 1980s and designed by Tod Williams Billie Tsien & Associates. Park Tower Realty and IBM were the clients for Two Federal Reserve Plaza. Weiskopf & Pickworth were structural engineers, Cosentini Associates were mechanical engineers, and Claude R. Engle was the lighting consultant.

TYCON TOWER

8000 Towers Crescent Drive | Vienna | VA
1985 | John Burgee Architects with Philip Johnson

Tycon Tower is a seventeen-story speculative office building in Tyson's Corner, a Virginia suburb of Washington, DC. It was designed to be one of three identical buildings, curved slabs in plan, backed up by a separate, curved parking garage. Only the east slab was built to Burgee/Johnson's design. As at 500 Boylston and the Crescent, a central bay rises into an arched frontispiece, extruded through the center of the top floor as a glass-roofed vault. The central bay is flanked by brick-clad cylinders set on a three-story, brick-faced plinth and terminating in horizontal brick-bands at the top of the building. A gridded metal-and-glass curtain wall is recessed behind the cylinders. Brick-faced spandrels interrupt the curtain wall at every other floor to give the building its outsized scale. The outsized arched frontispiece earned Tycon Tower its nickname: the Shopping Bag Building. Guldu & Fernández were structural engineers, Cosentini Associates were mechanical engineers, Claude R. Engle was the lighting consultant, and Zion & Breen Associates were the landscape architects.

190 SOUTH LA SALLE STREET BUILDING

190 South La Salle Street | Chicago | IL

1986 | John Burgee Architects with Philip Johnson and Shaw Associates

Designed for the John Buck Company, 190 South La Salle Street is a forty-story, 900,000-square-foot speculative office building in the heart of the financial district of the Chicago Loop. As at the 580 California Building in San Francisco, Johnson and Burgee grounded their postmodernism in the architectural history of Chicago, paying homage to Burnham & Root's Masonic Temple Building, a pioneer Chicago skyscraper of the 1890s, demolished in the 1930s and marked by big-scaled gables. Johnson and Burgee's building repeats the rhythms of neighboring skyscrapers in its horizontal coursing and vertical alignments. Allen Freeman praised it for the plasticity of its curtain wall, which echoes the materiality and sense of depth of adjoining buildings. The tall base of 190 South La Salle Street is faced with Imperial Red granite; the shaft is faced with a Spanish Pink granite. Burgee and Johnson employed double-height window divisions in the curtain wall panels beneath the roof gables, proportionally integrating them with the framing bays of the shaft. The simplified decoration and slightly playful curvature of the gable profiles add a note of postmodern whimsy that animates the design rather than reducing it to kitsch. The vaulted lobby paralleling La Salle Street is spatially grandiose and opulent in its finishes. An exedra at one end of the lobby contains Anthony Caro's sculpture *Chicago Fugue*. A tapestry by Helena Henmarck pays tribute to D. H. Burnham's Chicago Plan of 1909. Powell/Kleinschmidt designed the interiors of the building's major tenant, the law firm of Mayer, Brown & Platt, although Burgee/Johnson designed the firm's law library, which occupied the high top floor. Cohen, Barreto, Marchertas were the structural engineers for 190 South La Salle Street, Cosentini Associates were the mechanical engineers, and Claude R. Engle was the lighting consultant.

ONE ATLANTIC CENTER

1201 West Peachtree Street N.E. | Atlanta | GA

1987 | John Burgee Architects with Philip Johnson and Heery Architects and Engineers

The fifty-story One Atlantic Center/IBM Tower is an authoritative presence on the skyline of midtown Atlanta, just north of downtown and Peachtree Center. The tower's slender profile, subtly setback top, and copper-surfaced pyramidal roof cause it to figure strongly in its isolated setting. Johnson and Burgee contained three office floors in a supergrid of pink granite spandrels and piers of different widths. This overlay contributes to the tower's soaring aspect. Behind the building is a two-acre corporate park and a freestanding, architecturally coordinated parking garage joined to the tower by a continuous water-wall fountain. Although more conservative architecturally than the Transco Tower in Houston (Allen Freeman observed that One Atlantic Center is not "like" a 1920s skyscraper, it is a 1920s skyscraper), it fulfills a similar role in Atlanta by providing an urban focus for the midtown area. Had Burgee and Johnson's master plan for the other components of Atlantic Center been carried out, they would have blunted the singularity of the IBM Tower. Prentiss Properties and IBM were the developers of the tower. Datum Moore Partnership was the structural engineer, Blum Consulting were the mechanical and electrical engineers, Claude R. Engle was the lighting consultant, Zion & Breen Associates were the landscape architects, and CMS Collaborative were the fountain consultants.

MOMENTUM PLACE (NOW BANK ONE CENTER)

1717 Main Street | Dallas | TX

1987 | John Burgee Architects with Philip Johnson and HKS

The sixty-story, 1.53-million-square-foot Momentum Place was built by Cadillac Fairview Urban Development as headquarters for MCorp, the bank holding corporation that grew out of the Mercantile National Bank. It was constructed on a full-block site across Main Street from the Mercantile National Bank Building, once the tallest in Dallas, in the heart of downtown. In contrast to the restraint and purposefulness of 190 South La Salle Street and One Atlantic Center, Momentum Place is a postmodern extravaganza of external arch shapes and of mega-lomaniacal vaulted spaces inside. Insistent, overstated symmetries subvert the building's compositional authority; it lacks the arresting profiles of the United Bank Tower in Denver. Even so, the building faces Ervay Street with dignity. The monumental arched entrance — recycling similar portals from RepublicBank, 190 South La Salle, and One Atlantic Center — leads into a five-story-high, glass-vaulted pavilion containing a basement-level trading floor bridged by the entrance causeway. Glass vaulted spaces higher up in the tower contained opulently detailed and finished function rooms and offices for the bank. The Reagan-era excess embodied in Momentum Place deflated with the collapse of Texas's oil- and real estate–based economy. The MCorp system went bankrupt in 1989 and the building's next occupant, Bank One, had RTKL Interiors remodel its spaces in order to appear less ostentatious. The Datum/Moore Partnership was the structural engineer for Momentum Place, Cosentini Associates were mechanical engineers, Claude R. Engle was the lighting consultant, and CMS Collaborative was the fountain consultant.

ONE INTERNATIONAL PLACE, FORT HILL SQUARE

100 Oliver Street | Boston | MA

1987 | John Burgee Architects with Philip Johnson

Like the 500 Boylston Street building, Burgee and Johnson's twin-towered International

Place complex was received with intense public criticism in Boston, in this instance because

of its density. Designed for Donald J. Chiofaro and Theodore Oatis of the Chiofaro Company,

the complex consists of two cylindrical towers sprouting lower wings, arrayed on an almost

triangular site around a central, glass-roofed winter garden. The first and tallest tower, of

forty-six stories (with wings of twenty-seven stories and nineteen stories), was mocked for its

Palladian curtain wall, applied to the flat, granite-faced wall planes of the building in order

to contrast with a gridded, primarily glazed curtain wall on the faceted portions of the tower.

Burgee and Johnson reworked their design of the 101 California Building in San Francisco,

deforming cylindrical and rectangular geometries as the components of International Place

intersected. KKBNA McNamara/Salvia were structural engineers, Cosentini Associates were

mechanical engineers, John Ownby & Associates were electrical engineers, Claude R. Engle

was the lighting consultant, Zion & Breen Associates were the landscape architects, and CMS

Collaborative were the fountain consultants.

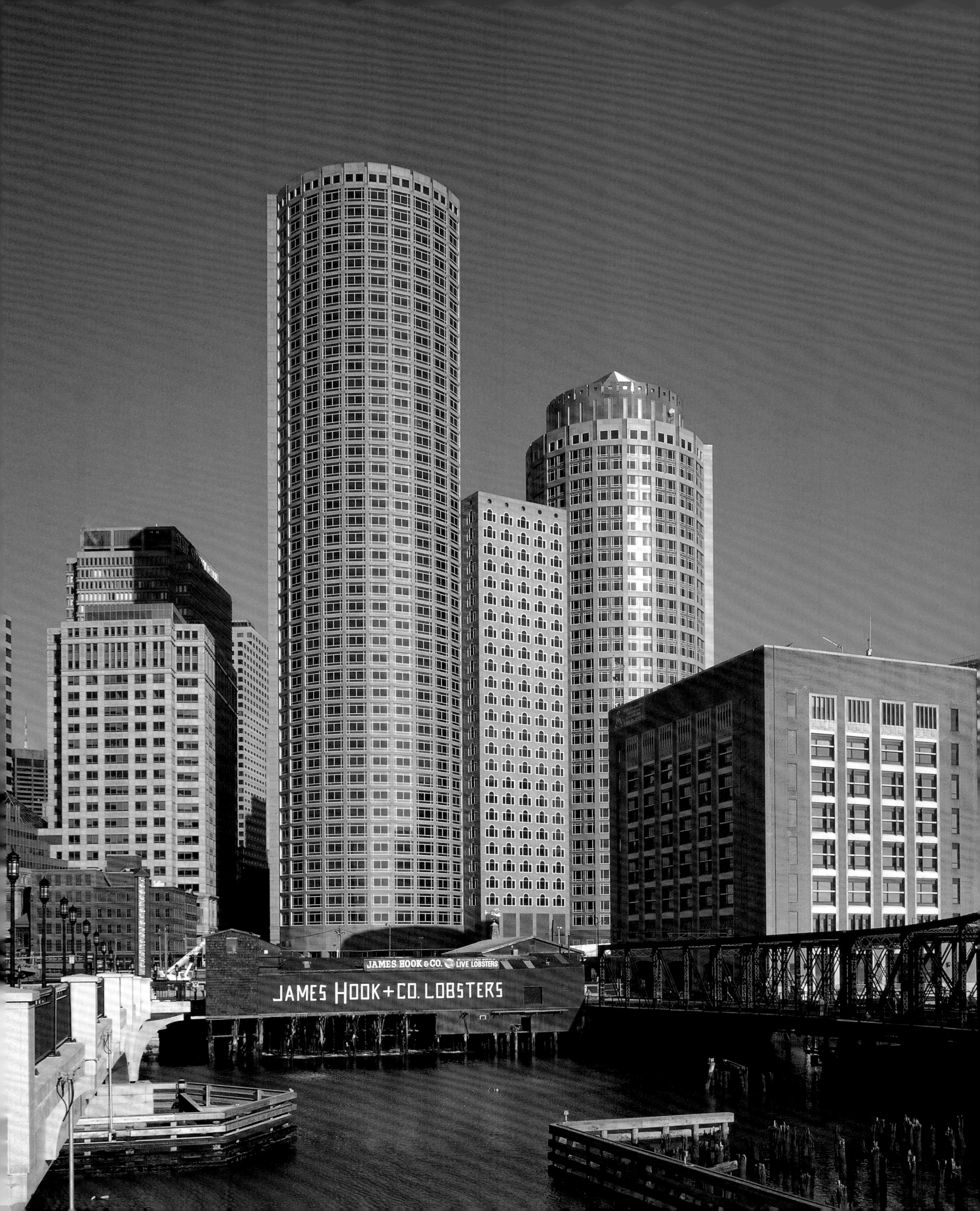
JAMES HOOK & CO. LIVE LOBSTERS
JAMES HOOK + CO. LOBSTERS

TWO INTERNATIONAL PLACE, FORT HILL SQUARE

High Street and Fort Hill Square | Boston | MA

1992 | John Burgee Architects, Philip Johnson Consultant

Also designed for the Chiofaro Company, Two International Place was built with no Palladian windows and a more emphatic pyramidal roof cap than was present in Burgee and Johnson's master plan design. The Turner Construction Company was the general contractor.

FRANKLIN SQUARE

1300 I Street, N.W. | Washington | DC

1989 | John Burgee Architects with Philip Johnson and Richard Fitzgerald & Partners

Like other office buildings in Washington, DC, the twelve-story, 505,000-square-foot Franklin Square office building was designed to fill the buildable envelope permitted by municipal planning regulations. Burgee and Johnson repeated the technique of contrasting solid wall planes, here faced with Indiana limestone and penetrated by rectangular window openings, with an aluminum and glass curtain wall recessed behind a screen of slender limestone-faced cylinders. The tall lobby replicates the feel of early twentieth-century classical building interiors. The frieze band of square-proportioned windows is quite similar to the frieze band of Tycon Tower, as are the cylinders. Franklin Square was built by Hines. It faces Franklin Square, a public park.

343 SANSOME STREET

343 Sansome Street | San Francisco | CA

1990 | John Burgee Architects, Philip Johnson Consultant and Kendall/Heaton Associates

Designed for Hines, the sixteen-story 343 Sansome Street office building is one of Burgee and Johnson's most restrained exercises in postmodern contextualism. Carefully aligned with neighboring buildings, it was designed to adhere to new city codes intended to conserve the scale, textures, and rhythms of downtown San Francisco. The building is capped by a publicly accessible roof garden. Three Forty-three Sansome exemplifies Mies van der Rohe's advice to Johnson that it is better to be good than original.

COMERICA TOWER AT DETROIT CENTER

500 Woodward Avenue | Detroit | MI

1991 | John Burgee Architects, Philip Johnson Consultant and
Kendall/Heaton Associates

Designed for Hines, the forty-five-story Comerica Tower was the tallest building in Detroit
when completed. Giant, multistory gables crown each of the tower's four faces. A granite-
faced supergrid frames double-height window wall apertures.

191 PEACHTREE TOWER

191 Peachtree Street N.E. | Atlanta | GA
1991 | John Burgee Architects, Philip Johnson Consultant and
Kendall/Heaton Associates

Wedged onto a block shared with older retail buildings in downtown Atlanta's Peachtree Center district, the fifty-story, 1.2-million-square-foot 191 Peachtree Tower was designed for Gerald D. Hines Interests. Burgee and Johnson contrasted a three-story supergrid with bounding wall planes of windows. Recessing the floor slab of the office tower at the centers of its long sides and notching its corners made the building seem taller and more slender, an effect enhanced by the pair of stepped, classically detailed lanterns that give the building its identity on the skyline. Flame-finished Rosa Dante granite was used to sheathe the exterior; this gives 191 Peachtree a strong sense of kinship to other Burgee/Johnson towers of the 1980s. The building is entered from Peachtree Street along one of its narrow sides through a six-story-high, glass-roofed court that is also connected to a retail arcade and the adjoining Ritz-Carlton Hotel. CBM Engineers were structural engineers, I. A. Naman+Associates were mechanical engineers, and Claude R. Engle was the lighting consultant.

CANADIAN BROADCASTING CENTRE

250 Front Street West | Toronto | Ontario | Canada
1992 | Bregman + Hamann Architects, Scott Associates Architects,
John Burgee Architects, Philip Johnson Consultant

Built by Cadillac Fairview Corporation as headquarters for the English-language division of the Canadian Broadcasting Corporation, the ten-story Canadian Broadcasting Centre was designed to contain offices and broadcasting studios for radio and television. It was Johnson and Burgee's first built example of the architecture of Deconstruction and it paid special tribute to the architecture of Peter Eisenman in its angled and tilted wall planes, layered wall grids, and slipped and skewed plan grids. Departures from the orthogonal articulate the layered spatial organization of the building and highlight the requirements for intensively serviced, acoustically insulated broadcasting spaces. The building is organized around the glass-roofed Barbara Frum Atrium. Burgee and Johnson used inflected panels of aluminum and glass curtain wall and bright red and green steel panel systems to identify the three large-volume broadcast studios on the roof and the elevator core in the Frum Atrium. The center also contains the CBC Museum, the Glenn Gould Studio, and other publicly accessible spaces. Quinn & Dressel Associates were structural engineers, Smith & Anderson Consulting Engineers were mechanical engineers, Mulvey & Banani International were electrical engineers, Vibron was the acoustical consultant, Moorhead Fleming Corban & Partners were the landscape architects, KJA Consultants were the elevator consultants, Rolfe Jenson & Associates were the life safety consultants, Rowan Williams Davies & Irwin were the environmental consultants, and Delcan Corporation was the traffic consultant. The Eastern Construction Company was the general contractor.

SCIENCE AND ENGINEERING LIBRARY

Ohio State University | 175 West 18th Avenue | Columbus | OH
1992 | John Burgee Architects, Philip Johnson Consultant
with Collins, Reimer & Gordon Architects

MATHEMATICS TOWER

Ohio State University | 231 West 18th Avenue | Columbus | OH
1992 | John Burgee Architects, Philip Johnson Consultant
with Collins, Reimer & Gordon Architects

In contrast to Peter Eisenman's Wexner Center for the Visual Arts at Ohio State University, the first major public building to advance a Deconstructionist position in the United States, Burgee and Johnson based their design of the university's four-story Science and Engineering Library and the two- and seven-story Mathematics Tower on the Armory, a reconstructed fragment of a historical campus building that Eisenman evoked in his design. As Johnson's associate John Manley observed, the layered application of round arches to the wall planes of the two brick-faced buildings and their stepped gables were redolent of Johnson/Burgee's earlier New Cleveland Play House. Korda Nemeth Engineering was the structural engineer and M-E Engineering was the mechanical engineer.

WILLIAM S. PALEY BUILDING, MUSEUM OF TELEVISION AND RADIO

23 West Fifty-second Street | New York | NY

1991 | John Burgee Architects, Philip Johnson Consultant

The "sliver" building emerged as a Manhattan architectural problem in the 1980s. The William S. Paley Building of the Museum of Television and Radio exemplifies the problem, and Burgee and Johnson's deft resolution of it. The museum is slotted onto a midblock site on a side street, such as those on which the Rockefeller Guest House and Asia House were built. It rises as a narrow sliver between older, much lower buildings. By setting the ten-story office tower back from the street face of the six-story museum block, Johnson and Burgee preserved the dominant height relationships along Fifty-second Street. Although their streamlined Jacobean architectural theme is unrelated to surrounding buildings, the composition of the limestone-faced exteriors and the proportions of windows-to-solid wall are so assured that Johnson and Burgee's eclecticism is not problematic. Chamfering the building's corners, which rise into piers, and recessing windows within the limestone-framed window grid give the building a strong urban presence and rescue it from the flimsiness characteristic of postmodern skyscrapers. Irwin Cantor was the structural engineer for the museum building, Cosentini Associates was the mechanical engineer, and Claude R. Engle was the lighting consultant. The building is named for William S. Paley, chairman of CBS, who founded the museum in 1975. In 1996, a West Coast branch of the museum was opened in Beverly Hills, California, in a building designed by Richard Meier & Partners.

CELEBRATION TOWN HALL

Market Street and Celebration Avenue | Celebration | FL
1996 | Philip Johnson, Ritchie & Fiore Architects and HKS

Robert A. M. Stern Architects and Cooper, Robertson & Partners were the master planners of Celebration, a 4,900-acre planned community developed by the Walt Disney Company outside Orlando, Florida, that opened in 1996. Robert Stern invited Johnson and other leading U.S. postmodern architects to design the major buildings of the community's commercial center, planned according to the principles of the Congress of New Urbanism. Johnson, Ritchie and Fiore's Town Hall is a small, two-story building containing the offices of the Disney Development Company, which manages Celebration, and a community meeting room. To highlight the building's civic status, Johnson and his associate Christian Bjone surrounded the core with slender, closely spaced concrete columns, lined three deep at the front portico. A turned stair, its proportions and profile recognizable from Johnson's Miesian period, is set inside the portico to provide access to the second floor. A low-pitched hip roof with broad overhangs affirms the Town Hall's intended Southern regional identity. Critiques of Celebration consistently mention residents' irritation with the Town Hall's triple front colonnade, an indication of Johnson's ability to affect bodily awareness with his architecture, if not always pleasurably. HKS Structural was the structural engineer and Blum Consulting Engineers were mechanical engineers.

AEGON CENTER

400 West Market Street | Louisville | KY

1993 | John Burgee Architects, Philip Johnson Consultant and Richard Fitzgerald & Partners

Built for Hines, this thirty-five-story, 633,650-square-foot office building was the tallest building in Louisville at the time of its completion. The modeling of the tower is based on the Nebraska State Capitol by Bertram Grosvenor Goodhue of 1932. The center includes a separate, five-story garage.

PUERTA DE EUROPA

Paseo de la Castellana and Avenida de Asturias and Calle M. Inurria | Madrid | Spain
1995 | John Burgee Architects, Philip Johnson Consultant with Pedro Sentieri and
Tomás Domínguez del Castillo y Juan Carlos Martín Baranda

The Puerta de Europa — the Gateway to Europe — is a pair of twenty-five-story office buildings that slant nearly fifteen degrees out of vertical alignment to frame the multilevel Paseo
de la Castellana at the Plaza de Castilla. A conflict with the routing of underground lines of
the Madrid metro, which prevented one of the towers from being built at the street line of its
site, occasioned the tilting profiles. Stainless steel was used to dramatize the bracing members
of the structural steel frames, which facilitate the slants. A secondary supergrid in red highlights the towers' somewhat ominous scale. In 1992, the Kuwait Investment Office, whose
Spanish agent, Grupo Torras, had commissioned the buildings, stopped construction because
of an economic scandal that had severe repercussions for the Spanish economy. The buildings'
height in the generally low-rise skyline of Madrid caused the skeletal towers to stand out,
provoking a caustic denunciation from Madrid's foremost architectural critic, Luis
Fernández-Galiano, of the temporarily deconstructed design, the architects, and the clients.
Fernández-Galiano unfavorably compared the buildings' emphasis on image and their tectonic
expediency to the conceptually and tectonically situated modern architecture characteristic of
Spain's leading architects in the 1980s, reflecting on how the towers represented the incursion of American market and architectural practices as Spain struggled with recession and
integration with global markets. Construction was resumed in 1994. Leslie E. Robertson
Associates were the structural engineers and Goymar Inginieros Consultores were the
mechanical engineers.

MILLENNIA WALK

1 Temasek Avenue | Suntec City | Singapore

1996 | John Burgee Architects, Philip Johnson Consultant and DP Architects

Millennia Walk is a multiuse complex that includes the forty-one-story Millennia Tower and the Ritz-Carlton Hotel by Kevin Roche John Dinkeloo & Associates. Burgee and Johnson's contribution is a 270,000-square-foot, multilevel retail mall marked by a series of truncated pyramids that graduate in size, culminating in the largest, above the fifty-foot-high Great Hall. The complex is faced in red granite. Leslie E. Robertson was the structural engineer, and Cosentini Associates were the mechanical engineers. Millennia Walk was a joint project of the Kajima Corporation and Pontiac Land Pte. Ltd. of Singapore.

© ALBERT LIM KS

© ALBERT LIM KS

PHILIP-JOHNSON-HAUS

Friedrichstraße 200 | Berlin | Germany

1997 | Philip Johnson, Ritchie & Fiore Architects and Pysall,
Stahrenberg & Partners

Designed for the investors Ronald S. Lauder and Abraham Rosenthal as part of a five-building complex, Das American Business Center am Checkpoint Charlie, the seven-story Philip-Johnson-Haus capitalized more on Johnsor's celebrity to attract tenants than his design. The building had to comply with Berlin's strict urban design codes: therefore its overlay of gray Brazilian granite on a glass curtain wall, its low height, operable windows, two interior court-yards, and roof garden. It was designed with interstitial service floors so that no suspended ceilings are required. An austere, gridded, three-story lobby pays homage to the early twentieth-century German architect Heinrich Tessenow. Johnson's rebellion against the expected is embodied in bays of curtain wall that seem to pivot outward on the diagonal. Leonhardt, Andrä & Partner were the structural engineers, and Flack & Kurtz/Integ were the mechanical engineers. Claes Oldenburg's *Houseball* was installed on the plaza behind the building.

Forty years after Johnson's master plan for the University of St. Thomas was accepted, his university chapel, designed in 1991 and dedicated to St. Basil the Great, patron of the Basilian Fathers, was completed. Built where the 1957 master plan called for a chapel to be located, the Chapel of St. Basil was larger and more formally assertive than Johnson's early proposals. Externally, a diagonally aligned screen wall, faced with polished black granite and containing a carillon, appears to slice through the square-planned chapel, cleaving its gold-leaf-surfaced dome into two unequal lobes outfitted with skylights. Entrance to the chapel is through a skewed, stucco-surfaced plane into a skylit interior vestibule, and from there into the fifty-five-foot-tall interior. Skylights focus awareness on the sanctuary and a seated votive statue in a side niche. Filtered daylight from above (as well as through a translucent wall cross framed in steel in the west wall) displays Johnson's proposed means of lighting the Rothko Chapel, designed in 1964 to be the university's chapel but built off-campus by Dominique and John de Menil after Johnson resigned the commission. Liturgical and devotional additions by the sculptor David Cargill are competing focuses of attention. Cagley, Conti & Jumper were structural engineers, CHP & Associates were mechanical, electrical, and plumbing engineers, McDonough Engineering Corporation was the civil engineer, Hoover & Keith were acoustical engineers, Engle Associates Lighting Design were lighting consultants, and Michael Dobbins made the furniture. The Linbeck Construction Corporation was the general contractor. Leo Linbeck, Jr., and his family were important supporters of the chapel project.

University of St. Thomas | 3800 Yoakum Boulevard | Houston | TX
1997 | Philip Johnson, Ritchie & Fiore Architects with
John Manley and Merriman Holt Architects

TRUMP INTERNATIONAL TOWER AND HOTEL

1 Central Park West | New York | NY

1997 | Philip Johnson, Ritchie & Fiore Architects and Costas Kondylis

For the Trump Organization, the Galbreath Company, and the General Electric Pension Trust, Philip Johnson, Ritchie & Fiore designed a new curtain-wall system, featuring brassy reflective glass, to replace the original curtain wall of the slender, forty-four-story, cruciform-planned Gulf & Western Building of 1968. This facilitated its transformation into an opulent hotel and condominium apartment building.

TRUMP PLACE

200, 180, and 160 Riverside Drive | New York | NY

1999–2001 | Philip Johnson/Alan Ritchie Architects and Costas Kondylis & Partners

Johnson and Ritchie, with Costas Kondylis, were architects for the first three residential towers constructed by the New York developer Donald Trump on a seventy-six-acre site between West Fifty-ninth and West Seventy-second Streets facing the Hudson River. Alexander Cooper & Associates were involved as urban design consultants in negotiating with residents of the area opposed to Trump's development plans. This led to the completed designs, which evoke the modernistic, setback apartment towers of Central Park West. Two Hundred Riverside Drive, at forty-six stories the tallest building, a 377-unit condominium apartment building completed in 1999, looks more like a midtown speculative office building of the 1960s with its cruciform tower, asymmetrical lower block, and extensively glazed curtain wall. One Eighty, a forty-story, 516-unit condominium apartment building completed in 1998, and the twin-towered One Sixty, a thirty-four-story, 455-unit rental apartment building completed in 2001, adhere more closely to the Central Park West models, although both are glassier. A fourth building, at 220, was under construction in 2002. Ysrael A. Seinuk was the structural engineer for One Sixty Riverside Drive, I. N. Robbins was the mechanical engineer, Bird Coffey Design Associates was the interior designer, and Bowers Lend Lease was the construction manager.

TURNING POINT

Case Western Reserve University | Bellflower Road | Cleveland | OH
1996 | Philip Johnson, Ritchie & Fiore Architects

Johnson's first sculpture was commissioned by Harvey Buchanan, professor of art history at Case Western Reserve University and curator of the university's John and Mildred Putnam Sculpture Collection, for installation on the university campus at a place called the Turning Point, between Mather Quad and a new university library. *Turning Point* is part of the Putnam Sculpture Collection, an installation of works at Case Western by artists with connections to Cleveland and Ohio. Johnson and his associate Elizabeth Murrell devised five pieces, constructed of polyester resin and fiberglass over structurally reinforced polyurethane foam. They are irregularly faceted, scooped, and overlapped shapes, seventeen to twenty feet in height, tilting inward to frame a passage between them. Buchanan characterized them as Stonehenge-like. *Turning Point* was fabricated by Merrifield-Roberts, Inc. It is formally related to a contemporaneous three-part work, *Vienna Trio*, which Johnson and Murrell produced for exhibition at the Österreichisches Museum für Angewandte Kunst in Vienna in 1996.

TIME SCULPTURE

Dante Square, Lincoln Center for the Performing Arts
West Sixty-fourth Street and Broadway | New York | NY
1999 | Philip Johnson/Alan Ritchie Architects

Time Sculpture is a four-sided irregular polygon, eighteen feet tall, cast in bronze. Each of its four faces contains an illuminated circular clock. It was originally designed for Lincoln Center Plaza but was erected in Dante Square instead, adjacent to the plaza, to placate public concern over installing works randomly in the plaza. The donors were Sonia and Gedalio Grinberg. Gedalio Grinberg was chairman of the Movado Group watch-making corporation. He paid Lincoln Center an annual fee in return for permission to erect the piece, which is fitted with Movado clocks.

FIRST UNION PLAZA

925 South Federal Highway | Boca Raton | FL

2000 | Philip Johnson/Alan Ritchie Architects

Designed for Songy Partners Limited, a real estate investment and development corporation, one of whose founders was a former officer of Hines, First Union Plaza is an office complex in central Boca Raton. Facing Federal Highway are seven-story and two-story office buildings, both rectangles in plan but with a concave curved plane hollowed out of one corner of the seven-story building and a convex plane attached to the front of the two-story building. The curved planes are constructed of aluminum-and-glass curtain-wall assemblies, which contrast with the repeating pattern of two-over-two windows punched into the solid wall planes of the taller building. The curved components are likened to wave formations, reflecting the site's proximity to the Atlantic Ocean.

JOHN THOMAS MEMORIAL AIDS BELL WALL

Cathedral of Hope | 5910 Cedar Springs Road | Dallas | TX

2000 | Philip Johnson/Alan Ritchie Architects

The Bell Wall, a shaped slab that is seventy-eight feet tall, is the first constructed increment of Johnson/Ritchie's design for the Cathedral of Hope. It was designed for the Rev. Michael Piazza, pastor of the congregation that describes itself as the world's largest lesbian, gay, bisexual, and transgendered church. The wall is to be part of an atrium in front of Johnson's 2,000-seat church building, called the Cathedral of Hope.

DDC DOMUS DESIGN COLLECTION

181 Madison Avenue | New York | NY

2000 | Philip Johnson/Alan Ritchie Architects

Johnson and Ritchie installed a showroom for high-style contemporary furniture in a three-story, 30,000-square-foot retail space in an early twentieth-century building in midtown Manhattan. They layered the loft-like space to create different spatial sequences and paths of movement. Tilted, jutting wall planes enclose discrete display spaces and spatially activate the main showroom. Donald Kaufman was the color consultant, Bladykus Engineering was the mechanical consultant, Claude R. Engle was the lighting consultant, and Certified Construction of New York was the contractor.

THE
TRYLONS
AT THE
CHRYSLER
CENTER

RETAIL/
SHOWROOM
SPACE
AVAILABLE

THE TRYLONS AT CHRYSLER CENTER

666 Third Avenue | New York | NY

2001 | Philip Johnson/Alan Ritchie and Adamson Associates Architects

In 1997 Tishman Speyer Properties bought the landmark Chrysler Building of 1930, an architecturally undistinguished annex at 666 Third Avenue built in 1951, and intervening property. Johnson/Ritchie were retained to expand, remodel, and upgrade 666 Third Avenue and design a link between it and the Chrysler Building. Johnson/Ritchie designed a dark, gridded curtain wall for 666 Third and redesigned its entrance lobby with faceted and shaped column covers and light-toned granite cladding. They produced a spatial construction, built with steel tubing and surfaced with reflective glass, called the Chrysler Trylons: three deflected pyramidal structures, irregular triangles in plan and eighty-five feet tall, that lead from East Forty-second Street into a three-level retail building between the two office buildings. Severud Associates was structural engineer, and the Turner Construction Company was construction manager. Beyer Blinder Belle were architects for the restoration of the Chrysler Building.

AMON CARTER MUSEUM ADDITION

3501 Camp Bowie Boulevard | Fort Worth | TX

2001 | Philip Johnson/Alan Ritchie Architects and Carter & Burgess

The need for expansion of the museum's gallery, office, and support spaces in the 1990s led to the decision to demolish the additions of 1964 and 1977, which occurred in 1999. Johnson and Ritchie replaced them with a rear annex, clad in Narjan Brown granite from Saudi Arabia. It contains nearly twice the volume of the earlier additions. The 1961 building was preserved and rehabilitated. The addition is organized internally around a skylit interior court, faced with fossilized limestone, which is directly accessible from Lancaster Avenue. David Dillon observed that the galleries suffer from lack of daylight (a condition mandated by the museum so that it could exhibit light-sensitive art works) and that the brown granite contrasts too insistently with the light-colored limestone. Ruth Carter Stevenson and the Amon Carter Museum were the clients for the addition. Rick Stewart was the director of the museum. Datum Engineering was the structural engineer, Blum Consulting Engineers were the mechanical, electrical, and plumbing engineers, Gordon Anson was the lighting consultant, L. Jane Mills Company designed the museum store interior, Richard Jensen Architects designed the art storage system, and Qunroe Associates were installation design consultants. The Linbeck Construction Company was the general contractor.

BIBLIOGRAPHY

PHILIP JOHNSON HOUSE
9 Ash Street
Cambridge, MA
1942, Philip Johnson with S. Clements Horsley

> "House in Cambridge, Mass., Philip Johnson, Architect,
S. Clements Horsley, Associate." *Architectural Forum* 79
(December 1943): 89–93.
> Jacobus, John M., Jr. *Philip Johnson*. Makers of Contemporary
Architecture. New York: George Braziller, 1962.
> Rettig, Robert Bell. *Guide to Cambridge Architecture: Ten
Walking Tours*. Cambridge: MIT Press, 1969, C-11.
> Bunting, Bainbridge, and Robert H. Nylander. *Report Four: Old
Cambridge*. Survey of Architectural History in Cambridge.
Cambridge: Cambridge Historical Commission, 1973, 130.
> *Philip Johnson: The Architect in His Own Words*. Edited by
Hilary Lewis and John O'Connor. New York: Rizzoli International
Publications, 1994.
> Cappellieri, Alba. *Philip Johnson: Dall'International Style al
Decostruttivismo*. Introduction by Vincent Scully. Naples:
Clean Edizioni, 1996, 46.
> Blake, Peter. *Philip Johnson*. Basel, Berlin, Boston: Birkhäuser,
1997, 26–28.
> Jenkins, Stover, and David Mohney. *The Houses of Philip Johnson*.
Afterword by Neil Levine. Photographs by Steven Brooke.
New York: Abbeville Press Publishers, 2001.

BARN
Townsend Farms
New London, OH
1944, Philip Johnson
destroyed

> Blake, Peter. *Philip Johnson*. Basel, Berlin, Boston: Birkhäuser,
1997, 29.

MR. AND MRS. RICHARD E. BOOTH HOUSE
Bedford Village, NY
1946, Philip C. Johnson

> Jenkins, Stover, and David Mohney. *The Houses of Philip Johnson*.
Afterword by Neil Levine. Photographs by Steven Brooke.
New York: Abbeville Press Publishers, 2001.

MR. AND MRS. EUGENE FARNEY HOUSE
Sagaponack, NY
1947, Philip C. Johnson

> Jacobus, John M., Jr. *Philip Johnson*. Makers of Contemporary
Architecture. New York: George Braziller, 1962.
> Blake, Peter. *Philip Johnson*. Basel, Berlin, Boston: Birkhäuser,
1997, 30–31.
> Gordon, Alastair. *Weekend Utopia: Modern Living in the Hamptons*.
New York: Princeton Architectural Press, 2001, 88–89.
> Jenkins, Stover, and David Mohney. *The Houses of Philip Johnson*.
Afterword by Neil Levine. Photographs by Steven Brooke.
New York: Abbeville Press Publishers, 2001.

GLASS HOUSE
New Canaan, CT
1949, Philip C. Johnson Associates

> Drexler, Arthur. "Architecture Opaque and Transparent: Philip
Johnson's Glass and Brick Houses in Connecticut," *Interiors* 109
(October 1949): 90–101.
> "Glass House in Connecticut: Philip C. Johnson's Home, New
Canaan." *House and Garden*, October 1949, 168–73.
> "Glass House." *Architectural Forum* 91 (November 1949): 74–79.
> "House at New Canaan, Connecticut." *Architectural Review*,
no. 645 (September 1950): 152–59.
> Hitchcock, Henry-Russell. "The Current Work of Philip Johnson."
Zodiac 8 (1961): 64–81.
> Jacobus, John M., Jr. *Philip Johnson*. Makers of Contemporary
Architecture. New York: George Braziller, 1962.
> "House of Glass Today." *House and Garden*, October 1965,
184–87.
> *Philip Johnson Architecture 1949–1965*. Introduction by
Henry-Russell Hitchcock. New York: Holt, Rinehart and Winston,
1966, 36–39.
> Stern, Robert. *New Directions in American Architecture*. New
York: George Braziller, 1969, 42–49.
> *Philip Johnson: Johnson House, New Canaan, Connecticut,
1949*. Edited and photographed by Yukio Futagawa; text by Brian
Robertson. Global Architecture 12, 1972.
> Noble, Charles. *Philip Johnson*. Photographs by Yukio Futagawa.
London: Thames and Hudson, 1972.
> Dean, Andrea O. "Honor Awards Go to Nine Buildings, the 25-Year
Award to a Glass House." *AIA Journal* 63 (May 1975): 26–27.
> Stern, Robert A. M. "The Evolution of Philip Johnson's Glass
House, 1947–1948." *Oppositions* 10 (Fall 1977): 56–67.
> Scully, Vincent. "Philip Johnson: The Glass House Revisited."
Architectural Digest 44 (November 1986): 116–25.
> Whitney, David, and Jeffrey Kipnis, editors. *Philip Johnson:
The Glass House*. New York: Pantheon Books, 1993.
> *Philip Johnson: The Architect in His Own Words*. Edited by
Hilary Lewis and John O'Connor. New York: Rizzoli International
Publications, 1994.
> Dean, Andrea Oppenheimer. "Reflections from a Glass House."
Preservation 48 (July–August 1996): 70–81.
> Cappellieri, Alba. *Philip Johnson: Dall'International Style
al Decostruttivismo*. Introduction by Vincent Scully. Naples:
Clean Edizioni, 1996, 47–54.
> Blake, Peter. *Philip Johnson*. Basel, Berlin, Boston: Birkhäuser,
1997, 32–39.
> Melchionne, Kevin. "Living in Glass Houses: Domesticity, Interior
Decoration, and Environmental Esthetics." *Journal of Aesthetics
and Art Criticism* 56 (Spring 1998): 191–200.
> Lewis, Hilary. "The Seat of Power." *Architecture* 89 (May 2000):
162–71.
> Ockman, Joan. "Glass House." In *World Architecture 1900–2000:
A Critical Mosaic. Volume 1: Canada and the United States*,
edited by Richard Ingersoll, 104–07. Vienna and New York: China
Architecture and Building Press and Springer Wien New York, 2000.
> Le Blanc, Sidney. *The Architecture Traveler: A Guide to 250 Key
20th-Century American Buildings*. New York: W. W. Norton &
Company, 2000, 84.

GUEST HOUSE
New Canaan, CT
1949, Philip C. Johnson Associates

> Drexler, Arthur. "Architecture Opaque and Transparent:
Philip Johnson's Glass and Brick Houses in Connecticut."
Interiors 109 (October 1949): 90–101.
> "Glass House in Connecticut: Philip C. Johnson's Home, New
Canaan." *House and Garden*, October 1949, 168–73.
> "Glass House." *Architectural Forum* 91 (November 1949): 74–79.
> "House at New Canaan, Connecticut." *Architectural Review*,
no. 645 (September 1950): 152–59.
> Jenkins, Stover, and David Mohney. *The Houses of Philip Johnson*.
Afterword by Neil Levine. Photographs by Steven Brooke.
New York: Abbeville Press Publishers, 2001.

GUEST HOUSE INTERIOR ALTERATIONS
New Canaan, CT
1953, Philip Johnson

> Gueft, Olga. "Pavilion in the Desert." *Interiors* 113 (July 1954):
70–71.
> Jacobus, John M., Jr. *Philip Johnson*. Makers of Contemporary
Architecture. New York: George Braziller, 1962.
> *Philip Johnson Architecture 1949–1965*. Introduction by
Henry-Russell Hitchcock. New York: Holt, Rinehart and Winston,
1966, 40–41.
> *Philip Johnson: The Architect in His Own Words*. Edited by
Hilary Lewis and John O'Connor. New York: Rizzoli International
Publications, 1994.
> Cappellieri, Alba. *Philip Johnson: Dall'International Style
al Decostruttivismo*. Introduction by Vincent Scully. Naples:
Clean Edizioni, 1996, 55–62.
> Blake, Peter. *Philip Johnson*. Basel, Berlin, Boston: Birkhäuser,
1997, 52–53.
> Jenkins, Stover, and David Mohney. *The Houses of Philip Johnson*.
Afterword by Neil Levine. Photographs by Steven Brooke.
New York: Abbeville Press Publishers, 2001.

PAVILION
New Canaan, CT
1962, Philip Johnson Associates

> "Johnson." *Perspecta* 7 (1961): 3–8.
> "Recent Work of Philip Johnson: Philip Johnson Pavilion,
New Canaan, Connecticut." *Architectural Record* 132
(July 1962): 126–27.
> "Pre-cast Pavilion." *Architectural Design* 32 (September 1962):
408.
> Jacobus, John M., Jr. *Philip Johnson*. Makers of Contemporary
Architecture. New York: George Braziller, 1962.
> Hitchcock, Henry-Russell. "Connecticut, U.S.A., in 1963."
Zodiac 13 (1964): 6–7.
> *Philip Johnson Architecture 1949–1965*. Introduction by
Henry-Russell Hitchcock. New York: Holt, Rinehart and Winston,
1966, 42–45.
> Stern, Robert. *New Directions in American Architecture*.
New York: George Braziller, 1969, 42–49.
> *Philip Johnson: The Architect in His Own Words*. Edited by
Hilary Lewis and John O'Connor. New York: Rizzoli International
Publications, 1994.
> Cappellieri, Alba. *Philip Johnson: Dall'International Style
al Decostruttivismo*. Introduction by Vincent Scully. Naples:
Clean Edizioni, 1996, 55–62.
> Blake, Peter. Philip Johnson. Basel, Berlin, Boston: Birkhäuser,
1997, 86–87.
> Jenkins, Stover, and David Mohney. *The Houses of Philip
Johnson*. Afterword by Neil Levine. Photographs by Steven
Brooke. New York: Abbeville Press Publishers, 2001.

PAINTING GALLERY
New Canaan, CT
1965, Philip Johnson
> O'Brien, G. "Down with Art." *New York Times Magazine*, 28 February 1965, 70–71.
> "Connecticut Bunker." *Architectural Forum* 124 (May 1966): 57.
> "Johnson Explains His Underground Museum." *Vogue*, May 1966, 200–01.
> Plessix, Francine du. "Philip Johnson Goes Underground." *Art in America* 54 (July–August 1966): 88–97.
> "Johnson Underground." *Progressive Architecture* 48 (April 1967): 146.
> Peter, John. "Philip Johnson's Suburban Museum." *Look*, 16 May 1967, 60–64.
> Hornbeck, James S. "Three Projects by Philip Johnson, Each Designed for a Hill: Sunken Hillside Gallery." *Architectural Record* 141 (June 1967): 146–47.
> Stern, Robert. *New Directions in American Architecture*. New York: George Braziller, 1969, 42–49.
> Cappellieri, Alba. *Philip Johnson: Dall'International Style al Decostruttivismo*. Introduction by Vincent Scully. Naples: Clean Edizioni, 1996, 55–62.
> Blake, Peter. *Philip Johnson*. Basel, Berlin, Boston: Birkhäuser, 1997, 106–07.
> Jenkins, Stover, and David Mohney. *The Houses of Philip Johnson*. Afterword by Neil Levine. Photographs by Steven Brooke. New York: Abbeville Press Publishers, 2001.

SCULPTURE GALLERY
New Canaan, CT
1970, Philip Johnson
> Dixon, John Morris. "Sculpture Under Glass." *Architectural Forum* 133 (December 1970): 22–25.
> "Art Under Glass." *Vogue*, 15 August 1971, 102–05.
> *Philip Johnson: The Architect in His Own Words*. Edited by Hilary Lewis and John O'Connor. New York: Rizzoli International Publications, 1994.
> Cappellieri, Alba. *Philip Johnson: Dall'International Style al Decostruttivismo*. Introduction by Vincent Scully. Naples: Clean Edizioni, 1996, 55–62.
> Blake, Peter. *Philip Johnson*. Basel, Berlin, Boston: Birkhäuser, 1997, 117–20.
> Jenkins, Stover, and David Mohney. *The Houses of Philip Johnson*. Afterword by Neil Levine. Photographs by Steven Brooke. New York: Abbeville Press Publishers, 2001.

LIBRARY/STUDY
New Canaan, CT
1980, Philip Johnson
> Wagner, Walter, Jr. "Architect's Retreat." *Architectural Record* 171 (July 1983): 114–19.
> *Philip Johnson: The Architect in His Own Words*. Edited by Hilary Lewis and John O'Connor. New York: Rizzoli International Publications, 1994.
> Cappellieri, Alba. *Philip Johnson: Dall'International Style al Decostruttivismo*. Introduction by Vincent Scully. Naples: Clean Edizioni, 1996, 55–62.
> Blake, Peter. *Philip Johnson*. Basel, Berlin, Boston: Birkhäuser, 1997, 165–66.
> Jenkins, Stover, and David Mohney. *The Houses of Philip Johnson*. Afterword by Neil Levine. Photographs by Steven Brooke. New York: Abbeville Press Publishers, 2001.

GHOST HOUSE
New Canaan, CT
1984, Philip Johnson
> *Philip Johnson: The Architect in His Own Words*. Edited by Hilary Lewis and John O'Connor. New York: Rizzoli International Publications, 1994.
> Cappellieri, Alba. *Philip Johnson: Dall'International Style al Decostruttivismo*. Introduction by Vincent Scully. Naples: Clean Edizioni, 1996, 55–62.
> Blake, Peter. *Philip Johnson*. Basel, Berlin, Boston: Birkhäuser, 1997, 198–99.
> Jenkins, Stover, and David Mohney. *The Houses of Philip Johnson*. Afterword by Neil Levine. Photographs by Steven Brooke. New York: Abbeville Press Publishers, 2001.

LINCOLN KIRSTEIN TOWER
New Canaan, CT
1985, Philip Johnson
> Bernier, Rosamond. "Improving His View." *House and Garden*, June 1986, 118–23.
> *Philip Johnson: The Architect in His Own Words*. Edited by Hilary Lewis and John O'Connor. New York: Rizzoli International Publications, 1994.
> Cappellieri, Alba. *Philip Johnson: Dall'International Style al Decostruttivismo*. Introduction by Vincent Scully. Naples: Clean Edizioni, 1996, 55–62.
> Blake, Peter. *Philip Johnson*. Basel, Berlin, Boston: Birkhäuser, 1997, 200–01.
> Jenkins, Stover, and David Mohney. *The Houses of Philip Johnson*. Afterword by Neil Levine. Photographs by Steven Brooke. New York: Abbeville Press Publishers, 2001.

GATE HOUSE
New Canaan, CT
1995, Philip Johnson
> *Philip Johnson: The Architect in His Own Words*. Edited by Hilary Lewis and John O'Connor. New York: Rizzoli International Publications, 1994.
> Dietsch, Deborah K. "Philip's Folly." *Architecture* 84 (November 1995): 74–79.
> Cappellieri, Alba. *Philip Johnson: Dall'International Style al Decostruttivismo*. Introduction by Vincent Scully. Naples: Clean Edizioni, 1996, 55–62.
> Kipnis, Jeffrey. *Philip Johnson: Recent Work*. Architectural Monographs No. 44. London: Academy Editions, 1996, 22–39.
> Blake, Peter. *Philip Johnson*. Basel, Berlin, Boston: Birkhäuser, 1997, 228–31.
> Jenkins, Stover, and David Mohney. *The Houses of Philip Johnson*. Afterword by Neil Levine. Photographs by Steven Brooke. New York: Abbeville Press Publishers, 2001.

DOG HOUSE
New Canaan, CT
1998, Philip Johnson
> Welch, Frank D. *Philip Johnson and Texas*. Austin: University of Texas Press, 2000.

MR. AND MRS. G. E. PAINE, JR., HOUSE
Wellsboro, NY
1949, Philip C. Johnson Associates
> Jenkins, Stover, and David Mohney. *The Houses of Philip Johnson*. Afterword by Neil Levine. Photographs by Steven Brooke. New York: Abbeville Press Publishers, 2001.

MR. AND MRS. BENJAMIN WOLF HOUSE
Newburgh, NY
1949, Philip C. Johnson Associates
> Jenkins, Stover, and David Mohney. *The Houses of Philip Johnson*. Afterword by Neil Levine. Photographs by Steven Brooke. New York: Abbeville Press Publishers, 2001.

MR. AND MRS. JOHN DE MENIL HOUSE
3363 San Felipe Road
Houston, TX
1950, Philip C. Johnson Associates with
Landis Gores and Cowell & Neuhaus
> "Art Collection and Home of the John de Menils in Houston's River Oaks." *Interiors* 123 (November 1963): 84–91.
> Sweeney, James Johnson. "Collectors' Home: In the John de Menils' House a Great Ranging Art Collection." *Vogue*, 1 April 1966, 184–91.
> Hewitt, Mark A. "Neoclassicism and Modern Architecture— Houston Style." *Cite, The Architecture and Design Review of Houston*, Fall 1984, 12–15.
> Bernier, Rosamond. "A Gift of Vision." *House and Garden*, July 1987, 10, 120–29.
> Tomkins, Calvin. "The Benefactor." *New Yorker*, 8 June 1998, 52–67.
> Viladas, Pilar. "Style: They Did It Their Way." *New York Times Magazine*, 10 October 1999, 81–94.
> Welch, Frank D. *Philip Johnson and Texas*. Austin: University of Texas Press, 2000.
> Jenkins, Stover, and David Mohney. *The Houses of Philip Johnson*. Afterword by Neil Levine. Photographs by Steven Brooke. New York: Abbeville Press Publishers, 2001.

GRACE RAINEY ROGERS ANNEX
The Museum of Modern Art
21 East Fifty-third Street
New York, NY
1951, Philip C. Johnson Associates with Landis Gores
1980, demolished
> "Three Approaches to Modern Architecture: 2. Modern Classicism." *Architectural Forum* 102 (May 1955): 146–48.
> Jacobus, John M., Jr. *Philip Johnson*. Makers of Contemporary Architecture. New York: George Braziller, 1962.
> Stern, Robert A. M., Thomas Mellins, and David Fishman. *New York 1960: Architecture and Urbanism Between the Second World War and the Bicentennial*. New York: Monacelli Press, 1995, 476–77.
> Blake, Peter. *Philip Johnson*. Basel, Berlin, Boston: Birkhäuser, 1997, 40–42.
> Reed, Peter. "The Space and the Frame: Philip Johnson as the Museum's Architect." In *Philip Johnson and the Museum of Modern Art*, edited by John Elderfield, 70–103. Studies in Modern Art 6. New York: The Museum of Modern Art, 1998.

**MRS. JOHN D. ROCKEFELLER 3RD
GUEST HOUSE**
242 East Fifty-second Street
New York, NY
1950, Philip C. Johnson with Landis Gores and Frederick C. Genz
> "Guest House." *Architectural Forum* 93 (August 1950): 84–87.
> Drexler, Arthur. "Town House." *Interiors* 110 (December 1950): 80–85.
> "A Patio Town House is Good Enough for New York's Top Families." *House + Home* 12 (October 1957): 130.
> Jacobus, John M., Jr. *Philip Johnson*. Makers of Contemporary Architecture. New York: George Braziller, 1962.
> *Philip Johnson Architecture 1949–1965*. Introduction by Henry-Russell Hitchcock. New York: Holt, Rinehart and Winston, 1966, 46–47.
> Goldberger, Paul. *The City Observed: New York*. New York: Vantage Books, 1979, 150–51.
> Stern, Robert A. M., Thomas Mellins, and David Fishman. *New York 1960: Architecture and Urbanism Between the Second World War and the Bicentennial*. New York: Monacelli Press, 1995, 304–06.
> Cappellieri, Alba. *Philip Johnson: Dall'International Style al Decostruttivismo*. Introduction by Vincent Scully. Naples: Clean Edizioni, 1996, 63–64.
> Blake, Peter. *Philip Johnson*. Basel, Berlin, Boston: Birkhäuser, 1997, 43–45.
> Reed, Peter. "The Space and the Frame: Philip Johnson as the Museum's Architect." In *Philip Johnson and the Museum of Modern Art*, edited by John Elderfield, 70–103. Studies in Modern Art 6. New York: The Museum of Modern Art, 1998.
> Viladas, Pilar. "Tea and Geometry." *New York Times Magazine*, 28 May 2000, 44–48.
> White, Norval, and Elliott Willensky. *AIA Guide to New York City*. 4th rev. ed. New York: Three Rivers Press, 2000, 310.
> Jenkins, Stover, and David Mohney. *The Houses of Philip Johnson*. Afterword by Neil Levine. Photographs by Steven Brooke. New York: Abbeville Press Publishers, 2001.

MR. AND MRS. HENRY FORD II HOUSE ADDITION
Southampton, NY
1950, Philip C. Johnson Associates with Landis Gores
> Gordon, Alastair. *Weekend Utopia: Modern Living in the Hamptons*. New York: Princeton Architectural Press, 2001, 89.
> Jenkins, Stover, and David Mohney. *The Houses of Philip Johnson*. Afterword by Neil Levine. Photographs by Steven Brooke. New York: Abbeville Press Publishers, 2001.

MR. AND MRS. RICHARD HODGSON HOUSE
Ponus Ridge Road
New Canaan, CT
1951, Philip C. Johnson Associates with Landis Gores
1956, addition, Philip C. Johnson Associates
> Haeberly, Mabel C. "Residence in New Canaan Soon to Shed 'Winter Wraps' to Display Modern Design." *New York Times*, 6 May 1951, sections 8–9, p. 1.
> "A Connecticut House for a Television Executive." *Architectural Record* 113 (March 1953): 156–61.
> Jacobus, John M., Jr. *Philip Johnson*. Makers of Contemporary Architecture. New York: George Braziller, 1962.
> *Philip Johnson Architecture 1949–1965*. Introduction by Henry-Russell Hitchcock. New York: Holt, Rinehart and Winston, 1966, 48–50.
> Noble, Charles. *Philip Johnson*. Photographs by Yukio Futagawa. London: Thames and Hudson, 1972.
> Cappellieri, Alba. *Philip Johnson: Dall'International Style al Decostruttivismo*. Introduction by Vincent Scully. Naples: Clean Edizioni, 1996, 65–66.
> Blake, Peter. *Philip Johnson*. Basel, Berlin, Boston: Birkhäuser, 1997, 46–47.
> Jenkins, Stover, and David Mohney. *The Houses of Philip Johnson*. Afterword by Neil Levine. Photographs by Steven Brooke. New York: Abbeville Press Publishers, 2001.

MR. AND MRS. GEORGE C. ONETO HOUSE
Irvington-on-Hudson, NY
1951, Philip C. Johnson Associates with Landis Gores
> "New Directions, 2: Philip Johnson: House on the Hudson." *Perspecta* 1 (1952): 26–28.
> "Beautiful Site, No Special Requirements." *Architectural Record* 120 (November 1956): 167–71.
> "Ease and Order in the Suburbs." *Architectural Record* 121 (mid-May 1957): 156–59.
> Jacobus, John M., Jr. *Philip Johnson*. Makers of Contemporary Architecture. New York: George Braziller, 1962.
> *Philip Johnson Architecture 1949–1965*. Introduction by Henry-Russell Hitchcock. New York: Holt, Rinehart and Winston, 1966, 51–55.
> Rowe, Colin. "Neo-'Classicism' and Modern Architecture I." In *The Mathematics of the Ideal Villa and Other Essays*. Cambridge: MIT Press, 1976, 119–38.
> Kroloff, Reed. "Oneto House." *Architecture* 85 (February 1996): 42–43.
> Blake, Peter. *Philip Johnson*. Basel, Berlin, Boston: Birkhäuser, 1997, 48–49.
> Goldberger, Paul. "Shock of the New: Surprising Additions to a 1951 Philip Johnson House." *Architectural Digest* 55 (February 1998): 176–83.
> Jenkins, Stover, and David Mohney. *The Houses of Philip Johnson*. Afterword by Neil Levine. Photographs by Steven Brooke. New York: Abbeville Press Publishers, 2001.

**MR. AND MRS. BURTON G. TREMAINE HOUSE ALTER-
ATIONS AND ADDITIONS**
Madison, CT
1952, Philip C. Johnson Associates
> "How to Turn an Old Barn into a Modern House." *House + Home* 6 (October 1954): 148–49.
> Housley, Kathleen L. *Emily Hall Tremaine: Collector on the Cusp*. Meriden, CT: Emily Hall Tremaine Foundation, 2001.
> Jenkins, Stover, and David Mohney. *The Houses of Philip Johnson*. Afterword by Neil Levine. Photographs by Steven Brooke. New York: Abbeville Press Publishers, 2001.

SCHLUMBERGER ADMINISTRATION BUILDING
Schlumberger-Doll Research Center
Old Quarry Road
Ridgefield, CT
1952, Philip C. Johnson Associates
> "This Small Suburban Administration Building Is Four Things to Four Men." *Architectural Forum* 99 (September 1953): 124–29.
> Jacobus, John M., Jr. *Philip Johnson*. Makers of Contemporary Architecture. New York: George Braziller, 1962.
> "Architectural Details 3. Philip Johnson: Administration Building for Schlumberger, Ridgefield, Connecticut, 1952." *Architectural Record* 135 (April 1964): 138–39.
> Blake, Peter. *Philip Johnson*. Basel, Berlin, Boston: Birkhäuser, 1997, 50–51.

MRS. ALICE BALL HOUSE
Oenoke Avenue
New Canaan, CT
1953, Philip C. Johnson Associates
> Jacobus, John M., Jr. *Philip Johnson*. Makers of Contemporary Architecture. New York: George Braziller, 1962.
> Jenkins, Stover, and David Mohney. *The Houses of Philip Johnson*. Afterword by Neil Levine. Photographs by Steven Brooke. New York: Abbeville Press Publishers, 2001.

ABBY ALDRICH ROCKEFELLER SCULPTURE GARDEN
The Museum of Modern Art
11 West Fifty-third Street
New York, NY
1953, Philip C. Johnson Associates with Landis Gores and George Hopkinson; James Fanning, landscape architect
> Anderson, John. "The Museum's Marble Piazze." *Interiors* 112 (June 1953): 98–99.
> "Museum Garden Is an Outdoor Living Room for Sculpture Display." *Architectural Forum* 99 (July 1953): 136–37.
> Jacobus, John M., Jr. *Philip Johnson*. Makers of Contemporary Architecture. New York: George Braziller, 1962.
> *Philip Johnson Architecture 1949–1965*. Introduction by Henry-Russell Hitchcock. New York: Holt, Rinehart and Winston, 1966, 96–97.
> Barr, Alfred H., Jr. "On Nelson Rockefeller and Modern Art." In *The Nelson A. Rockefeller Collection: Masterpieces of Modern Art*, edited by Dorothy Canning Miller, 23. New York: Hudson Hills Press, 1981.
> Kidder Smith, G. E. *The Architecture of the United States, Volume 1: New England and the Mid-Atlantic States*. Garden City, NY: Anchor Press/Doubleday, 1981, 544–47.
> Stern, Robert A. M., Thomas Mellins, and David Fishman. *New York 1960: Architecture and Urbanism Between the Second World War and the Bicentennial*. New York: Monacelli Press, 1995, 478–81.
> Cappellieri, Alba. *Philip Johnson: Dall'International Style al Decostruttivismo*. Introduction by Vincent Scully. Naples: Clean Edizioni, 1996, 67.
> Olin, Laurie D. "The Museum of Modern Art Garden: The Rise and Fall of a Modernist Landscape." *Journal of Garden History* 17 (April/June 1997): 140–62.
> Blake, Peter. *Philip Johnson*. Basel, Berlin, Boston: Birkhäuser, 1997, 54–57.
> Benes, Mirka. "A Modern Classic: The Abby Aldrich Sculpture Garden." In *Philip Johnson and the Museum of Modern Art*, edited by John Elderfield, 104–51. Studies in Modern Art 6. New York: The Museum of Modern Art, 1998.

**EAST WING, GARDEN WING, REMODELED SCULPTURE
GARDEN, AND UPPER TERRACE**
The Museum of Modern Art
New York, NY
1964, Philip Johnson Associates
1984, altered
> "M. O. M. A. Announces Spacious New Wing." *Progressive Architecture* 40 (December 1959): 74.
> Blake, Peter. "The Museum Explosion." *Art in America* 52, no. 2 (1964): 97–103.
> "Architectural Details 3. Philip Johnson: Museum of Modern Art, East Wing, New York City, New York." *Architectural Record* 135 (April 1964): 150–51.
> "Museum of Modern Art: A Study in Elegance by Johnson." *Progressive Architecture* 45 (July 1964): 64, 66.
> "Philip Johnson's Modern." *Interiors* 123 (July 1964): 92–95.
> "Johnson in New York." *Architectural Review*, no. 812 (October 1964): 235–36.
> Johnson, Philip. "Whence and Whither: The Processional Element in Architecture." *Perspecta* 9/10 (1965): 167–78.
> *Philip Johnson Architecture 1949–1965*. Introduction by Henry-Russell Hitchcock. New York: Holt, Rinehart and Winston, 1966, 98–99.
> "Camp Mies." *Progressive Architecture* 48 (December 1967): 128–29.
> Noble, Charles. *Philip Johnson*. Photographs by Yukio Futagawa. London: Thames and Hudson, 1972.
> Goldberger, Paul. *The City Observed: New York*. New York: Vantage Books, 1979, 173–74.
> Stern, Robert A. M., Thomas Mellins, and David Fishman. *New York 1960: Architecture and Urbanism Between the Second World War and the Bicentennial*. New York: Monacelli Press, 1995, 481–85.

> Olin, Laurie D. "The Museum of Modern Art Garden: The Rise and Fall of a Modernist Landscape." *Journal of Garden History* 17 (April/June 1997): 140–62.

> Blake, Peter. *Philip Johnson*. Basel, Berlin, Boston: Birkhäuser, 1997, 96–97.

> Benes, Mirka. "A Modern Classic: The Abby Aldrich Sculpture Garden." In *Philip Johnson and the Museum of Modern Art*, edited by John Elderfield, 104–51. Studies in Modern Art 6. New York: The Museum of Modern Art, 1998.

MR. AND MRS. ROBERT C. WILEY HOUSE
Sleepy Hollow Road
New Canaan, CT
1953, Philip C. Johnson Associates

> "Clear Cut Expression of the Double Life." *Architectural Record* 117 (June 1953): 167–72.

> Scully, Vincent J., Jr. "Archetype and Order in Recent American Architecture." *Art in America* 42 (December 1954): 251–61.

> "The Seven Crutches of Modern Architecture." *Perspecta* 3 (1955):44–45.

> Jacobus, John M., Jr. *Philip Johnson*. Makers of Contemporary Architecture. New York: George Braziller, 1962.

> "Architectural Details 3. Philip Johnson: The Robert Wiley House, New Canaan, Connecticut, 1953." *Architectural Record* 135 (April 1964): 140–41.

> *Philip Johnson Architecture 1949–1965*. Introduction by Henry-Russell Hitchcock. New York: Holt, Rinehart and Winston, 1966, 54–57.

> Schulze, Franz. *Philip Johnson: Life and Work*. New York: Alfred A. Knopf, 1994, 435n.

> Cappellieri, Alba. *Philip Johnson: Dall'International Style al Decostruttivismo*. Introduction by Vincent Scully. Naples: Clean Edizioni, 1996, 68–69.

> Blake, Peter. *Philip Johnson*. Basel, Berlin, Boston: Birkhäuser, 1997, 58–59.

> Jenkins, Stover, and David Mohney. *The Houses of Philip Johnson*. Afterword by Neil Levine. Photographs by Steven Brooke. New York: Abbeville Press Publishers, 2001.

MR. AND MRS. RICHARD S. DAVIS HOUSE
1780 Shoreline Drive
Wayzata, MN
1954, Philip C. Johnson Associates with Magney, Tussler & Setter

> Gueft, Olga. "Home for a Collector's Double Life." *Interiors* 113 (July 1954): 62–67.

> "What Patios Can Do for Your House: Indoor Gardens Can Be a Source of Light." *House + Home* 6 (August 1954): 110–15.

> Jacobus, John M., Jr. *Philip Johnson*. Makers of Contemporary Architecture. New York: George Braziller, 1962.

> Viladas, Pilar. "Outdoor Sculpture." *Progressive Architecture* 68 (December 1987): 60–67.

> Blake, Peter. *Philip Johnson*. Basel, Berlin, Boston: Birkhäuser, 1997, 60–61.

> Jenkins, Stover, and David Mohney. *The Houses of Philip Johnson*. Afterword by Neil Levine. Photographs by Steven Brooke. New York: Abbeville Press Publishers, 2001.

MR. AND MRS. WILLIAM A. M. BURDEN APARTMENT
820 Fifth Avenue
New York, NY
1954, Philip C. Johnson Associates

> Jenkins, Stover, and David Mohney. *The Houses of Philip Johnson*. Afterword by Neil Levine. Photographs by Steven Brooke. New York: Abbeville Press Publishers, 2001.

JOSEPH H. HIRSHHORN HOUSE
Blind River, Ontario, Canada
1955, Philip C. Johnson Associates

> Jenkins, Stover, and David Mohney. *The Houses of Philip Johnson*. Afterword by Neil Levine. Photographs by Steven Brooke. New York: Abbeville Press Publishers, 2001.

WILEY DEVELOPMENT COMPANY HOUSE
Sleepy Hollow Road
New Canaan, CT
1955, Philip C. Johnson Associates

> "Connecticut Development House Is Versatile." *Architectural Record* 118 (November 1955): 176–79.

> Jacobus, John M., Jr. *Philip Johnson*. Makers of Contemporary Architecture. New York: George Braziller, 1962.

> Jenkins, Stover, and David Mohney. *The Houses of Philip Johnson*. Afterword by Neil Levine. Photographs by Steven Brooke. New York: Abbeville Press Publishers, 2001.

METEOR CRATER PAVILION
Barringer Meteor Crater
Interstate 40 between Winslow and Flagstaff
Coconino County, AZ
1956, Philip C. Johnson Associates

> Hill, Gladwin. "Where the Meteor Scarred Arizona's Desert." *New York Times*, January 29, 1956, sect. 2, p. 31.

> Allaback, Sarah. *Mission 66 Visitor Centers: The History of a Building Type*. U.S. Department of the Interior, National Park Service, Cultural Resource Stewardship and Partnerships, Park Historic Structures and Cultural Landscapes Program. Washington, DC: GPO, 2000, 146.

> Housley, Kathleen L. *Emily Hall Tremaine: Collector on the Cusp*. Meriden, CT: Emily Hall Tremaine Foundation, 2001.

MR. AND MRS. ERIC H. BOISSONNAS HOUSE
Logan Road
New Canaan, CT
1956, Philip C. Johnson Associates

> Jordy, William H. "The Mies-less Johnson." *Architectural Forum* 111 (September 1959): 121.

> "Return to the Past." *Time*, 5 September 1960, 52–55.

> Hitchcock, Henry-Russell. "The Current Work of Philip Johnson." *Zodiac* 8 (1961): 64–81.

> Jacobus, John M., Jr. *Philip Johnson*. Makers of Contemporary Architecture. New York: George Braziller, 1962.

> *Philip Johnson Architecture 1949–1965*. Introduction by Henry-Russell Hitchcock. New York: Holt, Rinehart and Winston, 1966, 64–67.

> Noble, Charles. *Philip Johnson*. Photographs by Yukio Futagawa. London: Thames and Hudson, 1972.

> Cappellieri, Alba. *Philip Johnson: Dall'International Style al Decostruttivismo*. Introduction by Vincent Scully. Naples: Clean Edizioni, 1996, 70–71.

> Blake, Peter. *Philip Johnson*. Basel, Berlin, Boston: Birkhäuser, 1997, 62–64.

> Jenkins, Stover, and David Mohney. *The Houses of Philip Johnson*. Afterword by Neil Levine. Photographs by Steven Brooke. New York: Abbeville Press Publishers, 2001.

> Webb, Michael. *Modernism Reborn: Mid-Century American Houses*. Photographs by Roger Straus III. New York: Universe Publishing, 2001, 114–19.

CONGREGATION KNESES TIFERETH ISRAEL SYNAGOGUE
575 King Street
Port Chester, NY
1956, Philip C. Johnson Associates

> Scully, Vincent J., Jr. "Archetype and Order in Recent American Architecture." *Art in America* 42 (December 1954): 251–61.

> "K. T. I. Synagogue, Port Chester, N.Y." *Architectural Record* 117 (June 1955): 186–88.

> "K. T. I. Synagogue, Port Chester, N.Y." *Architectural Record* 120 (December 1956): 124–29.

> Jacobus, John M., Jr. *Philip Johnson*. Makers of Contemporary Architecture. New York: George Braziller, 1962.

> *Philip Johnson Architecture 1949–1965*. Introduction by Henry-Russell Hitchcock. New York: Holt, Rinehart and Winston, 1966, 58–60.

> Noble, Charles. *Philip Johnson*. Photographs by Yukio Futagawa. London: Thames and Hudson, 1972.

> Cappellieri, Alba. *Philip Johnson: Dall'International Style al Decostruttivismo*. Introduction by Vincent Scully. Naples: Clean Edizioni, 1996, 73–75.

> Blake, Peter. *Philip Johnson*. Basel, Berlin, Boston: Birkhäuser, 1997, 65–67.

MR. AND MRS. ROBERT C. LEONHARDT HOUSE
Lloyd's Neck, NY
1956, Philip C. Johnson Associates

> "United States of America: Lloyd's Neck, Long Island, New York." *Architectural Design* 29 (November 1960): 472–74.

> "Glass Living Pavilion Tops View." *Architectural Record* 131 (mid-May 1962): 110–113.

> Jacobus, John M., Jr. *Philip Johnson*. Makers of Contemporary Architecture. New York: George Braziller, 1962.

> *Philip Johnson Architecture 1949–1965*. Introduction by Henry-Russell Hitchcock. New York: Holt, Rinehart and Winston, 1966, 61–63.

> Cappellieri, Alba. *Philip Johnson: Dall'International Style al Decostruttivismo*. Introduction by Vincent Scully. Naples: Clean Edizioni, 1996, 72.

> Blake, Peter. *Philip Johnson*. Basel, Berlin, Boston: Birkhäuser, 1997, 68–69.

> Jenkins, Stover, and David Mohney. *The Houses of Philip Johnson*. Afterword by Neil Levine. Photographs by Steven Brooke. New York: Abbeville Press Publishers, 2001.

HARVEY RESIDENCE HALL
Seton Hill College
Seton Hill Drive
Greensburg, PA
1957, Philip C. Johnson Associates

> Kipnis, Jeffrey. *Philip Johnson: Recent Work*. Architectural Monographs No. 44. London: Academy Editions, 1996, 74–79.

MASTER PLAN, UNIVERSITY OF ST. THOMAS; STRAKE HALL, JONES HALL, AND WELDER HALL
3812-3900 Yoakum Boulevard
Houston, TX
1957–1959, Philip C. Johnson Associates with Bolton & Barnstone

> "The University of St. Thomas, Houston." *Architectural Record* 122 (August 1957): 137–38, 142–43.

> "First Units in the Fabric of a Closed Campus." *Architectural Record* 126 (September 1959): 180–82.

> Jordy, William H. "The Mies-less Johnson." *Architectural Forum* 111 (September 1959): 120.

> "The University of St. Thomas." *Liturgical Arts* 28 (November 1959): 15.

> Hitchcock, Henry-Russell. "The Current Work of Philip Johnson." *Zodiac* 8 (1961): 64–81.

> Jacobus, John M., Jr. *Philip Johnson*. Makers of Contemporary Architecture. New York: George Braziller, 1962.

> "Université St-Thomas, Houston: Auditorium et Salles de Cours." *L'Architecture d'Aujourd'hui* 107 (April–May 1963): 26–27.

> "Two Ways of Looking at Art in Houston: II Gallery of Fine Arts." *Interiors* 123 (November 1963): 97–99.

> "Processional Elements in Houston." *Architectural Record* 137 (June 1965): 159.

> *Philip Johnson Architecture 1949–1965*. Introduction by Henry-Russell Hitchcock. New York: Holt, Rinehart and Winston, 1966, 68–69.

> Noble, Charles. *Philip Johnson*. Photographs by Yukio Futagawa. London: Thames and Hudson, 1972.

> *Philip Johnson: The Architect in His Own Words*. Edited by Hilary Lewis and John O'Connor. New York: Rizzoli International Publications, 1994.

> Blake, Peter. *Philip Johnson*. Basel, Berlin, Boston: Birkhäuser, 1997, 70–71.

> Welch, Frank D. *Philip Johnson and Texas*. Austin: University of Texas Press, 2000.

NELSON A. ROCKEFELLER ART GALLERY
Seal Harbor, ME
1957, Philip C. Johnson Associates

> Lieberman, William S. *The Nelson A. Rockefeller Collection: Masterpieces of Modern Art*. Introduction by Nelson A. Rockefeller. New York: Hudson Hills Press, 1981, 18–19.

ASIA HOUSE
112 East Sixty-fourth Street
New York, NY
1959, Philip C. Johnson Associates
> "Alternative Elevations." *Architectural Review* 768
(February 1961): 81.
> Jacobus, John M., Jr. *Philip Johnson*. Makers of Contemporary
Architecture. New York: George Braziller, 1962.
> Noble, Charles. *Philip Johnson*. Photographs by Yukio Futagawa.
London: Thames and Hudson, 1972.
> Cook, John W., and Heinrich Klotz. *Conversations with
Architects*. New York: Praeger Publishers, 1973, 11–51.
> Goldberger, Paul. *The City Observed: New York*. New York:
Vantage Books, 1979, 235.
> Stern, Robert A. M., Thomas Mellins, and David Fishman.
*New York 1960: Architecture and Urbanism Between the Second
World War and the Bicentennial*. New York: Monacelli Press,
1995, 837–38.
> Cappellieri, Alba. *Philip Johnson: Dall'International Style al
Decostruttivismo*. Introduction by Vincent Scully. Naples:
Clean Edizioni, 1996, 76.
> Blake, Peter. *Philip Johnson*. Basel, Berlin, Boston: Birkhäuser,
1997, 72–73.
> White, Norval, and Elliott Willensky. *AIA Guide to New York
City*. 4th rev. ed. New York: Three Rivers Press, 2000, 391.

THE FOUR SEASONS
Seagram Building
99 East Fifty-second Street
New York, NY
1959, Philip Johnson with William Pahlmann Associates
> Jordy, William H. "The Mies-less Johnson." *Architectural Forum*
111 (September 1959): 122–23.
> "More Elegance at the House of Seagram." *Architectural Record*
126 (November 1959): 201–04.
> "The Four Seasons." *Interiors* 119 (December 1959): 80–85.
> "The Four Seasons: Collaborations for Elegance." *Progressive
Architecture* 40 (December 1959): 142–47.
> "Return to the Past." *Time,* 5 September 1960, 52–55.
> Hitchcock, Henry-Russell. "The Current Work of Philip Johnson."
Zodiac 8 (1961): 64–81.
> Jacobus, John M., Jr. *Philip Johnson*. Makers of Contemporary
Architecture. New York: George Braziller, 1962.
> *Philip Johnson Architecture 1949–1965*. Introduction by
Henry-Russell Hitchcock. New York: Holt, Rinehart and Winston,
1966, 70–71.
> Noble, Charles. *Philip Johnson*. Photographs by Yukio Futagawa.
London: Thames and Hudson, 1972.
> Goldberger, Paul. *The City Observed: New York*. New York:
Vantage Books, 1979, 161.
> Slavin, Maeve. "The Four Seasons at 25." *Interiors* 143
(July 1984): 128–29.
> "Seagram Building and Four Seasons Attain Landmark Status."
Interior Design 60 (November 1989): 66.
> *Philip Johnson: The Architect in His Own Words*. Edited by Hilary
Lewis and John O'Connor. New York: Rizzoli International
Publications, 1994.
> Stern, Robert A. M., Thomas Mellins, and David Fishman.
*New York 1960: Architecture and Urbanism Between the Second
World War and the Bicentennial*. New York: Monacelli Press,
1995, 348–51.
> Blake, Peter. *Philip Johnson*. Basel, Berlin, Boston: Birkhäuser,
1997, 74–77.

JOSEPH E. SEAGRAM & SONS EXECUTIVE OFFICES
Seagram Building
375 Park Avenue
New York, NY
58, Philip Johnson Associates, Phyllis B. Lambert, J. Gordon Carr, and
'l Associates
derson, John. "Seagram Building: Interiors in Keeping with a
asterpiece." *Interiors* 118 (December 1958): 76–81.

THE BRASSERIE
Seagram Building
100 East Fifty-third Street
New York, NY
1959, Philip Johnson with William Pahlmann Associates
1995, demolished
> "The Brasserie, in the Seagram Building, New York." *Interiors*
120 (December 1960): 94–95.

MUNSON-WILLIAMS-PROCTOR INSTITUTE
310 Genesee Street
Utica, NY
1960, Philip Johnson Associates with Bice & Baird
> Jordy, William H. "The Mies-less Johnson." *Architectural Forum*
111 (September 1959): 118.
> "The Perfect Professional Museum." *Architectural Forum* 113
(December 1960): 90–95.
> Hitchcock, Henry-Russell. "The Current Work of Philip Johnson."
Zodiac 8 (1961): 64–81.
> "Musée Munson-Williams-Proctor à Utica, États-Unis."
L'Architecture d'Aujourd'hui 100 (February–March 1962): 29–31.
> Jacobus, John M., Jr. *Philip Johnson*. Makers of Contemporary
Architecture. New York: George Braziller, 1962.
> "Architectural Details 3. Philip Johnson: Stairway, Museum of
Art, Munson-Williams-Proctor Institute, Utica, New York, 1960."
Architectural Record 135 (April 1964): 152–53.
> *Philip Johnson Architecture 1949–1965*. Introduction by
Henry-Russell Hitchcock. New York: Holt, Rinehart and Winston,
1966, 76–79.
> Noble, Charles. *Philip Johnson*. Photographs by Yukio Futagawa.
London: Thames and Hudson, 1972.
> Cappellieri, Alba. *Philip Johnson: Dall'International Style al
Decostruttivismo*. Introduction by Vincent Scully. Naples:
Clean Edizioni, 1996, 77–79.
> Blake, Peter. *Philip Johnson*. Basel, Berlin, Boston: Birkhäuser,
1997, 78–79.

NAHAL SOREQ NUCLEAR CENTER (MAMAG)
Nahal Soreq, Israel
1960, Philip Johnson Associates with Gideon Ziv
> Jordy, William H. "The Mies-less Johnson." *Architectural Forum*
111 (September 1959): 119.
> "Return to the Past." *Time,* 5 September 1960, 52–55.
> "Atoms for Israel." *Architectural Forum* 114 (April 1961):
130–31.
> Hitchcock, Henry-Russell. "The Current Work of Philip Johnson."
Zodiac 8 (1961): 64–81.
> "Réacteur Nucléaire a Rehovot, Israël." *L'Architecture
d'Aujourd'hui* 100 (February–March 1962): 32–33.
> Jacobus, John M., Jr. *Philip Johnson*. Makers of Contemporary
Architecture. New York: George Braziller, 1962.
> *Philip Johnson Architecture 1949–1965*. Introduction by
Henry-Russell Hitchcock. New York: Holt, Rinehart and Winston,
1966, 80–82.
> *Philip Johnson: The Architect in His Own Words*. Edited by Hilary
Lewis and John O'Connor. New York: Rizzoli International
Publications, 1994.
> Blake, Peter. *Philip Johnson*. Basel, Berlin, Boston: Birkhäuser,
1997, 80–81.
> Cohen, Avner. *Israel and the Bomb*. New York: Columbia
University Press, 1998.

ROOFLESS CHURCH
North Street
New Harmony, IN
1960, Philip Johnson Associates
> "Buildings in the News." *Architectural Record* 125
(June 1959): 13.
> Jordy, William H. "The Mies-less Johnson." *Architectural Forum*
111 (September 1959): 122.
> Moore, Robin H. "A Shrine by Philip Johnson." *Art in America* 47,
(no. 4 1959): 70–71.
> "Return to the Past." *Time,* 5 September 1960, 52–55.
> "Shingled Shrine." *Architectural Forum* 113 (September 1960):
128.
> "Culture, Religion and Architecture in Indiana." *Architectural
Record* 128 (October 1960): 15.

> Hitchcock, Henry-Russell. "The Current Work of Philip Johnson."
Zodiac 8 (1961): 64–81.
> Jacobus, John M., Jr. *Philip Johnson*. Makers of Contemporary
Architecture. New York: George Braziller, 1962.
> "Architectural Details 3. Philip Johnson: Roofless Church,
New Harmony, Indiana, 1960." *Architectural Record* 135
(April 1964): 142–43.
> *Philip Johnson Architecture 1949–1965*. Introduction by
Henry-Russell Hitchcock. New York: Holt, Rinehart and Winston,
1966, 72–75.
> Kidder Smith, G. E. *The Architecture of the United States,
Volume 2: The South and the Midwest*. Garden City, NY:
Anchor Press/Doubleday, 1981, 263–64.
> *Philip Johnson: The Architect in His Own Words*. Edited by
Hilary Lewis and John O'Connor. New York: Rizzoli International
Publications, 1994.
> Cappellieri, Alba. *Philip Johnson: Dall'International Style
al Decostruttivismo*. Introduction by Vincent Scully. Naples:
Clean Edizioni, 1996, 80–81.
> Blake, Peter. *Philip Johnson*. Basel, Berlin, Boston: Birkhäuser,
1997, 82–83.
> Celant, Germano. *Cattedrali d'Arte: Dan Flavin per Santa Maria
in Chiesa Rossa*. Milan: Fondazione Prada, 1997.
> Welch, Frank D. *Philip Johnson and Texas*. Austin: University of
Texas Press, 2000.

TAYLOR HALL, GARRISON HALL, AND ROTHSCHILD HALL
Sarah Lawrence College
Bronxville, NY
1960, Philip Johnson Associates
> "Recent Work of Philip Johnson: Dormitories at Sarah Lawrence
College, Bronxville, New York." *Architectural Record* 132
(July 1962): 118–19.
> Jacobus, John M., Jr. *Philip Johnson*. Makers of Contemporary
Architecture. New York: George Braziller, 1962.

ROBERT TOURRE HOUSE
Vaucresson, Hautes-de-Seine, France
1960, Philip Johnson Associates
> "L'Emozione della Geometria." *Abitare* 186 (July–August 1980):
16–21.
> Jenkins, Stover, and David Mohney. *The Houses of Philip Johnson*.
Afterword by Neil Levine. Photographs by Steven Brooke.
New York: Abbeville Press Publishers, 2001.

AMON CARTER MUSEUM OF WESTERN ART
(now the Amon Carter Museum)
3501 Camp Bowie Boulevard
Fort Worth, TX
1961, Philip Johnson Associates with Joseph R. Pelich
1964, addition, Joseph R. Pelich with Philip Johnson Associates
1999, demolished
1977, addition, Johnson/Burgee Architects
1999, demolished
> Jordy, William H. "The Mies-less Johnson." *Architectural Forum*
111 (September 1959): 117.
> *Inaugural Exhibition, Amon Carter Museum of Western Art*.
Fort Worth: Amon Carter Museum of Western Art, January 1961.
Remarks by Philip Johnson.
> "Portico on a Plaza." *Architectural Forum* 114 (March 1961):
86–88.
> Lynes, Russell. "Everything's Up to Date in Texas . . . But Me."
Harper's Magazine, May 1961, 38–42.
> "Building: The New Face of Texas." *Fortune* 64 (October 1961):
129–35.
> Jacobus, John M., Jr. *Philip Johnson*. Makers of Contemporary
Architecture. New York: George Braziller, 1962.
> "Architectural Details 3. Philip Johnson: Amon Carter Museum
of Western Art, 1961." *Architectural Record* 135 (April 1964):
144–45.

> Johnson, Philip. "Whence and Whither: The Processional Element in Architecture." *Perspecta* 9/10 (1965): 167–78.

> *Philip Johnson Architecture 1949–1965.* Introduction by Henry-Russell Hitchcock. New York: Holt, Rinehart and Winston, 1966, 83–85.

> Stern, Robert. *New Directions in American Architecture.* New York: George Braziller, 1969, 42–49.

> Noble, Charles. *Philip Johnson.* Photographs by Yukio Futagawa. London: Thames and Hudson, 1972.

> Kidder Smith, G. E. *The Architecture of the United States, Volume 3: The Plains States and the Far West.* Garden City, NY: Anchor Press/Doubleday, 1981, 659–60.

> Robertson, Kelly. "Museum Gets Facelift." *Texas Architect* 46 (July–August 1996): 23.

> Blake, Peter. *Philip Johnson.* Basel, Berlin, Boston: Birkhäuser, 1997, 84–85.

> Wright, George. *Monument for a City: Philip Johnson's Design for the Amon Carter Museum.* Fort Worth: Amon Carter Museum, 1997.

> Gunderson, W. Mark. "Johnson Redux." *Texas Architect* 49 (January–February 1999): 12–13.

> Fuller, Larry Paul, editor. *The American Institute of Architects Guide to Dallas Architecture with Regional Highlights.* New York: McGraw-Hill Construction Information Group, 1999, 192.

> Welch, Frank D. *Philip Johnson and Texas.* Austin: University of Texas Press, 2000.

COMPUTING LABORATORY
Brown University
180 George Street
Providence, RI
1961, Philip Johnson Associates with Conrad Green

> Jordy, William H. "The Mies-less Johnson." *Architectural Forum* 111 (September 1959): 117.

> Jacobus, John M., Jr. *Philip Johnson.* Makers of Contemporary Architecture. New York: George Braziller, 1962.

> "Recent Work of Philip Johnson: Computing Laboratory, Brown University, Providence, Rhode Island." *Architectural Record* 132 (July 1962): 124–25.

> "Université Brown à Providence: Batiment Memorial et de Laboratoire." *L'Architecture d'Aujourd'hui* 107 (April–May 1963): 24–25.

> Mitchell, Martha. "Computing Laboratory." In *Encyclopaedia Brunoniana.* Providence: Brown University Library, 1993.

MUSEUM FOR THE ROBERT WOODS BLISS COLLECTION OF PRE-COLUMBIAN ART
Dumbarton Oaks
1703 Thirty-second Street, N.W.
Washington, DC
1963, Philip Johnson Associates

> "Recent Work of Philip Johnson: Dumbarton Oaks Wing, Washington, D.C." *Architectural Record* 132 (July 1962): 120–21.

> "Pre-Columbian Art in a Post-Modern Museum." *Architectural Forum* 120 (March 1964): 106–11.

> "Architectural Details 3. Philip Johnson: Wing for Bliss Collection of Pre-Columbian Art, Dumbarton Oaks, Washington, D.C., 1963." *Architectural Record* 135 (April 1964): 146–47.

> "Philip Johnson and Post-Modern Architecture." *Architectural Review* 136 (July 1964): 4.

> Sherman, Stanley M. "Uncommon Ground: Dumbarton Oaks." *AIA Journal* 43 (March 1965): 36–40.

> *Philip Johnson Architecture 1949–1965.* Introduction by Henry-Russell Hitchcock. New York: Holt, Rinehart and Winston, 1966, 90–93.

> Whitehill, Walter Muir. Dumbarton Oaks: *The History of a Georgetown House and Garden.* Cambridge: The Belknap Press of Harvard University Press, 1967.

> Dean, Andrea O. "Mr. Johnson's Hidden Jewel of a Museum." *AIA Journal* 69 (May 1980): 52–57.

> Kidder Smith, G. E. *The Architecture of the United States, Volume 1: New England and the Mid-Atlantic States.* Garden City, NY: Anchor Press/Doubleday, 1981, 122–23.

> Scott, Pamela, and Antoinette J. Lee. *Buildings of the District of Columbia. Buildings of the United States.* New York: Oxford University Press, 1993, 413–14.

> *Philip Johnson: The Architect in His Own Words.* Edited by Hilary Lewis and John O'Connor. New York: Rizzoli International Publications, 1994.

> Weeks, Christopher. *AIA Guide to the Architecture of Washington, D.C.* Introduction by Francis D. Lethbridge. 3d ed. Baltimore: Johns Hopkins University Press, 1994, 253–54.

> Cappellieri, Alba. *Philip Johnson: Dall'International Style al Decostruttivismo.* Introduction by Vincent Scully. Naples: Clean Edizioni, 1996, 82.

> Blake, Peter. *Philip Johnson.* Basel, Berlin, Boston: Birkhäuser, 1997, 88–91.

MONASTERY WING, ST. ANSELM'S ABBEY
4501 South Dakota Avenue, N.E.
Washington, DC
1963, Philip Johnson Associates

> "Johnson." *Perspecta* 7 (1961): 3–6.

> "Concrete Shell Vaults a Church." *Engineering News-Record* 168 (11 January 1962): 27.

> "Recent Work of Philip Johnson: St. Anselm's Abbey, Washington, D.C." *Architectural Record* 132 (July 1962): 116–17.

SHELDON MEMORIAL ART GALLERY
University of Nebraska, Lincoln
Twelfth Street and R Street
Lincoln, NE
1963, Philip Johnson Associates with Hazen & Robinson

> "Johnson." *Perspecta* 7 New Haven: (1961): 3–5.

> "Recent Work of Philip Johnson: Sheldon Art Gallery, University of Nebraska, Lincoln, Nebraska." *Architectural Record* 132 (July 1962): 122–23.

> Jacobus, John M., Jr. *Philip Johnson.* Makers of Contemporary Architecture. New York: George Braziller, 1962.

> "An Art Gallery for a University Campus." *Architectural Record* 134 (August 1963): 129–31.

> "Art Gallery by Philip Johnson, Architect." *Arts + Architecture* 80 (August 1963): 18–21.

> *Philip Johnson Architecture 1949–1965.* Introduction by Henry-Russell Hitchcock. New York: Holt, Rinehart and Winston, 1966, 86–89.

> Noble, Charles. *Philip Johnson.* Photographs by Yukio Futagawa. London: Thames and Hudson, 1972.

> Jencks, Charles. "The Candid King Midas of New York Camp." *Architectural Association Quarterly* 5 (October/December 1973): 26–42.

> Kidder Smith, G. E. *The Architecture of the United States, Volume 3: The Plains States and the Far West.* Garden City, NY: Anchor Press/Doubleday, 1981, 479–80.

> Cappellieri, Alba. *Philip Johnson: Dall'International Style al Decostruttivismo.* Introduction by Vincent Scully. Naples: Clean Edizioni, 1996, 83.

> Blake, Peter. *Philip Johnson.* Basel, Berlin, Boston: Birkhäuser, 1997, 92–93.

MR. AND MRS. HENRY C. BECK, JR., HOUSE
10210 Strait Lane
Dallas, TX
1964, Philip Johnson Associates

> Blake, Peter. *Philip Johnson.* Basel, Berlin, Boston: Birkhäuser, 1997, 103–04.

> Fuller, Larry Paul, editor. *The American Institute of Architects Guide to Dallas Architecture with Regional Highlights.* New York: McGraw-Hill Construction Information Group, 1999, 145.

> Welch, Frank D. *Philip Johnson and Texas.* Austin: University of Texas Press, 2000.

> Jenkins, Stover, and David Mohney. *The Houses of Philip Johnson.* Afterword by Neil Levine. Photographs by Steven Brooke. New York: Abbeville Press Publishers, 2001.

MR. AND MRS. ERIC H. BOISSONNAS HOUSE
Cap Bénat, Côte d'Azur, France
1964, Philip Johnson Associates

> "Recent Work of Philip Johnson: Boissonnas Residence, Cap Bénat, France." *Architectural Record* 132 (July 1962): 128.

> Jacobus, John M., Jr. *Philip Johnson.* Makers of Contemporary Architecture. New York: George Braziller, 1962.

> Gueft, Olga. "The Villa Becomes an Acropolis." *Interiors* 125 (December 1965): 68–72.

> *Philip Johnson Architecture 1949–1965.* Introduction by Henry-Russell Hitchcock. New York: Holt, Rinehart and Winston, 1966, 94–95.

> Hornbeck, James S. "Three Projects by Philip Johnson, Each Designed for a Hill: Riviera House on a Hilltop." *Architectural Record* 141 (June 1967): 148–50.

> "Overlooking the Mediterranean: A House of Six Pavilions." *House and Garden,* August 1967, 114–17.

> Blake, Peter. *Philip Johnson.* Basel, Berlin, Boston: Birkhäuser, 1997, 94–95.

> Jenkins, Stover, and David Mohney. *The Houses of Philip Johnson.* Afterword by Neil Levine. Photographs by Steven Brooke. New York: Abbeville Press Publishers, 2001.

NEW YORK STATE THEATER
Lincoln Center for the Performing Arts
New York, NY
1964, Philip Johnson Associates

> Jordy, William H. "The Mies-less Johnson." *Architectural Forum* 111 (September 1959): 114–17.

> Jacobus, John M., Jr. *Philip Johnson.* Makers of Contemporary Architecture. New York: George Braziller, 1962.

> "Critical Trialogue on Johnson's Lincoln Center Theater." *Progressive Architecture* 45 (May 1964): 58–59.

> "Theater Glamour Again." *Architectural Record* 135 (May 1964): 137–44.

> Gueft, Olga. "Philip Johnson's Neo-Classic" and Wilson, Forrest. "Some Details of Elegance." *Interiors* 123 (July 1964): 85–91.

> Johnson, Philip. "At Lincoln Center." *Art in America* 52, no. 4 (1964): 122–27.

> Smith, C. Ray. "Johnson's Interior Details." *Progressive Architecture* 46 (March 1965): 196–99.

> Johnson, Philip. "Whence and Whither: The Processional Element in Architecture." *Perspecta* 9/10 (1965): 167–78.

> *Philip Johnson Architecture 1949–1965.* Introduction by Henry-Russell Hitchcock. New York: Holt, Rinehart and Winston, 1966, 100–05.

> Stern, Robert. *New Directions in American Architecture.* New York: George Braziller, 1969, 42–49.

> Noble, Charles. *Philip Johnson.* Photographs by Yukio Futagawa. London: Thames and Hudson, 1972.

> Cook, John W., and Heinrich Klotz. *Conversations with Architects.* New York: Praeger Publishers, 1973, 11–51.

> Smith, C. Ray. *Supermannerism: New Attitudes in Post-Modern Architecture.* New York: E. P. Dutton, 1977, 171.

> Goldberger, Paul. *The City Observed: New York.* New York: Vantage Books, 1979, 195–98.

> Young, Edgar D. *Lincoln Center: The Building of an Institution.* New York: New York University Press, 1980, 87, 154–57, 180–88, 206–08.

> Bloom, Martin. "Cultural Colossi: Lincoln Center at 19." *AIA Journal* 70 (August 1981): 32–39.

> "Theater Gets Hearing Aids." *Engineering News-Record* 208 (15 April 1982): 16.

> *Philip Johnson: The Architect in His Own Words.* Edited by Hilary Lewis and John O'Connor. New York: Rizzoli International Publications, 1994.

> Stern, Robert A. M., Thomas Mellins, and David Fishman. *New York 1960: Architecture and Urbanism Between the Second World War and the Bicentennial.* New York: Monacelli Press, 1995, 677–84, 690–95.

> Cappellieri, Alba. *Philip Johnson: Dall'International Style al Decostruttivismo.* Introduction by Vincent Scully. Naples: Clean Edizioni, 1996, 34–88.

> Blake, Peter. *Philip Johnson.* Basel, Berlin, Boston: Birkhäuser, 1997, 98–100.

> Blumenthal, Ralph. "Lincoln Center Gets $1.5 Billion Renovation Plan." *New York Times,* 5 December 1999, sect. A, p. 1.

> White, Norval, and Elliott Willensky. *AIA Guide to New York City.* 4th rev. ed. New York: Three Rivers Press, 2000, 318–19.

LINCOLN CENTER PLAZA AND FOUNTAIN

Lincoln Center for the Performing Arts

New York, NY

1964, Philip Johnson Associates

> *Philip Johnson: The Architect in His Own Words.* Edited by
Hilary Lewis and John O'Connor. New York: Rizzoli International
Publications, 1994.

> Stern, Robert A. M., Thomas Mellins, and David Fishman. *New
York 1960: Architecture and Urbanism Between the Second
World War and the Bicentennial.* New York: Monacelli Press,
1995, 710–12.

NEW YORK STATE PAVILION

1964–1965 World's Fair

Flushing Meadows–Corona Park

Queens, NY

1964, Philip Johnson and Richard Foster

1982, interior renovation, Johnson/Burgee Architects

> "32 Jacks Raise 2,000-Ton Roof" and "The Pavilions: With
Structures Like These, Who Needs Exhibits?" *Engineering
News-Record* 171 (31 October 1963): 15, 22–29.

> Schmertz, Mildred F. "Architecture at the New York World's
Fair." *Architectural Record* 136 (July 1964): 143–50.

> Johnson, Philip. "Young Artists at the Fair and at Lincoln
Center." *Art in America* 52, no. 4 (1964): 112–21.

> Johnson, Philip. "Whence and Whither: The Processional Element
in Architecture." *Perspecta* 9/10 (1965): 167–78.

> *Philip Johnson Architecture 1949–1965.* Introduction by
Henry-Russell Hitchcock. New York: Holt, Rinehart and Winston,
1966, 106–09.

> Noble, Charles. *Philip Johnson.* Photographs by Yukio Futagawa.
London: Thames and Hudson, 1972.

> Smith, C. Ray. *Supermannerism: New Attitudes in Post-Modern
Architecture.* New York: E. P. Dutton, 1977, 170–71.

> *Philip Johnson: The Architect in His Own Words.* Edited by Hilary
Lewis and John O'Connor. New York: Rizzoli International
Publications, 1994.

> Stern, Robert A. M., Thomas Mellins, and David Fishman. *New
York 1960: Architecture and Urbanism Between the Second
World War and the Bicentennial.* New York: Monacelli Press,
1995, 1034–38.

> Cappellieri, Alba. *Philip Johnson: Dall'International Style al
Decostruttivismo.* Introduction by Vincent Scully. Naples:
Clean Edizioni, 1996, 89–90.

> Blake, Peter. *Philip Johnson.* Basel, Berlin, Boston: Birkhäuser,
1997, 101–02.

> White, Norval, and Elliott Willensky. *AIA Guide to New York City.*
4th rev. ed. New York: Three Rivers Press, 2000, 830.

EPIDEMIOLOGY AND PUBLIC HEALTH BUILDING

Yale University

50 College Street

New Haven, CT

1964, Philip Johnson and The Office of Douglas Orr

> *Philip Johnson Architecture 1949–1965.* Introduction by
Henry-Russell Hitchcock. New York: Holt, Rinehart and Winston,
1966, 110–11.

> Holden, Reuben A. *Yale: A Pictorial History.* New Haven:
Yale University Press, 1967, 285.

> Noble, Charles. *Philip Johnson.* Photographs by Yukio Futagawa.
London: Thames and Hudson, 1972.

> Cook, John W., and Heinrich Klotz. *Conversations with Architects.*
New York: Praeger Publishers, 1973, 11–51.

> Metz, Don. *New Architecture in New Haven.* Rev. ed. Cambridge:
MIT Press, 1973, 12–13.

> Brown, Elizabeth Mills. *New Haven: A Guide to Architecture and
Urban Design.* New Haven: Yale University Press, 1976, 144.

> Scully, Vincent. *American Architecture and Urbanism.* Rev. ed.
New York: Henry Holt and Company, Inc., 1988, 246–48.

> Pinnell, Patrick. *The Campus Guide: Yale University.* New York:
Princeton Architectural Press, 1999, 172–73.

MR. AND MRS. JAMES GEIER HOUSE

9100 Kugler Mill Road

Cincinnati, OH

1965, Philip Johnson

> "Johnson Underground." *Progressive Architecture* 48 (April
1967): 146.

> Johnson, Philip. "Beyond Monuments." *Architectural Record* 138
(January–February 1973): 67.

> "Johnson's 'Mound Architecture.' " *AIA Journal* 67 (November
1978): 38–39.

> Langsam, Walter E. *Great Houses of the Queen City.* Photographs
by Alice Weston. Cincinnati: Cincinnati Museum Center, 1997.

> Blake, Peter. *Philip Johnson.* Basel, Berlin, Boston: Birkhäuser,
1997, 105.

> Jenkins, Stover, and David Mohney. *The Houses of Philip Johnson.*
Afterword by Neil Levine. Photographs by Steven Brooke. New
York: Abbeville Press Publishers, 2001.

KLINE BIOLOGY TOWER

Yale University

Sachem Street

New Haven, CT

1965, Philip Johnson and Richard Foster

> "Recent Work of Philip Johnson: Kline Science Center, Yale
University, New Haven." *Architectural Record* 132 (July 1962):
114–15.

> Jacobus, John M., Jr. *Philip Johnson.* Makers of Contemporary
Architecture. New York: George Braziller, 1962.

> "Architectural Details 3. Philip Johnson: Kline Science Center,
Yale University, New Haven, Connecticut." *Architectural Record*
135 (April 1964): 148–49.

> Hitchcock, Henry-Russell. "Connecticut, U.S.A., in 1963."
Zodiac 13 (1964): 17.

> Johnson, Philip. "Whence and Whither: The Processional Element
in Architecture." *Perspecta* 9/10 (1965): 167–78.

> *Philip Johnson Architecture 1949–1965.* Introduction by
Henry-Russell Hitchcock. New York: Holt, Rinehart and Winston,
1966, 114–15.

> Burns, James T., Jr. "Locus for Gown, Focus for Town."
Progressive Architecture 48 (February 1967): 90–97.

> Hornbeck, James S. "Three Projects by Philip Johnson, Each
Designed for a Hill: The Kline Tower at Yale." *Architectural
Record* 141 (June 1967): 140–45.

> Holden, Reuben A. *Yale: A Pictorial History.* New Haven: Yale
University Press, 1967, 295.

> "Corners: The Classical Corner." *Progressive Architecture* 49
(August 1968): 92.

> Stern, Robert. *New Directions in American Architecture.*
New York: George Braziller, 1969, 42–49.

> Noble, Charles. *Philip Johnson.* Photographs by Yukio Futagawa.
London: Thames and Hudson, 1972.

> Cook, John W., and Heinrich Klotz. *Conversations with Architects.*
New York: Praeger Publishers, 1973, 11–51.

> Metz, Don. *New Architecture in New Haven.* Rev. ed. Cambridge:
MIT Press, 1973, 56–57.

> Brown, Elizabeth Mills. *New Haven: A Guide to Architecture and
Urban Design.* New Haven: Yale University Press, 1976, 144.

> Scully, Vincent. *American Architecture and Urbanism.* Rev. ed.
New York: Henry Holt and Company, Inc., 1988, 194–95.

> Cappellieri, Alba. *Philip Johnson: Dall'International Style al
Decostruttivismo.* Introduction by Vincent Scully. Naples:
Clean Edizioni, 1996, 91–93.

> Blake, Peter. *Philip Johnson.* Basel, Berlin, Boston: Birkhäuser,
1997, 110–12.

> Pinnell, Patrick. *The Campus Guide: Yale University.* New York:
Princeton Architectural Press, 1999, 164–65.

KLINE GEOLOGY LABORATORY

Yale University

210 Whitney Avenue

New Haven, CT

1964, Philip Johnson and Richard Foster

> "Recent Work of Philip Johnson: Kline Science Center, Yale
University, New Haven." *Architectural Record* 132 (July 1962):
114–15.

> "Griswold's Memorial." *Architectural Review,* no.799
(September 1963): 149–50.

> Hitchcock, Henry-Russell. "Connecticut, U.S.A., in 1963."
Zodiac 13 (1964): 17–21.

> "Kline Geology Laboratory." *Architectural Design* 34 (April
1964): 174–75.

> Burns, James T., Jr. "Locus for Gown, Focus for Town."
Progressive Architecture 48 (February 1967): 90–97.

> Holden, Reuben A. *Yale: A Pictorial History.* New Haven: Yale
University Press, 1967, 293.

> Noble, Charles. *Philip Johnson.* Photographs by Yukio Futagawa.
London: Thames and Hudson, 1972.

> Metz, Don. *New Architecture in New Haven.* Rev. ed. Cambridge:
MIT Press, 1973, 60–61.

> Brown, Elizabeth Mills. *New Haven: A Guide to Architecture and
Urban Design.* New Haven: Yale University Press, 1976, 144.

> Scully, Vincent. *American Architecture and Urbanism.* Rev. ed.
New York: Henry Holt and Company, Inc., 1988, 194–95.

> Pinnell, Patrick. *The Campus Guide: Yale University.* New York:
Princeton Architectural Press, 1999, 167.

KLINE CHEMISTRY LABORATORY

Yale University

Prospect Street

New Haven, CT

1965, Philip Johnson and Richard Foster

> Burns, James T., Jr. "Locus for Gown, Focus for Town."
Progressive Architecture 48 (February 1967): 90–97.

> Holden, Reuben A. *Yale: A Pictorial History.* New Haven:
Yale University Press, 1967, 294.

> Pinnell, Patrick. *The Campus Guide: Yale University.* New York:
Princeton Architectural Press, 1999, 164–65.

**HENRY L. MOSES INSTITUTE MONTEFIORE HOSPITAL
(now Montefiore Medical Center)**

111 East Two Hundred Tenth Street

The Bronx, NY

1965, Philip Johnson

> "Research Raised on High: Research Tower 2: It Stands Out."
Architectural Forum 125 (October 1966): 75–77.

> *Philip Johnson Architecture 1949–1965.* Introduction by
Henry-Russell Hitchcock. New York: Holt, Rinehart and Winston,
1966, 112–13.

> Noble, Charles. *Philip Johnson.* Photographs by Yukio Futagawa.
London: Thames and Hudson, 1972.

> Stern, Robert A. M., Thomas Mellins, and David Fishman. *New
York 1960: Architecture and Urbanism Between the Second
World War and the Bicentennial.* New York: Monacelli Press,
1995, 947.

> Blake, Peter. *Philip Johnson.* Basel, Berlin, Boston: Birkhäuser,
1997, 108–09.

> White, Norval, and Elliott Willensky. *AIA Guide to New York City.*
4th rev. ed. New York: Three Rivers Press, 2000, 603.

O. C. BAILEY LIBRARY

Hendrix College
1600 Washington Avenue
Conway, AR
1967, Philip Johnson and Wittenberg, Delony & Davidson
1998, demolished
> Smith, Herbert L., Jr. "Four Just-Completed Buildings by Philip Johnson." *Architectural Record* 146 (December 1969): 92–93.
> Kidder Smith, G. E. *The Architecture of the United States, Volume 3: The Plains States and the Far West.* Garden City, NY: Anchor Press/Doubleday, 1981, 57–58.

KUNSTHALLE BIELEFELD

Artur-Ladebeck-Straße 5
Bielefeld, Germany
1968, Philip Johnson with Architekt Professor Käsar F. Pinnau
> "Johnson Exports a Small Museum." *Progressive Architecture* 46 (May 1965): 200–01.
> "Johnson Kunsthalle." *Architectural Forum* 129 (September 1968): 66.
> "Zwei Kunsthallen: Art Gallery, Bielefeld: Philip Johnson, Architect." *Architectural Review,* no.865 (March 1969): 119–21.
> Smith, Herbert L., Jr. "Four Just-Completed Buildings by Philip Johnson." *Architectural Record* 146 (December 1969): 94–95.
> Blake, Peter. *Philip Johnson.* Basel, Berlin, Boston: Birkhäuser, 1997, 114–15.

RADIO WRVA STUDIO

200 North Twenty-second Street
Richmond, VA
1968, Budina & Freeman; Philip Johnson, consulting architect
> Smith, Herbert L., Jr. "Four Just-Completed Buildings by Philip Johnson." *Architectural Record* 146 (December 1969): 96.

MR. AND MRS. DAVID LLOYD KREEGER HOUSE
(now Kreeger Museum)

2401 Foxhall Road, N.W.
Washington, DC
1968, Philip Johnson and Richard Foster
> "La Maison Kreeger à Washington." *L'Oeil* 168 (December 1968): 60–63.
> "In Washington, D.C.: Art Museum Designed for Living." *House Beautiful,* February 1969, 58–65.
> Smith, Herbert L., Jr. "Four Just-Completed Buildings by Philip Johnson." *Architectural Record* 146 (December 1969): 87–91.
> Sharpe, Margy R., editor. *The Collection of Mr. and Mrs. David Lloyd Kreeger.* Washington, DC: privately printed, 1976.
> Scott, Pamela, and Antoinette J. Lee. *Buildings of the District of Columbia, Buildings of the United States.* New York: Oxford University Press, 1993, 396.
> Weeks, Christopher. *AIA Guide to the Architecture of Washington, D.C.* Introduction by Francis D. Lethbridge. 3d ed. Baltimore: Johns Hopkins University Press, 1994, 219.
> Blake, Peter. "The Kreeger." *Interior Design* 66 (June 1995): 90–95.
> Blake, Peter. *Philip Johnson.* Basel, Berlin, Boston: Birkhäuser, 1997, 113.
> Jenkins, Stover, and David Mohney. *The Houses of Philip Johnson.* Afterword by Neil Levine. Photographs by Steven Brooke. New York: Abbeville Press Publishers, 2001.

JOHN F. KENNEDY MEMORIAL

600 Main Street
Dallas, TX
1970, Philip Johnson
> "The Empty Room." *Time,* 24 December 1965, 38.
> Stern, Robert. *New Directions in American Architecture.* New York: George Braziller, 1969, 42–49.
> Kidder Smith, G. E. *The Architecture of the United States, Volume 3: The Plains States and the Far West.* Garden City, NY: Anchor Press/Doubleday, 1981, 644–45.
> Blake, Peter. *Philip Johnson.* Basel, Berlin, Boston: Birkhäuser, 1997, 116.
> Fuller, Larry Paul, editor. *The American Institute of Architects Guide to Dallas Architecture with Regional Highlights.* New York: McGraw-Hill Construction Information Group, 1999, 19.
> Del Monte, Betsy. "JFK Memorial Restored." *Texas Architect* 50 (September–October 2000): 16–17.
> Welch, Frank D. *Philip Johnson and Texas.* Austin: University of Texas Press, 2000.

ALBERT AND VERA LIST ART BUILDING

Brown University
64 College Street
Providence, RI
1971, Philip Johnson with Samuel Glaser & Partners
> Goldberger, Paul. "Form and Procession." *Architectural Forum* 138 (January–February 1973): 48.
> Blake, Peter. *Philip Johnson.* Basel, Berlin, Boston: Birkhäuser, 1997, 121–22.

THE ART MUSEUM OF SOUTH TEXAS

1902 North Shoreline Drive
Corpus Christi, TX
1972, Philip Johnson and John Burgee with Howard Barnstone and Eugene Aubry
> "Three New Museums in Texas." *Art in America* 60 (September–October 1972): 52–53.
> Goldberger, Paul. "Form and Procession." *Architectural Forum* 138 (January–February 1973): 41–45.
> Johnson, Philip. *Johnson/Burgee: Architecture.* Text by Nory Miller, photographs by Richard Payne. New York: Random House, 1979, 10–17.
> Cappellieri, Alba. *Philip Johnson: Dall'International Style al Decostruttivismo.* Introduction by Vincent Scully. Naples: Clean Edizioni, 1996, 94–95.
> Lessoff, Alan. "An Art Museum for South Texas, 1944–1980." In *Legacy: A History of the Art Museum of South Texas.* Corpus Christi: Art Museum of South Texas, 1997, 24–53.
> Blake, Peter. *Philip Johnson.* Basel, Berlin, Boston: Birkhäuser, 1997, 123–26.
> Welch, Frank D. *Philip Johnson and Texas.* Austin: University of Texas Press, 2000.

BURDEN HALL

Harvard Business School
Harvard University
Soldiers Field
Boston, MA
1972, Philip Johnson and John Burgee
> Goldberger, Paul. "Form and Procession." *Architectural Forum* 138 (January–February 1973): 50.
> Johnson, Philip. *Johnson/Burgee: Architecture.* Text by Nory Miller, photographs by Richard Payne. New York: Random House, 1979, 18–19.
> Shand-Tucci, Douglas. *The Campus Guide: Harvard University.* New York: Princeton Architectural Press, 2001, 303.

ROY R. NEUBERGER MUSEUM OF ART

State University of New York, Purchase
735 Anderson Hill Road
Purchase, NY
1972, Philip Johnson and John Burgee
> "Academic Village: State University College, Purchase, New York; Art Museum." *Architectural Forum* 133 (November 1970): 39.
> Goldberger, Paul. "Form and Procession." *Architectural Forum* 138 (January–February 1973): 46.
> Johnson, Philip. *Johnson/Burgee: Architecture.* Text by Nory Miller, photographs by Richard Payne. New York: Random House, 1979, 20–25.
> Barnes, Edward Larrabee. *Edward Larrabee Barnes, Architect.* Introduction by Peter Blake. New York: Rizzoli International Publications, 1994, 122–29.

TISCH HALL

New York University
40 West Fourth Street
New York, NY
1972, Philip Johnson and Richard Foster
> Stern, Robert A. M., Thomas Mellins, and David Fishman. *New York 1960: Architecture and Urbanism Between the Second World War and the Bicentennial.* New York: Monacelli Press, 1995, 241.
> White, Norval, and Elliott Willensky. *AIA Guide to New York City.* 4th rev. ed. New York: Three Rivers Press, 2000, 121.

FAÇADE OF ANDRÉ AND BELLA MEYER PHYSICS HALL

New York University
4 Washington Place
New York, NY
1972, Philip Johnson and Richard Foster
> Perry, Ellen. "An Urban Problem: The People Object." *Progressive Architecture* 47 (June 1966): 180–93.
> Stern, Robert A. M., Thomas Mellins, and David Fishman. *New York 1960: Architecture and Urbanism Between the Second World War and the Bicentennial.* New York: Monacelli Press, 1995, 241.
> White, Norval, and Elliott Willensky. *AIA Guide to New York City.* 4th rev. ed. New York: Three Rivers Press, 2000, 122.

ELMER HOLMES BOBST LIBRARY

New York University
70 Washington Square South
New York, NY
1972, Philip Johnson and Richard Foster
> Perry, Ellen. "An Urban Problem: The People Object." *Progressive Architecture* 47 (June 1966): 180–93.
> Goldberger, Paul. "Form and Procession." *Architectural Forum* 138 (January–February 1973): 45, 49.
> "Two Libraries by Philip Johnson Open." *Progressive Architecture* 54 (February 1973): 32, 34.
> Smith, C. Ray. *Supermannerism: New Attitudes in Post-Modern Architecture.* New York: E. P. Dutton, 1977, 266–68.
> Goldberger, Paul. *The City Observed: New York.* New York: Vantage Books, 1979, 76.
> *Philip Johnson: The Architect in His Own Words.* Edited by Hilary Lewis and John O'Connor. New York: Rizzoli International Publications, 1994.
> Stern, Robert A. M., Thomas Mellins, and David Fishman. *New York 1960: Architecture and Urbanism Between the Second World War and the Bicentennial.* New York: Monacelli Press, 1995, 236–41.
> Cappellieri, Alba. *Philip Johnson: Dall'International Style al Decostruttivismo.* Introduction by Vincent Scully. Naples: Clean Edizioni, 1996, 96–97.
> Blake, Peter. *Philip Johnson.* Basel, Berlin, Boston: Birkhäuser, 1997, 127–28.
> White, Norval, and Elliott Willensky. *AIA Guide to New York City.* 4th rev. ed. New York: Three Rivers Press, 2000, 121.

HAGOP KERVORKIAN CENTER FOR NEAR EASTERN STUDIES

New York University
50 Washington Square South
New York, NY
1973, Philip Johnson and Richard Foster
> Goldberger, Paul. "Form and Procession." *Architectural Forum* 138 (January–February 1973): 45, 49.
> Goldberger, Paul. *The City Observed: New York.* New York: Vantage Books, 1979, 76.
> Stern, Robert A. M., Thomas Mellins, and David Fishman. *New York 1960: Architecture and Urbanism Between the Second World War and the Bicentennial.* New York: Monacelli Press, 1995, 241–42.
> Blake, Peter. *Philip Johnson.* Basel, Berlin, Boston: Birkhäuser, 1997, 129.
> White, Norval, and Elliott Willensky. *AIA Guide to New York City.* 4th rev. ed. New York: Three Rivers Press, 2000, 123.

IDS CENTER

80 Eighth Street South
Minneapolis, MN
1973, Philip Johnson and John Burgee and Edward F. Baker Associates
> "Core's Shape, Plastic Design Join for High Economy." *Engineering News-Record* 187 (4 November 1971): 26–27.
> Goldberger, Paul. "Form and Procession." *Architectural Forum* 138 (January–February 1973): 32–38.
> Johnson, Philip. "A There There." *Architectural Forum* 139 (November 1973): 38–39.
> "Grist and Gusto." *Architectural Forum* 139 (December 1973): 40–42.
> "Thinking Too Big." *Forbes,* 15 June 1974, 30–31.
> Smith, C. Ray. "The Marquette Inn's Crystal Clarity." *Interiors* 135 (April 1975): 64–71.
> "I.D.S. Center, Minneapolis. Architects: Philip Johnson and John Burgee and Edward F. Baker Associates, Inc., a joint venture." *AIA Journal* 63 (May 1975): 42–43.

> "The Problems Get Worse at IDS." *Business Week*, 15 March 1976, 100–06.

> Gebhard, David, and Tom Martinson. *A Guide to the Architecture of Minnesota*. Minneapolis: University of Minnesota for the University Gallery of the University of Minnesota and the Minnesota Society of Architects, 1977, 31.

> Marcus, Clare Cooper. "Evaluation: A Tale of Two Spaces." *AIA Journal* 67 (August 1978): 34–39.

> Canty, Donald. "Evaluation: Single Complex City Core." *AIA Journal* 68 (June 1979): 52–59.

> Johnson, Philip. *Johnson/Burgee: Architecture*. Text by Nory Miller, photographs by Richard Payne. New York: Random House, 1979, 26–33.

> Goldberger, Paul. *The Skyscraper*. New York: Alfred A. Knopf, 1981, 123–24.

> Kidder Smith, G. E. *The Architecture of the United States, Volume 3: The Plains States and the Far West*. Garden City, NY: Anchor Press/Doubleday, 1981, 370–72.

> Baymiller, Joanna. "Should a 12-Year-Old Building Become a Historic Landmark?" *Architecture* 73 (August 1984): 11.

> *Philip Johnson: The Architect in His Own Words*. Edited by Hilary Lewis and John O'Connor. New York: Rizzoli International Publications, 1994.

> Cappellieri, Alba. *Philip Johnson: Dall'International Style al Decostruttivismo*. Introduction by Vincent Scully. Naples: Clean Edizioni, 1996, 98–100.

> Blake, Peter. *Philip Johnson*. Basel, Berlin, Boston: Birkhäuser, 1997, 130–33.

BOSTON PUBLIC LIBRARY ADDITION
Boylston Street and Exeter Street
Boston, MA
1972, Philip Johnson and John Burgee and Architects Design Group

> "Orthotropic Bridges Used in Library." *Engineering News-Record* 186 (10 June 1971): 32.

> Goldberger, Paul. "Form and Procession." *Architectural Forum*. 138 (January–February 1973): 45–46, 48, 51–53.

> "Two Libraries by Philip Johnson Open." *Progressive Architecture* 54 (February 1973): 32.

> Eldredge, Joseph J. *Architecture Boston*. Introduction by Walter Muir Whitehill. Barre: Barre Publishing, 1976, 70–72.

> Johnson, Philip. *Johnson/Burgee: Architecture*. Text by Nory Miller, photographs by Richard Payne. New York: Random House, 1979, 34–37.

> Kidder Smith, G. E. *The Architecture of the United States, Volume 1: New England and the Mid-Atlantic States*. Garden City, NY: Anchor Press/Doubleday, 1981, 245.

> Lyndon, Donlyn. T*he City Observed: Boston: A Guide to the Architecture of the Hub*. New York: Vantage Books, 1982, 170–71.

> Southworth. Susan, and Michael Southworth. *AIA Guide to Boston*. 2d ed. Chester, CT: Globe Pequot Press, 1992, 230.

> *Philip Johnson: The Architect in His Own Words*. Edited by Hilary Lewis and John O'Connor. New York: Rizzoli International Publications, 1994.

> Cappellieri, Alba. *Philip Johnson: Dall'International Style al Decostruttivismo*. Introduction by Vincent Scully. Naples: Clean Edizioni, 1996, 100–02.

> Blake, Peter. *Philip Johnson*. Basel, Berlin, Boston: Birkhäuser, 1997, 134–37.

NIAGARA FALLS CONVENTION AND CIVIC CENTER
305 South Fourth Street
Niagara Falls, NY
1974, Philip Johnson and John Burgee

> "Arch Truss Provides Low-Profile Clear Span." *Engineering News-Record* 189 (10 August 1972): 23.

> Johnson, Philip. "Beyond Monuments." *Architectural Forum* 138 (January–February 1973): 54–57.

> Stephens, Suzanne. "Second Honeymoon." *Progressive Architecture* 59 (August 1978): 80–81.

> Johnson, Philip. *Johnson/Burgee: Architecture*. Text by Nory Miller, photographs by Richard Payne. New York: Random House, 1979, 38–43.

> Kidder Smith, G. E. *The Architecture of the United States, Volume 1: New England and the Mid-Atlantic States*. Garden City, NY: Anchor Press/Doubleday, 1981, 446–47.

> Blake, Peter. *Philip Johnson*. Basel, Berlin, Boston: Birkhäuser, 1997, 138–39.

FORT WORTH WATER GARDEN
Fourteenth Street and Houston Street
Fort Worth, TX
1974, Johnson/Burgee Architects

> "Water Gardens Aim at Revitalizing Downtown Areas." *Engineering News-Record* 190 (7 June 1973): 13.

> Papademetriou, Peter C. "Big Splash in Fort Worth." *Progressive Architecture* 56 (January 1975): 22–23.

> Sumner, Jane. "Peace in the Gardens." *D: The Magazine of Dallas* 4 (November 1977): 111.

> Johnson, Philip. *Johnson/Burgee: Architecture*. Text by Nory Miller, photographs by Richard Payne. New York: Random House, 1979, 44–51.

> Kidder Smith, G. E. *The Architecture of the United States, Volume 3: The Plains States and the Far West*. Garden City, NY: Anchor Press/Doubleday, 1981, 663–65.

> *Philip Johnson: The Architect in His Own Words*. Edited by Hilary Lewis and John O'Connor. New York: Rizzoli International Publications, 1994.

> Blake, Peter. *Philip Johnson*. Basel, Berlin, Boston: Birkhäuser, 1997, 140–42.

> Fuller, Larry Paul, editor. *The American Institute of Architects Guide to Dallas Architecture with Regional Highlights*. New York: McGraw-Hill Construction Information Group, 1999, 182.

> Welch, Frank D. *Philip Johnson and Texas*. Austin: University of Texas Press, 2000.

MORNINGSIDE HOUSE
1000 Pelham Parkway South
The Bronx, NY
1974, Johnson/Burgee Architects

> Johnson, Philip. *Johnson/Burgee: Architecture*. Text by Nory Miller, photographs by Richard Payne. New York: Random House, 1979, 52–53.

> Stern, Robert A. M., Thomas Mellins, and David Fishman. *New York 1960: Architecture and Urbanism Between the Second World War and the Bicentennial*. New York: Monacelli Press, 1995, 751–53.

> White, Norval, and Elliott Willensky. *AIA Guide to New York City*. 4th rev. ed. New York: Three Rivers Press, 2000, 620.

ONE POST OAK CENTRAL
2000 Post Oak Boulevard
Houston, TX
1975, Johnson/Burgee Architects and S. I. Morris Associates

> Papademetriou, Peter. "Deco-rating Houston's Skyline." *Progressive Architecture* 58 (January 1977): 32.

> Johnson, Philip. *Johnson/Burgee: Architecture*. Text by Nory Miller, photographs by Richard Payne. New York: Random House, 1979, 64–67.

> *Philip Johnson: The Architect in His Own Words*. Edited by Hilary Lewis and John O'Connor. New York: Rizzoli International Publications, 1994.

> Blake, Peter. *Philip Johnson*. Basel, Berlin, Boston: Birkhäuser, 1997, 143–44.

TWO POST OAK CENTRAL
1980 Post Oak Boulevard
Houston, TX
1979, Johnson/Burgee Architects and Richard Fitzgerald & Partners

> Johnson, Philip. *Johnson/Burgee: Architecture*. Text by Nory Miller, photographs by Richard Payne. New York: Random House, 1979, 64–67.

AVERY FISHER HALL INTERIOR
Lincoln Center for the Performing Arts
New York, NY
1976, Johnson/Burgee Architects

> Abercrombie, Stanley. "Johnson and Burgee: Avery Fisher Hall." *Interiors* 136 (February 1977): 98–101.

> Ryder, Sharon Lee. "Music to My Ears?" *Progressive Architecture* 58 (March 1977): 64–69.

> Johnson, Philip. *Johnson/Burgee: Architecture*. Text by Nory Miller, photographs by Richard Payne. New York: Random House, 1979, 68–69.

> Blake, Peter. *Philip Johnson*. Basel, Berlin, Boston: Birkhäuser, 1997, 145–46.

PENNZOIL PLACE
711 Louisiana Street
Houston, TX
1976, Johnson/Burgee Architects and S. I. Morris Associates

> "Space Frames, 117 Ft High, to Cover Plazas." *Engineering News-Record* 188 (29 June 1972): 12.

> Goldberger, Paul. "Form and Procession." *Architectural Forum* 138 (January–February 1973): 37–39.

> "Seven-Story A-Frame Stiffens Tops of Sloped 38-Story Towers." *Engineering News-Record* 193 (11 July 1974): 23.

> "Hines Changes Houston's Skyline Profitably." *Business Week*, 19 April 1976, 114–15.

> Goldberger, Paul. "High Design at a Profit." *New York Times Magazine*, 14 November 1976, 76–79.

> Marlin, William. "Pennzoil Place." *Architectural Record* 160 (November 1976): 101–10.

> Huxtable, Ada Louise. "Pennzoil: Houston's Towering Achievement." In *Kicked a Building Lately?* New York: Quadrangle/New York Times Book Company, 1976, 67–71.

> "Pennzoil Place, Houston. Johnson/Burgee and S. I. Morris Associates." *AIA Journal* 66 (May 1977): 48–49.

> "Project Pennzoil." *Interior Design* 48 (June 1977): 134–45.

> Papademetriou, Peter. "Is 'Wow!' Enough?" *Progressive Architecture* 58 (August 1977): 66–72.

> Canty, Donald. "Progressive Architecture, Architectural Record; Some Images They Conveyed in 1977: Pennzoil Place." *AIA Journal* 67 (mid-May 1978): 144–45.

> Johnson, Philip. *Johnson/Burgee: Architecture*. Text by Nory Miller, photographs by Richard Payne. New York: Random House, 1979, 54–63.

> Kidder Smith, G. E. *The Architecture of the United States, Volume 3: The Plains States and the Far West*. Garden City, NY: Anchor Press/Doubleday, 1981, 579–95.

> Pastier, John. "Evaluation: Pennzoil as Sculpture and Symbol." *AIA Journal* 71 (June 1982): 38–43.

> *Philip Johnson: The Architect in His Own Words*. Edited by Hilary Lewis and John O'Connor. New York: Rizzoli International Publications, 1994.

> Cappellieri, Alba. *Philip Johnson: Dall'International Style al Decostruttivismo*. Introduction by Vincent Scully. Naples: Clean Edizioni, 1996, 103–04.

> Blake, Peter. *Philip Johnson*. Basel, Berlin, Boston: Birkhäuser, 1997, 147–50.

> Le Blanc, Sidney. *The Architecture Traveler: A Guide to 250 Key 20th-Century American Buildings*. New York: W. W. Norton & Company, 2000, 149.

CENTURY CENTER
120 South St. Joseph Street
South Bend, IN
1976, Johnson/Burgee Architects

> Johnson, Philip. *Johnson/Burgee: Architecture*. Text by Nory Miller, photographs by Richard Payne. New York: Random House, 1979, 70–77.

> Hoyt, Charles K. "The Performing and Visual Arts Join Civic Functions in an Important New Multi-Use Center." *Architectural Record* 169 (April 1981): 118–23.

GENERAL AMERICAN LIFE INSURANCE COMPANY BUILDING
700 Market Street
St. Louis, MO
1976, Johnson/Burgee Architects
> Gordon, Barclay F. "Three Designs by Johnson/Burgee: General American Life Insurance Building." *Architectural Record* 164 (July 1978): 80–83.
> Johnson, Philip. *Johnson/Burgee: Architecture*. Text by Nory Miller, photographs by Richard Payne. New York: Random House, 1979, 84–93.
> Peters, Frank, and George McCue. *A Guide to the Architecture of St. Louis*. Columbia: University of Missouri Press, 1989, 38.
> Cappellieri, Alba. *Philip Johnson: Dall'International Style al Decostruttivismo*. Introduction by Vincent Scully. Naples: Clean Edizioni, 1996, 105–06.

THANKS-GIVING SQUARE
Pacific Street and Ervay Street
Dallas, TX
1976, Johnson/Burgee Architects
1996, addition, Philip Johnson, Ritchie and Fiore Architects
> "Chapel Wall Cantilevers Off Itself in Spiral Climb Over Truck Depot." *Engineering News-Record* 197 (19 August 1976): 24–25.
> Sumner, Jane. "The Park That Peter Built." *D: The Magazine of Dallas* 4 (November 1977): 108–11.
> Johnson, Philip. *Johnson/Burgee: Architecture*. Text by Nory Miller, photographs by Richard Payne. New York: Random House, 1979, 94–101.
> Kidder Smith, G. E. *The Architecture of the United States, Volume 3: The Plains States and the Far West*. Garden City, NY: Anchor Press/Doubleday, 1981, 652–53.
> Ingersoll, Richard. "In the Capital of White Noise." *Texas Architect* 40 (January–February 1990): 36–41.
> *Philip Johnson: The Architect in His Own Words*. Edited by Hilary Lewis and John O'Connor. New York: Rizzoli International Publications, 1994.
> Cappellieri, Alba. *Philip Johnson: Dall'International Style al Decostruttivismo*. Introduction by Vincent Scully. Naples: Clean Edizioni, 1996, 107–08.
> Blake, Peter. *Philip Johnson*. Basel, Berlin, Boston: Birkhäuser, 1997, 151–53.
> Fuller, Larry Paul, editor. *The American Institute of Architects Guide to Dallas Architecture with Regional Highlights*. New York: McGraw-Hill Construction Information Group, 1999, 29.
> Welch, Frank D. *Philip Johnson and Texas*. Austin: University of Texas Press, 2000.

FINE ARTS CENTER
(now Dorothy and Dexter Baker Center for the Arts)
Muhlenberg College
2400 Chew Street
Allentown, PA
1977, Johnson/Burgee Architects and Wallace & Watson Associates
> Goldberger, Paul. "Form and Procession." *Architectural Forum* 138 (January–February 1973): 47.
> Nairn, Janet. "College Buildings: A Starkly Elegant Form Provides Strong Artistic Expression at the Fine Arts Center, Muhlenberg College." *Architectural Record* 162 (November 1977): 109–11.
> Johnson, Philip. *Johnson/Burgee: Architecture*. Text by Nory Miller, photographs by Richard Payne. New York: Random House, 1979, 78–83.
> Blake, Peter. *Philip Johnson*. Basel, Berlin, Boston: Birkhäuser, 1997, 154–55.

80 FIELD POINT ROAD BUILDING
80 Field Point Road
Greenwich, CT
1978, Johnson/Burgee Architects
> Johnson, Philip. *Johnson/Burgee: Architecture*. Text by Nory Miller, photographs by Richard Payne. New York: Random House, 1979, 102–05.

FAÇADE OF 1001 FIFTH AVENUE
1001 Fifth Avenue
New York, NY
1978, Johnson/Burgee Architects and Philip Birnbaum & Associates
> Johnson, Philip. *Johnson/Burgee: Architecture*. Text by Nory Miller, photographs by Richard Payne. New York: Random House, 1979, 106–07.
> Cappellieri, Alba. *Philip Johnson: Dall'International Style al Decostruttivismo*. Introduction by Vincent Scully. Naples: Clean Edizioni, 1996, 109.
> Blake, Peter. *Philip Johnson*. Basel, Berlin, Boston: Birkhäuser, 1997, 156–57.
> White, Norval, and Elliott Willensky. *AIA Guide to New York City*. 4th rev. ed. New York: Three Rivers Press, 2000, 620.

TERRACE THEATER
Kennedy Center for the Performing Arts
Washington, DC
1979, Johnson/Burgee Architects
> Johnson, Philip. *Johnson/Burgee: Architecture*. Text by Nory Miller, photographs by Richard Payne. New York: Random House, 1979, 108–09.
> Dean, Andrea O. "Cultural Colossi: Kennedy Center at 10." *AIA Journal* 70 (August 1981): 24–31.

FAÇADE OF MARSHALL FIELD & COMPANY
(now Saks Fifth Avenue)
Galleria
5115 Westheimer Road
Houston, TX
1979, Johnson/Burgee Architects and S. I. Morris Associates
Dallas Galleria
13250 Dallas Parkway
Dallas, TX
1983, Johnson/Burgee Architects
> Papademetriou, Peter. "Johnson-Oldenburg Duet Cancelled." *Progressive Architecture* 60 (August 1979): 23–24.
> Van Bruggen, Coosje, and Claes Oldenburg. *Claes Oldenburg: Large-Scale Projects, 1977–1980*. New York: Rizzoli International Publications, Inc., 1980, 68–75.
> Johnson, Philip, and John Burgee. *Philip Johnson/John Burgee Architects 1979–1985*. Introduction by Carleton Knight III. New York: Rizzoli International Publications, 1985, 38–39.
> Blake, Peter. *Philip Johnson*. Basel, Berlin, Boston: Birkhäuser, 1997, 158–59.
> Fuller, Larry Paul, editor. *The American Institute of Architects Guide to Dallas Architecture with Regional Highlights*. New York: McGraw-Hill Construction Information Group, 1999, 162.
> Welch, Frank D. *Philip Johnson and Texas*. Austin: University of Texas Press, 2000.

CRYSTAL CATHEDRAL
Garden Grove Community Church
12141 Lewis Street
Garden Grove, CA
1980, Johnson/Burgee Architects with Albert C. Martin Associates
> Severud-Perrone-Sturm-Pastier, John. "An Evangelist of Unusual Architectural Aspirations." *AIA Journal* 68 (May 1979): 48–55.
> Fischer, Robert E. "The Crystal Cathedral: Embodiment of Light and Nature." *Architectural Record* 168 (November 1980): 77–85.
> Goldstein, Barbara. "New Crystal Palace." *Progressive Architecture* 61 (December 1980): 76–83.
> Jacqz, Margot. "Crystal Gem." *Interiors* 140 (December 1980): 42–43.
> "Garden Grove Community Church." *Architecture + Urbanism* 126 (March 1981): 5–9.
> Pastier, John. "Soaring Space Wrapped in Metal and Glass." *AIA Journal* 70 (mid-May 1981): 148–57.
> Moore, Charles, Peter Becker, and Regula Campbell. *The City Observed: Los Angeles: A Guide to Its Architecture and Landscapes*. New York: Vintage Books, 1984, 62–63.
> Johnson, Philip, and John Burgee. *Philip Johnson/John Burgee Architects 1979–1985*. Introduction by Carleton Knight III. New York: Rizzoli International Publications, 1985, 14–21.
> *Philip Johnson: The Architect in His Own Words*. Edited by Hilary Lewis and John O'Connor. New York: Rizzoli International Publications, 1994.
> Cappellieri, Alba. *Philip Johnson: Dall'International Style al Decostruttivismo*. Introduction by Vincent Scully. Naples: Clean Edizioni, 1996, 110–12.
> Blake, Peter. *Philip Johnson*. Basel, Berlin, Boston: Birkhäuser, 1997, 160–63.
> Le Blanc, Sidney. *The Architecture Traveler: A Guide to 250 Key 20th-Century American Buildings*. New York: W. W. Norton & Company, 2000, 56.

CREAN TOWER AND MARY HOOD CHAPEL
Garden Grove Community Church
Garden Grove, CA
1990, Philip Johnson and Gin Wong Associates
> "Crystal Cathedral Tower, Garden Grove, California, 1990." *Architecture + Urbanism* 247 (April 1991): 11–15.
> *Philip Johnson: The Architect in His Own Words*. Edited by Hilary Lewis and John O'Connor. New York: Rizzoli International Publications, 1994.
> Cappellieri, Alba. *Philip Johnson: Dall'International Style al Decostruttivismo*. Introduction by Vincent Scully. Naples: Clean Edizioni, 1996, 135–36.

TATA THEATRE, NATIONAL CENTRE FOR THE PERFORMING ARTS
Dorabji Tata Road, Nariman Point
Mumbai, India
1980, Johnson/Burgee Architects with Patell & Batliwala
> "Johnson/Burgee and Harris Team Up, Again, to Design a Hall for Indian Music in Bombay." *Architectural Record* 169 (March 1981): 41.
> Stephens, Suzanne. "Bombay." *Progressive Architecture* 62 (March 1981): 76–81.
> Cappellieri, Alba. *Philip Johnson: Dall'International Style al Decostruttivismo*. Introduction by Vincent Scully. Naples: Clean Edizioni, 1996, 113.

ONE SUGARLAND OFFICE PARK
15200 Southwest Freeway
Sugar Land, TX
1981, Johnson/Burgee Architects and Richard Fitzgerald & Partners
> Johnson, Philip, and John Burgee. *Philip Johnson/John Burgee Architects 1979–1985*. Introduction by Carleton Knight III. New York: Rizzoli International Publications, 1985, 86–91.
> Welch, Frank D. *Philip Johnson and Texas*. Austin: University of Texas Press, 2000.

101 CALIFORNIA STREET BUILDING
101 California Street
San Francisco, CA
1982, Johnson/Burgee Architects and Kendall/Heaton Associates
> "Recent Work of Johnson/Burgee." *Architecture + Urbanism* 126 (March 1981): 25–26.
> "Concrete Redesign Cuts Sawtooth Tower's Cost." *Engineering News-Record* 208 (11 March 1982): 30.
> Woodbridge, Sally B., and John B. Woodbridge. *Architecture San Francisco: The Guide*. New York: Charles Scribner's Sons, 1982, 31.
> "John Burgee Architects with Philip Johnson: 101 California." *GA Document* 12 (January 1985): 72–75.
> Johnson, Philip, and John Burgee. *Philip Johnson/John Burgee Architects 1979–1985*. Introduction by Carleton Knight III. New York: Rizzoli International Publications, 1985, 54–61.
> *Philip Johnson: The Architect in His Own Words*. Edited by Hilary Lewis and John O'Connor. New York: Rizzoli International Publications, 1994.
> Cappellieri, Alba. *Philip Johnson: Dall'International Style al Decostruttivismo*. Introduction by Vincent Scully. Naples: Clean Edizioni, 1996, 115.
> Blake, Peter. *Philip Johnson*. Basel, Berlin, Boston: Birkhäuser, 1997, 167–69.

PEORIA CIVIC CENTER
201 Southwest Jefferson Avenue
Peoria, IL
1982, Johnson/Burgee Architects and Lankton Ziegele Terry & Associates
> Johnson, Philip, and John Burgee. *Philip Johnson/John Burgee Architects 1979–1985*. Introduction by Carleton Knight III. New York: Rizzoli International Publications, 1985, 22–27.

NEIMAN-MARCUS
Stockton Street and Geary Street
San Francisco, CA
1982, Johnson/Burgee Architects
> Woodbridge, Sally. "Eat Your Heart Out, San Francisco." *Progressive Architecture* 60 (May 1979): 28.
> Woodbridge, Sally B., and John B. Woodbridge. *Architecture San Francisco: The Guide*. New York: Charles Scribner's Sons, 1982, 5.
> Johnson, Philip, and John Burgee. *Philip Johnson/John Burgee Architects 1979–1985*. Introduction by Carleton Knight III. New York: Rizzoli International Publications, 1985, 92–95.
> *Philip Johnson: The Architect in His Own Words*. Edited by Hilary Lewis and John O'Connor. New York: Rizzoli International Publications, 1994.
> Koerble, Barbara. "Buy Design: Stanley Marcus on the Architecture of Merchandising." *Cite 35: The Architecture and Design Review of Houston* (Fall 1996): 28–30.
> Cappellieri, Alba. *Philip Johnson: Dall'International Style al Decostruttivismo*. Introduction by Vincent Scully. Naples: Clean Edizioni, 1996, 114.
> O'Connor, Michael J. "100% Off." *Architecture* 88 (March 1999): 71.

TRANSCO TOWER AND WATER WALL
(now Williams Tower)
2800 Post Oak Boulevard
Houston, TX
1983, Johnson/Burgee Architects and Morris Aubry Architects
1984, Water Wall, Johnson/Burgee Architects and Richard Fitzgerald & Partners
> "10,000 Cu-Yd Mat Placed." *Engineering News-Record* 208 (7 January 1982): 19.
> Murphy, Jim. "It Towers." *Progressive Architecture* 65 (February 1984): 94–97.
> Russell, Beverly. "Powerful Tower." *Interiors* 144 (December 1984): 132–43.
> "John Burgee Architects with Philip Johnson: Transco Tower." *GA Document* 12 (January 1985): 97–109.
> Stern, Robert A. M. "Four Towers." *Architecture + Urbanism* 172 (January 1985): 43–48, 49–59.
> Brady, Steve. *Presence: The Transco Tower*. Text by Ann Holmes. Houston: Herring Press, 1985.
> Johnson, Philip, and John Burgee. *Philip Johnson/John Burgee Architects 1979–1985*. Introduction by Carleton Knight III. New York: Rizzoli International Publications, 1985, 72–79.

> *Philip Johnson: The Architect in His Own Words*. Edited by Hilary Lewis and John O'Connor. New York: Rizzoli International Publications, 1994.
> Cappellieri, Alba. *Philip Johnson: Dall'International Style al Decostruttivismo*. Introduction by Vincent Scully. Naples: Clean Edizioni, 1996, 129.
> Blake, Peter. *Philip Johnson*. Basel, Berlin, Boston: Birkhäuser, 1997, 170–73.
> Le Blanc, Sidney. *The Architecture Traveler: A Guide to 250 Key 20th-Century American Buildings*. New York: W. W. Norton & Company, 2000, 169.
> Welch, Frank D. *Philip Johnson and Texas*. Austin: University of Texas Press, 2000.

NEW CLEVELAND PLAY HOUSE
8500 Euclid Avenue
Cleveland, OH
1983, Johnson/Burgee Architects with Collins & Rimer
> Dixon, John Morris. "Teatro Simpatico." *Progressive Architecture* 65 (February 1984): 82–85.
> Johnson, Philip, and John Burgee. *Philip Johnson/John Burgee Architects 1979–1985*. Introduction by Carleton Knight III. New York: Rizzoli International Publications, 1985, 96–104.
> Cleveland Chapter, American Institute of Architects. *Guide to Cleveland Architecture*. Cleveland: Cleveland Chapter, American Institute of Architects, 1991, 4.4.
> Blake, Peter. *Philip Johnson*. Basel, Berlin, Boston: Birkhäuser, 1997, 174–75.

UNITED BANK OF COLORADO TOWER AND PLAZA
(now Wells Fargo Center)
1700 Lincoln Street
Denver, CO
1983, Johnson/Burgee Architects and Morris Aubry Architects
> "Recent Work of Johnson/Burgee." *Architecture + Urbanism* 126 (March 1981): 17–20.
> "John Burgee Architects with Philip Johnson: One United Bank Center." *GA Document* 12 (January 1985): 62–65.
> Johnson, Philip, and John Burgee. *Philip Johnson/John Burgee Architects 1979–1985*. Introduction by Carleton Knight III. New York: Rizzoli International Publications, 1985, 80–85.
> Noel, Thomas J. *Buildings of Colorado*. Buildings of the United States. New York: Oxford University Press, 1997, 54.

REPUBLICBANK CENTER
(now Bank of America Center)
700 Louisiana Street
Houston, TX
1984, Johnson/Burgee and Kendall/Heaton Associates
> "Texas Crews Toss Off a Mat." *Engineering News-Record* 208 (27 May 1982): 14.
> "Frame Contorts Around Gables, Older Building." *Engineering News-Record* 211 (14 July 1983): 30–33.
> Ferguson, John. "RepublicBank Houston." *Texas Architect* 34 (January–February 1984): 56–60.
> Viladas, Pilar. "Gothic Romance." *Progressive Architecture* 65 (February 1984): 86–93.
> "John Burgee Architects with Philip Johnson: RepublicBank Center." *GA Document* 12 (January 1985): 80–87.
> Stern, Robert A. M. "Four Towers." *Architecture + Urbanism* 172 (January 1985): 35–42, 49–59.
> Johnson, Philip, and John Burgee. *Philip Johnson/John Burgee Architects 1979–1985*. Introduction by Carleton Knight III. New York: Rizzoli International Publications, 1985, 105–17.
> *Philip Johnson: The Architect in His Own Words*. Edited by Hilary Lewis and John O'Connor. New York: Rizzoli International Publications, 1994.
> Cappellieri, Alba. *Philip Johnson: Dall'International Style al Decostruttivismo*. Introduction by Vincent Scully. Naples: Clean Edizioni, 1996, 126–27.
> Blake, Peter. Philip Johnson. Basel, Berlin, Boston: Birkhäuser, 1997, 180–85.
> Welch, Frank D. *Philip Johnson and Texas*. Austin: University of Texas Press, 2000.

PPG PLACE
Third and Fourth Avenues and Market Street
Pittsburgh, PA
1984, Johnson/Burgee Architects
> Toker, Franklin K. B. S. "PJ and PPG: A Date with History." *Progressive Architecture* 60 (July 1979): 60–61.
> "PPG Industries." *Architecture + Urbanism* 126 (March 1981): 21–24.
> "Gothic Detail Makes Glazing Tough." *Engineering News-Record* 209 (23 December 1982): 26–30.
> "Spires of PPG's Glass Tower Inspire Creative Methods." *Engineering News-Record* 211 (15 September 1983): 14.
> Boles, Daralice D. "Turned to Stone." *Progressive Architecture* 65 (February 1984): 76–79.
> Canty, Donald. "Historicist Spired 'City of Glass' Around a Plaza." *Architecture* 74 (May 1984): 242–51.
> Rastorfer, Darl. "Reflections on a Curtain Wall." *Architectural Record* 172 (October 1984): 192–99.
> "John Burgee Architects with Philip Johnson: PPG Corporate Headquarters." *GA Document* 12 (January 1985): 66–71.
> Stern, Robert A. M. "Four Tower." *Architecture + Urbanism* 172 (January 1985): 29–34, 49–59.
> Johnson, Philip, and John Burgee. *Philip Johnson/John Burgee Architects 1979–1985*. Introduction by Carleton Knight III. New York: Rizzoli International Publications, 1985, 62–71.
> Kidney, Walter C. *Landmark Architecture: Pittsburgh and Allegheny County*. Pittsburgh: Pittsburgh History and Landmarks Foundation, 1985.
> Houstoun, Laurence, Jr. "80s Retrospective: PPG's Unpopulated Places." *Architecture* 78 (December 1989): 60–63.
> *Philip Johnson: The Architect in His Own Words*. Edited by Hilary Lewis and John O'Connor. New York: Rizzoli International Publications, 1994.
> Cappellieri, Alba. *Philip Johnson: Dall'International Style al Decostruttivismo*. Introduction by Vincent Scully. Naples: Clean Edizioni, 1996, 124–25.
> Blake, Peter. *Philip Johnson*. Basel, Berlin, Boston: Birkhäuser, 1997, 176–79.

DADE COUNTY CULTURAL CENTER
(now Metro-Dade Cultural Center in Miami)
101 West Flagler Street
Miami, FL
1983, Johnson/Burgee Architects with Connell, Metcalf & Eddy
> Gordon, Barclay F. "Three Designs by Johnson/Burgee: Dade County Cultural Center, Miami." *Architectural Record* 164 (July 1978): 86–88.
> "New Smoke System Needed." *Engineering News-Record* 210 (9 June 1983): 13.
> Greer, Nora Richter. "History and Culture in Miami: They Are Joined in a New Johnson Complex." *Architecture* 73 (April 1984): 66–71.
> Johnson, Philip, and John Burgee. *Philip Johnson/John Burgee Architects 1979–1985*. Introduction by Carleton Knight III. New York: Rizzoli International Publications, 1985, 28–37.
> Blake, Peter. *Philip Johnson*. Basel, Berlin, Boston: Birkhäuser, 1997, 190–91.

AT&T BUILDING (now Sony Plaza)
550 Madison Avenue
New York, NY
1984, Johnson/Burgee Architects and Simmons Architects
> Gordon, Barclay F. "Three Designs by Johnson/Burgee: Headquarters for American Telephone & Telegraph, New York City." *Architectural Record* 164 (July 1978): 84–85.
> "AT&T." *Progressive Architecture* 60 (July 1979): 57.
> "Behind a 'Renaissance' Tower: A Contemporary Structure That Lets It Work." *Architectural Record* 168 (October 1980): 106–11.
> Knight, Carleton, III. "Significant Clients: Ma Bell Builds Big." *Architecture* 72 (June 1983): 60–75.
> Doubilet, Susan. "Not Enough Said." *Progressive Architecture* 65 (February 1984): 70–75.
> Banham, Reyner. "AT&T Building: The Post Post-Déco Skyscraper." *Architectural Review* no. 1050 (August 1984): 25–27.
> Geran, Monica. "ISD: American Telephone & Telegraph." *Interior Design* 55 (October 1984): 278–85.

> "John Burgee Architects with Philip Johnson: AT&T Headquarters." *GA Document* 12 (January 1985): 26–33.

> Stern, Robert A. M. "Four Towers." *Architecture + Urbanism* 172 (January 1985): 19–22, 49–59.

> Canty, Donald. "AT&T: The Tower, the Skyline, and the Street." *Architecture* 74 (February 1985): 46–55.

> Johnson, Philip, and John Burgee. *Philip Johnson/John Burgee Architects 1979–1985*. Introduction by Carleton Knight III. New York: Rizzoli International Publications, 1985, 40–53.

> Branch, Mark Alden. "From Highboy to Boom Box." *Progressive Architecture* 75 (July 1994): 100–05.

> *Philip Johnson: The Architect in His Own Words*. Edited by Hilary Lewis and John O'Connor. New York: Rizzoli International Publications, 1994.

> Cappellieri, Alba. *Philip Johnson: Dall'International Style al Decostruttivismo*. Introduction by Vincent Scully. Naples: Clean Edizioni, 1996, 116–23.

> Blake, Peter. *Philip Johnson*. Basel, Berlin, Boston: Birkhäuser, 1997, 192–95.

> Le Blanc, Sidney. *The Architecture Traveler: A Guide to 250 Key 20th-Century American Buildings*. New York: W. W. Norton & Company, 2000, 171.

> White, Norval, and Elliott Willensky. *AIA Guide to New York City*. 4th rev. ed. New York: Three Rivers Press, 2000, 297.

580 CALIFORNIA BUILDING
500–580 California Street
San Francisco, CA
1984, Johnson/Burgee and Kendall/Heaton Associates

> Johnson, Philip, and John Burgee. *Philip Johnson/John Burgee Architects 1979–1985*. Introduction by Carleton Knight III. New York: Rizzoli International Publications, 1985, 118–23.

> *Philip Johnson: The Architect in His Own Words*. Edited by Hilary Lewis and John O'Connor. New York: Rizzoli International Publications, 1994.

> Cappellieri, Alba. *Philip Johnson: Dall'International Style al Decostruttivismo*. Introduction by Vincent Scully. Naples: Clean Edizioni, 1996, 128.

> Blake, Peter. *Philip Johnson*. Basel, Berlin, Boston: Birkhäuser, 1997, 196–97.

TWO FEDERAL RESERVE PLAZA
33 Maiden Lane
New York, NY
1985, Johnson/Burgee Architects

> "Federal Reserve Plaza." *Architecture + Urbanism* 172 (January 1985): 23.

> "John Burgee Architects with Philip Johnson: One Federal Reserve Plaza at 33 Maiden Lane." *GA Document* 12 (January 1985): 22–23.

> Johnson, Philip, and John Burgee. *Philip Johnson/John Burgee Architects 1979–1985*. Introduction by Carleton Knight III. New York: Rizzoli International Publications, 1985, 124–29.

> Blake, Peter. "Art Pit." *Interior Design* 59 (August 1988): 156–61.

> Cappellieri, Alba. *Philip Johnson: Dall'International Style al Decostruttivismo*. Introduction by Vincent Scully. Naples: Clean Edizioni, 1996, 130.

> White, Norval, and Elliott Willensky. *AIA Guide to New York City*. 4th rev. ed. New York: Three Rivers Press, 2000, 40–41.

FIVE HUNDRED BOYLSTON STREET BUILDING
500 Boylston Street
Boston, MA
1985, John Burgee Architects with Philip Johnson and Kendall/Heaton Associates

> "John Burgee Architects with Philip Johnson: New England Life." *GA Document* 12 (January 1985): 24.

> Johnson, Philip, and John Burgee. *Philip Johnson/John Burgee Architects 1979–1985*. Introduction by Carleton Knight III. New York: Rizzoli International Publications, 1985, 148–51.

> Miller, Naomi, and Keith Morgan. *Boston Architecture 1975–1990*. Munich: Prestel-Verlag, 1990, 152–53.

> Southworth, Susan and Michael Southworth. *AIA Guide to Boston*. 2d ed. Chester, CT: Globe Pequot Press, 1992, 250–52.

> *Philip Johnson: The Architect in His Own Words*. Edited by Hilary Lewis and John O'Connor. New York: Rizzoli International Publications, 1994.

> Cappellieri, Alba. *Philip Johnson: Dall'International Style al Decostruttivismo*. Introduction by Vincent Scully. Naples: Clean Edizioni, 1996, 132–33.

> Blake, Peter. *Philip Johnson*. Basel, Berlin, Boston: Birkhäuser, 1997, 202–05.

ARCHITECTURE BUILDING
University of Houston
Houston, TX
1985, John Burgee Architects with Philip Johnson and Morris Aubry Architects

> Johnson, Philip, and John Burgee. *Philip Johnson/John Burgee Architects 1979–1985*. Introduction by Carleton Knight III. New York: Rizzoli International Publications, 1985, 136–39.

> Freeman, Allen. "Architecture School Patterned on an 18th-Century Precedent." *Architecture* 75 (March 1986): 84–87.

> Kaliski, John, "Master Johnson's House of Education." *Cite, The Architecture and Design Review of Houston*, Summer 1986, 16–18.

> Sorkin, Michael. "The Real Thing." *Architectural Record* 174 (September 1986): 78–85.

> *Philip Johnson: The Architect in His Own Words*. Edited by Hilary Lewis and John O'Connor. New York: Rizzoli International Publications, 1994.

> Blake, Peter. *Philip Johnson*. Basel, Berlin, Boston: Birkhäuser, 1997, 206–09.

> Le Blanc, Sidney. *The Architecture Traveler: A Guide to 250 Key 20th-Century American Buildings*. New York: W. W. Norton & Company, 2000, 179.

> Welch, Frank D. *Philip Johnson and Texas*. Austin: University of Texas Press, 2000.

THE CRESCENT
Cedar Springs Road and Pearl Street
Dallas, TX
1985, John Burgee Architects with Philip Johnson and Shepherd+Boyd USA

> "Computers 'Iron Out' the Crescents." *Engineering News-Record* 215 (5 December 1985): 22–25.

> Johnson, Philip, and John Burgee. *Philip Johnson/John Burgee Architects 1979–1985*. Introduction by Carleton Knight III. New York: Rizzoli International Publications, 1985, 130–33.

> Sorkin, Michael. "The Real Thing." *Architectural Record* 174 (September 1986): 78–85.

> Henderson, Justin. "The Hotel Crescent Court in Dallas Is Inspired by the Grand Hotels of the 19th Century." *Interiors* 148 (November 1988): 35–36.

> Fuller, Larry Paul, editor. *The American Institute of Architects Guide to Dallas Architecture with Regional Highlights*. New York: McGraw-Hill Construction Information Group, 1999, 60.

> Welch, Frank D. *Philip Johnson and Texas*. Austin: University of Texas Press, 2000.

TYCON TOWER
8000 Towers Crescent Drive
Vienna, VA
1985, John Burgee Architects with Philip Johnson

> Johnson, Philip, and John Burgee. *Philip Johnson/John Burgee Architects 1979–1985*. Introduction by Carleton Knight III. New York: Rizzoli International Publications, 1985, 142–45.

53RD AT THIRD BUILDING (Lipstick Building)
885 Third Avenue
New York, NY
1986, John Burgee Architects with Philip Johnson

> "Huge Steel Columns Carry Oval High-Rise." *Engineering News-Record* 212 (5 April 1984): 23–24.

> "53rd at Third Building." *Architecture + Urbanism* 172 (January 1985): 23.

> "John Burgee Architects with Philip Johnson: 53rd at Third." *GA Document* 12 (January 1985): 23.

> "Compact Columns Steady Ellipse." *Engineering News-Record* 215 (5 September 1985): 22–24.

> Johnson, Philip, and John Burgee. *Philip Johnson/John Burgee Architects 1979–1985*. Introduction by Carleton Knight III. New York: Rizzoli International Publications, 1985, 134–35.

> Sorkin, Michael. "The Real Thing." *Architectural Record* 174 (September 1986): 78–85.

> *Philip Johnson: The Architect in His Own Words*. Edited by Hilary Lewis and John O'Connor. New York: Rizzoli International Publications, 1994.

> Cappellieri, Alba. *Philip Johnson: Dall'International Style al Decostruttivismo*. Introduction by Vincent Scully. Naples: Clean Edizioni, 1996, 131.

> Blake, Peter. *Philip Johnson*. Basel, Berlin, Boston: Birkhäuser, 1997, 186–89.

> White, Norval, and Elliott Willensky. *AIA Guide to New York City*. 4th rev. ed. New York: Three Rivers Press, 2000, 309–10.

190 SOUTH LA SALLE STREET BUILDING
190 South La Salle Street
Chicago, IL
1986, John Burgee Architects with Philip Johnson and Shaw Associates

> Zotti, Ed. "Speculations on La Salle Street." *Inland Architect* 29 (September/October 1985): 24–25.

> Johnson, Philip, and John Burgee. *Philip Johnson/John Burgee Architects 1979–1985*. Introduction by Carleton Knight III. New York: Rizzoli International Publications, 1985, 152–55.

> Abercrombie, Stanley. "P/K vs PM." *Interior Design* 59 (May 1988): 234–45.

> Freeman, Allen. "A Tale of Four New Towers and What They Tell of Trends." *Architecture* 77 (May 1988): 124–30.

> Sinkevitch, Alice, editor. *AIA Guide to Chicago*. San Diego: Harcourt Brace & Company, 1993, 80.

> Sirefman, Susanna. *Chicago: A Guide to the Recent Architecture*. London: Artemis, Ltd., 1994, 176–77.

> Cappellieri, Alba. *Philip Johnson: Dall'International Style al Decostruttivismo*. Introduction by Vincent Scully. Naples: Clean Edizioni, 1996, 134.

> Wolfe, Gerard R. *Chicago In and Around the Loop: Walking Tours of Architecture and History*. New York: McGraw-Hill, 1996, 34, 36.

> Blake, Peter. *Philip Johnson*. Basel, Berlin, Boston: Birkhäuser, 1997, 210–12.

ONE ATLANTIC CENTER
1201 West Peachtree Street N.E.
Atlanta, GA
1987, John Burgee Architects with Philip Johnson and Heery Architects and Engineers

> Johnson, Philip, and John Burgee. *Philip Johnson/John Burgee Architects 1979–1985*. Introduction by Carleton Knight III. New York: Rizzoli International Publications, 1985, 160–63.

> Freeman, Allen. "A Trip Back to the 20's in Atlanta." *Architecture* 77 (January 1988): 56–59.

> Gournay, Isabelle. *AIA Guide to the Architecture of Atlanta*. Athens: University of Georgia Press, 1993, 121.

> Blake, Peter. *Philip Johnson*. Basel, Berlin, Boston: Birkhäuser, 1997, 213–15.

MOMENTUM PLACE
(now Bank One Center)
1717 Main Street
Dallas, TX
1987, John Burgee Architects with Philip Johnson and HKS
> "John Burgee Architects with Philip Johnson: Mercantile Center."
GA Document 12 (January 1985): 25.
> Johnson, Philip, and John Burgee. *Philip Johnson/John Burgee
Architects 1979–1985*. Introduction by Carleton Knight III.
New York: Rizzoli International Publications, 1985, 140–41.
> Tilley, Ray Don. "Trading Under a Barrel of Light." *Texas
Architect* 38 (November–December 1988): 25.
> Baker, James R. "Bank One and Interiors of the 1990s." *Texas
Architect* 41 (July–August 1991): 17–19.
> Fuller, Larry Paul, editor. *The American Institute of Architects
Guide to Dallas Architecture with Regional Highlights*.
New York: McGraw-Hill Construction Information Group, 1999, 60.
> Welch, Frank D. *Philip Johnson and Texas*. Austin: University of
Texas Press, 2000.

ONE INTERNATIONAL PLACE, FORT HILL SQUARE
100 Oliver Street
Boston, MA
1987, John Burgee Architects with Philip Johnson
> "Past Aids $360-Million Job." *Engineering News-Record* 210
(10 February 1983): 40.
> Sorkin, Michael. "Tower Hungry." *Skyline* (March 1983): 20–21.
> "Fort Hill Square." *Architecture + Urbanism* 172 (January
1985): 24.
> "John Burgee Architects with Philip Johnson: Fort Hill Square."
GA Document 12 (January 1985): 24.
> Johnson, Philip, and John Burgee. *Philip Johnson/John Burgee
Architects 1979–1985*. Introduction by Carleton Knight III.
New York: Rizzoli International Publications, 1985, 146–47.
> Miller, Naomi, and Keith Morgan. *Boston Architecture
1975–1990*. Munich: Prestel-Verlag, 1990, 98–99.
> Southworth, Susan and Michael Southworth. *AIA Guide to
Boston*. 2d ed. Chester, CT: Globe Pequot Press, 1992, 97–98.
> *Philip Johnson: The Architect in His Own Words*. Edited by Hilary
Lewis and John O'Connor. New York: Rizzoli International
Publications, 1994.
> Blake, Peter. *Philip Johnson*. Basel, Berlin, Boston: Birkhäuser,
1997, 216–17.

TWO INTERNATIONAL PLACE, FORT HILL SQUARE
High Street and Fort Hill Square
Boston, MA
1992, John Burgee Architects, Philip Johnson Consultant
> Miller, Naomi, and Keith Morgan. *Boston Architecture
1975–1990*. Munich: Prestel-Verlag, 1990, 98–99.
> Southworth, Susan, and Michael Southworth. *AIA Guide to
Boston*. 2d ed. Chester, CT: Globe Pequot Press, 1992, 97–98.

FRANKLIN SQUARE
1300 I Street, N.W.
Washington, DC
1989, John Burgee Architects with Philip Johnson and Richard Fitzgerald &
Partners
> Canty, Don, "Controlled Classicism Downtown."
Architectural Record 178 (February 1990): 101.

COMERICA TOWER AT DETROIT CENTER
500 Woodward Avenue
Detroit, MI
1991, John Burgee Architects, Philip Johnson Consultant and Kendall/Heaton
Associates
> Nathan, Scott A. "Downtown Detroit to Get Hines/Burgee Tower."
Inland Architect 33 (September–October 1989): 21.

191 PEACHTREE TOWER
191 Peachtree Street N.E.
Atlanta, GA
1991, John Burgee Architects, Philip Johnson Consultant and Kendall/Heaton
Associates
> Gournay, Isabelle. *AIA Guide to the Architecture of Atlanta*.
Athens: University of Georgia Press, 1993, 50.
> Blake, Peter. *Philip Johnson*. Basel, Berlin, Boston: Birkhäuser,
1997, 218–19.

CANADIAN BROADCASTING CENTRE
250 Front Street West
Toronto, Ontario, Canada
1992, Bregman + Hamann Architects, Scott Associates Architects,
John Burgee Architects, Philip Johnson Consultant
> "CBC Centre, Toronto." *The Canadian Architect* 36
(March 1991): 39–44.
> Blake, Peter. *Philip Johnson*. Basel, Berlin, Boston: Birkhäuser,
1997, 220–21.

SCIENCE AND ENGINEERING LIBRARY
Ohio State University
175 West 18th Avenue
Columbus, OH
1992, John Burgee Architects, Philip Johnson Consultant with
Collins, Reimer & Gordon Architects

MATHEMATICS TOWER
Ohio State University
231 West 18th Avenue
Columbus, OH
1992, John Burgee Architects, Philip Johnson Consultant with
Collins, Reimer & Gordon Architects
> Blake, Peter. *Philip Johnson*. Basel, Berlin, Boston: Birkhäuser,
1997, 222–23.

WILLIAM S. PALEY BUILDING,
MUSEUM OF TELEVISION AND RADIO
23 West Fifty-second Street
New York, NY
1991, John Burgee Architects, Philip Johnson Consultant
> Albrecht, Donald. "Museum of Television and Radio Opens in New
York." *Architecture* 80 (November 1991): 27.
> "Philip Johnson John Burgee Architects." *Architecture +
Urbanism* 268 (January 1993): 22–29.
> *Philip Johnson: The Architect in His Own Words*. Edited by
Hilary Lewis and John O'Connor. New York: Rizzoli International
Publications, 1994.
> Cappellieri, Alba. *Philip Johnson: Dall'International Style
al Decostruttivismo*. Introduction by Vincent Scully. Naples:
Clean Edizioni, 1996, 137–38.
> Blake, Peter. *Philip Johnson*. Basel, Berlin, Boston: Birkhäuser,
1997, 224–25.
> White, Norval, and Elliott Willensky. *AIA Guide to New York City*.
4th rev. ed. New York: Three Rivers Press, 2000, 292–93.

PUERTA DE EUROPA
Paseo de la Castellana and Avenida de Asturias and Calle M. Inurria
Madrid, Spain
1995, John Burgee Architects, Philip Johnson Consultant with Pedro Sentieri
and Tomás Domínguez del Castillo y Juan Carlos Martín Baranda
> Cohen, Roger. "Big Wallets and Little Supervision." *New York
Times*, 28 September 1993, sect. D, p. 1.
> "Puerta de Europa, Madrid, España." *Zodiac* 15 (May–August
1996): 166–71.
> Vitta, Maurizio. "Le torri che pendono." *L'Arca* 109
(November 1996): 32–41.
> Kipnis, Jeffrey. *Philip Johnson: Recent Work*. Architectural
Monographs No. 44. London: Academy Editions, 1996, 112–23.

> Blake, Peter. *Philip Johnson*. Basel, Berlin, Boston: Birkhäuser,
1997, 226–27.
> Fernández-Galiano, Luis. "El declive de la rosa: Las torres del
KIO como símbolo de una crisis." *Arquitectura Viva* 69
(November–December 1999): 32–33.

CELEBRATION TOWN HALL
Market Street and Celebration Avenue
Celebration, FL
1996, Philip Johnson, Ritchie & Fiore Architects and HKS
> "Celebration." *Zodiac* 15 (March–August 1996): 172–73.
> Field, Marcus. "Mickey Meets Plato." *Blueprint* 133 (November
1996): 28–31.
> Blake, Peter. *Philip Johnson*. Basel, Berlin, Boston: Birkhäuser,
1997, 232–33.
> Frantz, Douglas, and Catherine Collins. *Celebration USA: Living in
Disney's Brave New Town*. New York: Henry Holt & Company, 1999.
> Ross, Andrew. *The Celebration Chronicles*. New York: Ballantine
Books, 1999.

MILLENIA WALK
1 Temasek Avenue, Suntec City
Singapore
1996, John Burgee Architects, Philip Johnson Consultant and DP Architects
> Blake, Peter. *Philip Johnson*. Basel, Berlin, Boston: Birkhäuser,
1997, 234–35.
> Powell, Robert. *Singapore: Architecture of a Global City*.
Singapore: Archipelago Press, 2000.

TURNING POINT
Case Western Reserve University
Bellflower Road
Cleveland, OH
1996, Philip Johnson, Ritchie & Fiore Architects
> Kipnis, Jeffrey. *Philip Johnson: Recent Work*. Architectural
Monographs No. 44. London: Academy Editions, 1996, 16–21.
> *Philip Johnson: Turning Point*. Edited by Peter Noever. Vienna:
Springer-Verlag Wien, 1996.

PHILIP-JOHNSON-HAUS
Friedrichstraße 200
Berlin, Germany
1997, Philip Johnson, Ritchie & Fiore Architects and Pysall, Stahrenberg &
Partners
> *Philip Johnson: The Architect in His Own Words*. Edited by
Hilary Lewis and John O'Connor. New York: Rizzoli International
Publications, 1994.
> Cappellieri, Alba. *Philip Johnson: Dall'International Style
al Decostruttivismo*. Introduction by Vincent Scully. Naples:
Clean Edizioni, 1996, 148.
> Blake, Peter. *Philip Johnson*. Basel, Berlin, Boston: Birkhäuser,
1997, 236–37.
> "Philip Johnson Haus." *Bauwelt* 89 (13 March 1998): 534–35.
> Demmele, Matthias. "The Philip Johnson House, Friedrichstrasse
200." In *Bauwelt Berlin Annual: Chronology of Building Events,
1996 to 2001*, edited by Martina Düttmann and Felix Zwoch,
vol.2, pp. 40–47. Basel, Berlin, Boston: Birkhäuser Verlag, 1998.
> Schulz, Bernhard. "Chronik." *Baumeister* 96 (January 1999):
6–7.

CHAPEL OF ST. BASIL
University of St. Thomas
3800 Yoakum Boulevard
Houston, TX
1997, Philip Johnson, Ritchie & Fiore Architects with John Manley and Merriman Holt Architects
> Moorhead, Gerald. "Scenes from a Mall." *Cite 27: The Architecture and Design Review of Houston*, Fall 1991, 8–9.
> *Philip Johnson: The Architect in His Own Words*. Edited by Hilary Lewis and John O'Connor. New York: Rizzoli International Publications, 1994.
> Kroloff, Reed. "St. Basil's Chapel, University of St. Thomas, Houston, Texas, Philip Johnson, Ritchie & Fiore, Architects, in association with John Manley and Merriman Holt Architects." *Architecture* 85 (March 1996): 52–53.
> Cappellieri, Alba. *Philip Johnson: Dall'International Style al Decostruttivismo*. Introduction by Vincent Scully. Naples: Clean Edizioni, 1996, 143–44.
> Kipnis, Jeffrey. *Philip Johnson: Recent Work*. Architectural Monographs No. 44. London: Academy Editions, 1996, 86–92.
> Welch, Frank D. "Long Time Coming." *Texas Architect* 47 (September–October 1997): 82–83.
> Blake, Peter. *Philip Johnson*. Basel, Berlin, Boston: Birkhäuser, 1997, 238–39.
> Welch, Frank D. *Philip Johnson and Texas*. Austin: University of Texas Press, 2000.

TRUMP INTERNATIONAL TOWER AND HOTEL
1 Central Park West
New York, NY
1997, Philip Johnson, Ritchie & Fiore Architects and Costas Kondylis
> Sullivan, Ann C. "Recladding Modern Buildings." *Architecture* 84 (November 1995): 119–21.
> Webster, Jonathan. "Johnson's Trump Card." *Architect's Journal* 203 (6 June 1996): 22–23.
> Cramer, Ned. "Urbanism Trumped on Columbus Circle." *Architecture* 85 (July 1996): 51.
> White, Norval, and Elliott Willensky. *AIA Guide to New York City*. 4th rev. ed. New York: Three Rivers Press, 2000, 316.

TIME SCULPTURE
Dante Square, Lincoln Center for the Performing Arts
West Sixty-fourth Street and Broadway
New York, NY
1999, Philip Johnson/Alan Ritchie Architects
> Blumenthal, Ralph. "Debating a Sculpture with Four Faces." *New York Times*, 9 July 1996, sect. C, p. 11.
> "Protests Over New Face in Public Park." *New York Times*, 19 April 1998, sect. 14, p. 7.
> "Mixed Notices for Clock Sculpture." *New York Times*, 30 May 1999, sect. 14, p. 5.

TRUMP PLACE
200, 180, and 160 Riverside Drive
New York, NY
1998–2001, Philip Johnson/Alan Ritchie Architects and Costas Kondylis & Partners
> *Philip Johnson: The Architect in His Own Words*. Edited by Hilary Lewis and John O'Connor. New York: Rizzoli International Publications, 1994.
> Pogreben, Robin. "Protests Supplanted by Praise: Trump Place Becomes Real, and Even Popular." *New York Times*, 25 June 1999, sect. B, p. 2.
> White, Norval, and Elliott Willensky. *AIA Guide to New York City*. 4th rev. ed. New York: Three Rivers Press, 2000, 325–26.

CHAIN LINK PAVILION
Westchester County, NY
1999, Philip Johnson/Alan Ritchie Architects
> Newhouse, Victoria. "Garden Variety." *Architectural Digest* 57 (October 2000): 242–45.

DDC DOMUS DESIGN COLLECTION
181 Madison Avenue
New York, NY
2000, Philip Johnson/Alan Ritchie Architects
> Urbach, Henry. "Stage Set." *Interior Design* 71 (September 2000): 268–71.

JOHN THOMAS MEMORIAL AIDS BELL WALL
Cathedral of Hope
5910 Cedar Springs Road
Dallas, TX
2000, Philip Johnson/Alan Ritchie Architects
> Welch, Frank D. *Philip Johnson and Texas*. Austin: University of Texas Press, 2000.

THE TRYLONS AT CHRYSLER CENTER
666 Third Avenue
New York, NY
2001, Philip Johnson/Alan Ritchie Architects and Adamson Associates Architects
> White, Norval, and Elliott Willensky. *AIA Guide to New York City*. 4th rev. ed. New York: Three Rivers Press, 2000, 276.

AMON CARTER MUSEUM ADDITION
3501 Camp Bowie Boulevard
Fort Worth, TX
2001, Philip Johnson/Alan Ritchie Architects and Carter & Burgess
> Gunderson, W. Mark. "Johnson Redux." *Texas Architect* 49 (January–February 1999): 12–13.
> Welch, Frank D. *Philip Johnson and Texas*. Austin: University of Texas Press, 2000.
> Dillon, David. "Amon Carter Museum, Fort Worth, Texas." *Architectural Record* 189 (November 2001): 146–49.

ACKNOWLEDGMENTS

THE ANCHORAGE FOUNDATION OF TEXAS

SCALER FOUNDATION

THE LOUISA STUDE SAROFIM FOUNDATION

GERALD D. HINES